CONFUCIAN GOVERNMENTALITY AND SOCIALIST AUTOCRACY IN CONTEMPORARY CHINA

Chih-yu Shih

First published in Great Britain in 2025 by

Bristol University Press
University of Bristol
1-9 Old Park Hill
Bristol
BS2 8BB
UK
t: +44 (0)117 374 6645
e: bup-info@bristol.ac.uk

Details of international sales and distribution partners are available at bristoluniversitypress.co.uk

© Bristol University Press 2025

British Library Cataloguing in Publication Data
A catalogue record for this book is available from the British Library

ISBN 978-1-5292-3890-7 hardcover
ISBN 978-1-5292-3891-4 paperback
ISBN 978-1-5292-3892-1 ePub
ISBN 978-1-5292-3893-8 ePdf

The right of Chih-yu Shih to be identified as author of this work has been asserted by him in accordance with the Copyright, Designs and Patents Act 1988.

All rights reserved: no part of this publication may be reproduced, stored in a retrieval system, or transmitted in any form or by any means, electronic, mechanical, photocopying, recording, or otherwise without the prior permission of Bristol University Press.

Every reasonable effort has been made to obtain permission to reproduce copyrighted material. If, however, anyone knows of an oversight, please contact the publisher.

The statements and opinions contained within this publication are solely those of the author and not of the University of Bristol or Bristol University Press. The University of Bristol and Bristol University Press disclaim responsibility for any injury to persons or property resulting from any material published in this publication.

Bristol University Press works to counter discrimination on grounds of gender, race, disability, age and sexuality.

Cover design: Andrew Ward
Front cover image: Alamy/INTERFOTO

Contents

List of Figures and Tables — iv
About the Author — v
Acknowledgments — vi
Preface — vii

Introduction: Autocracy and Its People — 1

1   People's Hearts as the Regime of Regimes — 16
2   Restoring Normalcy during Involution — 39
3   Governing Hong Kong by Loving the Nation — 56
4   Pandemic Nationalism from Wuhan to across China (co-authored with Pichamon Yeophantong) — 73
5   Xi Jinping's Quest for Acceptance — 88
6   Relational Democracy of Confucianism — 106
7   A Pluriversal Dialogue with Ubuntu (co-authored with Raoul Bunskoek) — 126

Conclusion: Balancing Dominance and Belonging — 146

Appendix: The Diagrammatic Logic of Counter-governmentality — 152
References — 158
Index — 208

List of Figures and Tables

Figures

A.1	Demand for and supply of counter-governmentality	153
A.2	Supply and demand of counter-governmentality during involution under liberal democracy	154
A.3	Hong Kong, 2014 and 2019	154
A.4	Nationalist supply for counter-governmentality	155
A.5	Xi Jinping's counter-governmentality before and after 2012	156
A.6	Self-restraint as governmentality in relational democracy	156
A.7	Pluriversal relations between governmentalities	157

Tables

6.1	The Chinese R&B factor: other-orientation	119
6.2	The first Taiwanese R&B factor: unity	120
6.3	The second Taiwanese R&B factor: restraint	121
7.1	Mini-pluriversalism	140

About the Author

Chih-yu Shih teaches China studies, anthropology of knowledge, and international relations theory at Tongji University (Shanghai) and National Taiwan University (Taipei). Determined to recollect and re-present intellectual heritage in the Global South, he has devoted his academic career for the past 35 years to researching, teaching, and writing on the cultural and political agency of human society. Professor Shih's publications consistently challenge the mainstream views on the law of human behaviour and gather evidence of human relations from ethnic communities, developing countries, people in poverty, and so on. In his writings, Shih pays attention to the cultural meanings of civilizational components such as religion, language, ecology, and institution. He practises a multi-sited methodology reified through primarily field interviews, oral history, and archive research. He coached intermural basketball (in the political science league) with 10 national champions under his belt and is himself still a standing player in the Evergreen League. His research on comparative intellectual history of China and Chinese studies can be accessed at http://www.china-studies.taipei/.

Acknowledgments

Chapter 3 is a revised version of 'Loving Hong Kong: Unity and Solidarity in the Politics of Belonging', *Telos*, 202, Spring 2023: 43–65, https://doi.org/10.3817/0323202043.

Chapter 4 is a revised version of 'A Relational Reflection of Pandemic Nationalism', *Journal of Chinese Political Science*, 26, 2021: 549–72, https://doi.org/10.1007/s11366-021-09736-5, co-authored with Pichamon Yeophantong.

Chapter 7 is a revised version of a draft co-authored with Raoul Bunskoek.

The responsibility for these chapters' contents is completely the author's own.

Preface

My book proposes an alternative political science agenda that centres on governmentality, especially autocratic governmentality, to interrogate the relations between the governing regimes and their people. I aim to reveal the fallacy of posing democracy against autocracy and the irrelevance of promoting democratization in order to guide political science research.

The governmentality of a regime, democratic and autocratic alike, exists in the cooperation and coordination of its members and, therefore, depends on how they belong to the regime. Without shared belonging, they act in different degrees of alienation unpredictably. In addition to belonging, the balance between regime dominance and grassroots participation is the other component that informs the regime's capacity for survival and governance. The conditions of belonging and dominance are not the concerns of contemporary political science, which is instead premised upon the separation of the state and society and obsessed with the transition from autocracy to democracy. Moving beyond referencing democratization is a critical first step toward reconsidering democracy and democratic recession.

I have tried out some of the ideas of the book in their early stages in several institutes. I listened to the feedback from colleagues and friends at the Department of Global Studies at Ryukoku University, the Japan Association of South China Studies, the Leiden Asia Center, the Research Institute of Global Chinese and Area Studies at Huaqiao University, the INFRAGLOB project of the University of Bayreuth, the East Asia Barometers of National Taiwan University, the Research Center for Japanese Studies at Tsinghua University, the School of Political Science and International Relations at Tongji University, the Educational and Research Center for China Studies and Cross-Taiwan Strait Relations of the Department of Political Science at National Taiwan University, and the Institute of China Studies at the University of Malaya.

I wrote a couple of draft chapters under the generous support of a few visiting grants by the Alliance of Research on East Asia Ruhr (in affiliation with the Faculties of East Asia at the Ruhr University of Bochum and the Institute of East Asian Studies at the University of Duisburg-Essen), the Numata Fellowship, and the Department of Area Studies at the University of Tokyo.

Introduction: Autocracy and Its People

Reconsidering autocracy and democracy

This book relies on Confucianism to explore contemporary socialist governmentality in China. Instead of discussing Confucianism, socialism, and liberalism as ideas and reviewing their compatibility or potential for integration (see, for example, Chan 2014; Deng & Smith 2018; Miao 2021; Hong 2022), this book asks how, empirically as well as theoretically, China's autocratic practices have strategized these great ideas in different contexts as reification, revision, or resistance in terms of the human relations of dominance and belonging. Chinese autocracy has been incomprehensible to a social science that is preoccupied with liberal assumptions about the rights of nature, particularly since the literature does not attend to the relational governmentality through which the autocrat and the people constitute each other. This book integrates Chinese autocratic governmentality into a cosmological translation that is informed by the hearts of the people to enable the self-unlearning of the socialist autocrats and their liberal watchers and create a more inclusive, non-binary understanding of both autocracy and democracy worldwide.

The following chapters seek to unlearn Confucianism as well as liberalism, move beyond individualist social sciences, and substitute a relational lens for the binary of democracy and autocracy. Within these pluriversal sensibilities, the limitation of employing liberal democracy as a reference and state and society as an analytical frame to study China in English-language literature will loom apparent. Granted that contemporary social sciences understand democracy and autocracy as valid categories, these chapters suggest that they involve the same processes – belonging and dominance – being constituted by distinctive yet overlapping relational processes in terms of governmentality, genealogy of knowledge, and cosmology. These chapters are similarly conducive to the unlearning of other paralleling binaries – such as the state versus society, the self versus the other, or China versus the West – to appreciate the relational complication behind each. In the end, studying Chinese autocracy preaches that autocracy and democracy are not as they have been conventionally conceived.

Preparing people for belonging to communities

During my visiting scholarship at Duisburg-Essen University in 2022, I often visited the swimming pool of Queeranbang in Bochum. This large pool had sufficient capacity to provide ten swimming lanes, but there was only one, running down the centre of the pool. Cables running across the width of the pool on either side of this central lane separated off the shallow end, so that learners and a small number of people who had not come to swim could walk around or chat safely while in the pool. This was inconvenient for the majority of the swimmers, who had to dive under the cable each time they swam the length of the pool, but all readily yielded to the needs of the few. Later, in the six-lane municipal Guilini Pool in Bruges, which had three open lanes for those who wished to walk and three for those who wished to swim lengths, an embarrassingly slow swimmer like me was still strongly advised to use the lengths lane, so I yielded to this. There, the competitive swimmers seemed readily to tolerate me as I swam slowly, obstructing their path.

Such an arrangement would have not arisen in my hometown of Taipei. Generally, there is only one lane in the pool that is reserved for those who are learning to swim or walking, and those swimming lengths often encroach even on this, if the other lanes are crowded. Alternatively, the ward pool at Komaba of Meguro, Tokyo, attracts a good number of older people who walk in the open water, so two-thirds of the pool is reserved for them, with a temperature of 31.5 degrees for all. Competitive swimmers go elsewhere. In short, based on my limited experiences in an East Asian neighbourhood, the preferences of the majority seemed to prevail over those of the minority in the name of communal interest, until I witnessed the arrangements at the Queeranbang and Guilini pools.

A question worth exploring is how a community provides for a minority and protects them from the majority – equal rights versus equal treatment. In Queeranbang and Guilini, attending to each other's special needs promotes equal rights. In my society, in contrast, minority groups yield, lest the acknowledgment of a minority otherwise alludes to the existence of the many and disallows any claim that the community represents an existential unit. If all of the people are of the same kind, rights enable them to support each other as if they were supporting themselves. If all are considered different, selflessness rather than rights is necessary to enable them to remain together. The style of practising selflessness is likely to emphasize integration rather than participation within the field of public management.

The practice whereby people yield to each other in Bochum and Bruges while, in contrast, minorities yield to the majority in Taipei and

Komaba, attests to the existence of a community (Harell et al 2022). In these two cases, a community is either an aggregate of equal, identical individuals or a unity that is devoid of individuality. In a nutshell, affirmative action is commonly practised but respectively attests to the existence and nonexistence of entitlement. If yielding to special needs constitutes the value and urge of those who yield, all are simultaneously entitled to claim to be special in order for all to remain the same human being. However, if yielding reflects the sensibilities of a unitary communal interest, individuals are not responsible for caring for one another. Still, a minority will receive equivalent treatment in order for the community to affirm its members' sense of belonging and remain convincingly integral. Both kinds of yielding – acknowledging and renouncing rights to claim special needs – rely on the assumption that the people yield and belong in a mutually acceptable, ready way. This requires governmentality, and governmentality must likewise predispose the political leadership, including autocrats, to yield.

Solidarity versus unity

That all should care for special needs, as rights, reflects a culture of solidarity (Rorty 1989; Trey 1998; Habermas 2001; Brewster 2020; Einwohner et al 2021). I define solidarity as 'the felt obligation of the members of an imagined community to enable one another's consensual entitlement'. Solidarity ensures that equality is accompanied by equity and that equity attests to belonging. Belonging through solidarity informs the communitarian approach to liberalism (Eztioni 1993; Huang 1994; Manners 2013; Sangiovanni 2013; Motsamai 2019; Metz 2022). Communitarian liberalism, likewise, considers individual human rights as essential to community life. For rights are shared goods (Sandel 1998; Taylor 1999), and both communitarianism and liberalism caution against the abuse of authoritarian power (Bell 1995; Hall 2011). To that extent, John Locke (Kramer 1997) and Adam Smith (1759) are both communitarians, given their vigilance with regard to public goods, defined by the aggregation of interests that are claimed and can be counted.

In contrast (but not necessarily in conflict) with this, a majority that practises a culture of unity prioritizes the unitary collective interests (for example, African unity or nationalism, Nkrumah 1971; Bankie & Mchombu 2008). I define unity as 'the felt obligation of the members of an imagined community to align with one another to conceal incongruent self-concerns'. The unitary public interest calls for joint leadership, real or fabricated, to ensure and symbolize unity; for example, the culture of unity under Confucianism seeks a trustworthy leader or an imagined common ancestor who, arguably, has no private interests to symbolize unity, according to an empirical study (Linda & Wang 2019), as this is unnecessary for those enjoying equal rights. A people can relatively easily identify with their community because the shared trust in its leader, who reassures all that there is no need to worry about one's own and others' selfishness, constitutes the relational identity of the people (Limb 2022). For Confucians, leadership embodies the Heavenly Mandate and Heaven gives life to all phenomena, hence being relational and selfless (Pye 1985; Bell 2006; Ames 2021). Belonging to the community substitutes for the entitlement to rights in informing the people's sense of security and the leaders' obligation to attenuate their self-interests (Huntington 1968; Gerschewski 2018; Parry et al 2019; Kennedy 2021).

All are related, either through equal rights, acknowledged by each attending to everyone's 'special needs', or indirectly through the same treatment by the common leader, regardless of their 'differences'. I distinguish 'being special' from 'being different'. Being special refers to 'an uneven capacity of the same people to claim an entitlement', while being different to 'the implausibility of becoming the same people'. Solidarity enables equity in the former case. In the latter case, mutual belonging through a common leader can disregard differences, promote inclusivity and equity (Ai & Wang 2020; Gotsis 2022), and release their people from the anxiety of being excluded or the duty of caring for different others. Anyone, once distinguished from others, would be entitled to differential treatment within a culture of solidarity. On the contrary, any individual so distinguished would lose their belonging – that is the legitimacy to claim equal treatment – in a culture of unity (Oguejiofor 2009). If not, they would ruin 'the people's' assurance of belonging.

In short, the urge for solidarity assumes that all are the same, albeit special. On the other hand, striving for unity reflects the awareness and caution that all are different. The former is a relational belief that obliges mutual caring. The latter recognizes the implausibility of mutual caring and calls for a selfless leader to relate to and calm all.

By granting a minimum right to claim a special need, communitarianism and solidarity consciousness inform each other. Communitarianism continues to be inclined toward limited government and its consent by the ruled. Averting the claims of special needs, the culture of unity, conversely, tends to inspire the collectivist and autocratic aspect of governance (Murove 2020). Everyone feels a sense of togetherness due to a shared resemblance: the community either protects or silences the special needs of all. That said, group consciousness anywhere is usually composed of a different mix of both relational configurations. All communities are hybrids of solidarity through the entitlement to claim special needs and unity via the leadership to ensure belonging (Hofstede 2001; Tong, Toppinen & Wang 2021), but the way in which these are combined, the disposition toward one rather than the other, and the contingencies that enable a shift from one to the other are culturally prepared and contextually bred. While the tendency is for a group to rely mainly on one of the two in order to remain integral, imposing harsh measures to reproduce one disposition might prompt the other to rise among the members of the victim's group unpredictably.

Interrogating the role of the people within autocracy

This book is about Chinese autocracy. The initial puzzle of my research primarily arises from reading academic literature in English, which neglects the role of the people in an autocracy and provides an incentive to fill the lacuna (Jacobs 1991). However, I will neither romanticize the agency of the people for resistance nor the potential of autocracy to offer good governance. Both can be true. Even so, I think it is important to interrogate a neglected question: why does an autocracy, whose leader usually comes from the people, exist in this broad, deep relation to make the autocrat care for and fear the people at the same time in their practice of unity?

Autocracy can be either Confucian, socialist, or both (Wang & Nahm 2019; Jacoby & Cheng 2020). Confucianism is a hierarchical culture while socialism is an egalitarian ideology. That said, Confucianism prioritizes equal treatment between commoners while forfeiting their affluence, despite the fact that affluence constitutes the first principle of Confucian governance. Both Confucianism and socialism can suffer involution but are capable of recovery (Ang 2018), with the people always appearing discursively in collectivity and as the ultimate judge of legitimacy in the background (Fatenkov 2005). On the one hand, individuals, alongside the shadow of being 'different' (that is, private or unable to belong), form a silenced category, at most. On the other, silenced but occasionally (and unpredictably) active as a collective to cause change, the people within an autocracy play both a legitimating and a delegitimating role (Kang 2022).

Nevertheless, in the Chinese premodern as well as contemporary discourses, the people can judge and act, even under an autocracy. Modern liberalism's misperception of autocracy has to do with its failure to recognize the people's existential being. This book will discuss how this 'people discourse' can constitute autocratic governmentality in various ways (Borgström 1980; Ang 2016a). Therefore, the people are not merely a silenced category. In other words, autocracy is not as simple as being ruled by An Autocrat, who is external or superior to the collectivity of their people (Kendall-Taylor, Franz & Wright 2020). With people both as a discourse and in their practices of living, this book complicates the understanding of autocracy and collapses the familiar binary of democracy and autocracy into the same processes of belonging and dominance.

The common sense of a liberal society disallows the symbiosis of the two systems, democracy and autocracy (see, for example, Olson 1991; Marcus 2001; Brumberg 2002; Diamond 2003; Zakaria 2003). Rather, from the perspective of liberalism, they sit at opposite ends of the same spectrum.

A communitarian or liberal democracy protects the rights of the people, while an autocracy fails to acknowledge any rights at all. Under the Confucian lens, however, an autocrat symbolizes unity. To unite the people successfully, autocracy must attend to the totality of welfare, its balanced distribution between the different groups, and grievance alleviation (Lueders 2022). Typically, the peculiar privileges provided for various minorities, aimed eventually at delivering equal treatment, require affirmative, exceptional arrangements. Privileges allude to differences with regard to need and responsibility and convince all that the communal interest is an inclusive project. The Confucian question of how to prepare rulers to rule and hold them responsible for failing to deliver rightful benevolence, in terms of either rights or treatment, is a challenge that is also familiar to liberal democracy, which likewise suffers cleavages, corruption, and stratification.

What is unique about democracy, then? Philosophically, democracy means government by the consent of the governed. This is romantic, though. In the political world, the consent of the masses to their government is, by all means, speculative, ex post facto, performative, or even fictional. In practice, therefore, democracy on the ground concerns the idea and will of society continuously to enforce limited government, hence communitarian, liberal, and even populist democracy (Adamidis 2021). Nevertheless, there also exists illiberal democracy, which lacks the value of limited government despite sharing several institutional features, such as elections, opposition, privately owned media, private property, and so on (Zakaria 1997). However, within an illiberal democracy, political correctness prevents the institutions from checking and balancing each other, as they should. Rights are disposable for those members who – for ethnic, religious, economic, and ideological reasons – have failed to gain the trust of the incumbent (Harell et al 2022), who, and whose families, can be in power for a very long period of time (or, indeed, permanently so).

Therefore, these familiar grievances about il/liberal democracy point to the plagues of colonialism, fundamentalism, class, partisanship, and masculinity (Ling 2017; 2000; Dahl 2018; Helman, Malherbe & Kaminer 2019; Massey 2022). Colonialism nurtured the evolution of modern democracy at the expense of the indigenous population (Sabelo 2023). The same applies to the disadvantages experienced by women (Ahrens & Kantola 2022), whose reproductive work the democratic processes marginalize and depreciate. The critics also find that the class cleavage of capitalism, built within modern democracies, privileges the elitist strata and perpetuates the unequal capacity to claim and enjoy rights (Bennett, Brouwer & Claassen 2022). Moreover, the postcolonial ages witnessed an exodus of migrants, who have become the source of racism and ethnic cleavage that ruin community solidarity everywhere (Grande 2022). These reflections would not completely awaken the liberals. Still, liberalism can see that a plausible solution lies in certain, sincere communitarian reform, for example, deliberative democracy or civic nationalism. 'The people' remains the prerogative discourse of liberal democracy, despite the considerable hypocrisy of this. Therefore, the criticism has failed to incentivize an interrogation of the role of the people within autocracy.

Translating democracy in the pluriversal world

The comparative democratic transition is a popular academic as well as policy agenda, that assumes that the term 'democracy' may constitute an anchor, an established lens, or at least an independent valence to inform a shared destiny (Baloyra 2019; Oleinikova 2019; Joffé 2022). However, no such anchor has ever existed in practice. Instead, a cosmology of the state of nature and the rights of nature, evolving from specific geo-cultural and religious (that is, European and Christian) conditions, imbues and adapts the subsequent democracy. Like all other cosmologies, it makes assumptions about the relations between humans, nature, and the supernatural in a quest for monotheistic/Abrahamic transcendence, with the consequence of estranging democracy from a world of multiple cosmologies (Svetelj 2018; Luyaluka 2020; Martin 2020; Tarkhan 2020; Steinberg 2022), especially those unassociated with the trajectory of Reformation, secularization, and the separation of church and state.

Collecting and comparing examples of where terms like 'democracy' or 'the people' have been used differently is a particularly challenging task when dealing with another cultural system that is estranged from the contemporary democracy discourse. To devise a way of translating 'democracy' across cultural divides involves exploring how a value-laden, colonial lens of democracy understands those who are strangers to it and what terms might be employed to translate it for them (Doerr 2020; Meijen 2020; Connors & Ukrist 2021). In that sense, a translation that aims unilaterally to preach ideas defeats the purpose of the translation. A translation that enables unlearning on both sides contributes to a pluriversal coexistence between perceived strangers. That is why a critical translation must be reflexive and abstract in the first place if it is to be stranger-friendly. This amounts to the necessity of translating cosmological beliefs, as an initial step (Tieku 2012).

Critical translation means translating the meaning of a term in one language into a different language, which is so abstract that certain prototypical messages can be picked up at the other end that attain meanings in the latter's linguistic logic. These abstract messages, being devoid of any cultural or historical background, are unlikely to be assimilatory. In the second stage, they can then be re-translated into the first system for subscribers to appreciate how different their familiar concepts, values, or logic can feel once rid of their relational contexts and transcend self-limitation (Capan, dos

Reis & Grasten 2021; Kallio 2022). Critical translation between cosmologies is essential to appreciate the limit of any claim to democracy and facilitate unlearning of how seemingly distinctive cosmologies have already mutually constituted each other, especially since colonial/postcolonial encounters.

A pluriversal deconstruction of democracy through critical translation can entail a relational texture of democracy (Laszlo 1963). In other words, democracy at each site attests to the sharing of a prior cosmological imagination between individuals as entitlements-holders (Xu 2018; Nicolaisen 2020; Adebanwi 2022). As the claim to universal value proceeds through globalization and decolonization, there will be no single version of democracy that remains unchanged. Instead, multiple sensibilities cohabit. Depending on its colonial legacies, every democracy practically will privilege certain people rather than making all equal. With a social science preoccupied with transition to or from autocracy, these legacies compel it to compare and judge all in terms of their otherness. In contrast, pluriversal reflections complicate the dynamics of dominance and belonging, topics that were always intrinsic and familiar to what contemporary social scientists misconceive in the binary of democracy versus autocracy.

Although this book does not discuss the history of Western political thought, a brief note on its relevance to pluriversal democracy might prove useful at this point. Pluriversalism in terms of political thought deconstructs the binary. The coexistence and overlap between Confucianism and liberalism arise initially from the necessity of theorizing the state of nature, to say the least. The difference lies in their approaches to coping with natural human desires. While Confucianism endeavours to neutralize desires, camouflaging and taming them in the leadership circle, but allowing them among the masses of the subaltern population, liberalism regulates them by means of a social contract between equal individuals. Even so, the social contract theory fully reveals the ambivalence toward the dominance of the governing authorities, reified for example in the Hobbesian Leviathan and Rousseau's 'general will' (Talmon 1952; Chapman 1956; Owen 2005). Hobbes rationalized the exchange of individual freedom for security provided by Leviathan; Rousseau moralized the collective pursuit of goodness conditioned upon equality. Setting their incongruent philosophical interests aside, they could all simultaneously inspire what we today call democracy and autocracy. After all, the binary was not their concern, which entailed making respective sense of community, belonging, and governability based on a particular formulation of the state of nature.

Meanwhile, in the Western 'liberal democracy', which emerged from the traditions of the state of nature, the 'social contract' obliges the people to look after their own interests by limiting the power of the government; Confucianism, however, considers that all living creatures owe their birth to heaven and earth, where a metaphor of a 'natural contract' is a plausible fit.

This natural contract obliges the prince to look after the people's interests by predicting that Heaven, rather than the consenting constituency, will remove his Heavenly Mandate if he fails to display benevolence. Between these lines, the ambivalence is as apparent as in Leviathan or the general will. In the case of a retrieved mandate, the people's agency is not informed by their rights to limit the prince's power but, in the name of Heaven, their readiness to disengage – exerting disaffection, hiding information, shifting loyalty, turning idle, or even migrating elsewhere. These are the most frightening when their incentive is to wait for a replacement rather than seeking to make a change through participation. As a result, their action is unpredictable, because the autocrat is uncertain about the force and direction of their arousal, what triggers it, and when it will be triggered. Therefore, an autocrat facing unpredictable developments can feel isolated in a way that an elected leader rarely does, hence Confucius' warning to princes that 'the people' is the body of autocracy (recorded in Chapter Ziyi of the *Book of Rites*), which the latter cannot live without nor from which they can be alienated. In a nutshell, a Confucian autocrat must desire to belong.

The essence of Confucianism is to prepare autocrats to desire to belong by, as essential to their survival, refraining from abusing their dominance. The Confucian cosmology reveals how and why the prince and his people were related in a far more complicated system than simply one of top-down control or an indistinguishable type of authoritarianism. As a result of their different cosmological configurations, contemporary liberals cannot help but anticipate the Chinese people's eventual rise to limit the power of their government (see, for example, White 1993; Goldman 2005; Fukuyama 2012). In contrast, the Chinese political view is alerted to liberalism's encouragement of private interests to rival one another, to the neglect of a concerted, collective interest (Lee 2017; Ames 2020; Yan 2021; Qin 2022). For Confucianism, Heaven appears to relinquish the duty of rulers to love all children at liberal sites as if they were unrelated to the rulers. That said, plenty of examples in the Confucian historical documents and literature, as well as governance practice, echo the liberal kind of thinking on humankind's entitlement to security and autonomy (Shih 1999; Chan 2011; Gao & Walayat 2021; Jiang 2021; Kwak 2022).

Combined, liberalism and Confucianism point to an arguably democratic desire for a common style of policy making that is exempt from a monopoly (see further, Chapter 1). Despite this, in a practical sense, this ostensibly universal definition of democracy accommodates the pluriversal relationalities that allude to different values. This book engages experimentally in a critical translation between liberal democracy and Confucian sensibilities of the hearts of people by revealing their contrasting relational cosmologies, for each to embark upon an epistemological tour of the other's practices and so appreciate the value of the other in uncovering the unnoticed potential of and limitation on the practices of the self, that is, self-un/learning. The level of abstraction in the ensuing chapters will remain high due to this overall commitment to critical translation and unlearning.

Methodology: a relational approach

An individualist/rationalist approach considers solidarity as choices or preferences. In that case, all parties resemble each other in some fundamental way, and even strangers are familiar rather than absolute. There is no worry about coexistence between strangers. The only issue remaining would appear to be how to protect one against encroachment by the other. However, there is the inevitable assumption that others will think and act in the same way as oneself, not least in terms of all being the children of God and subscribing to the law of nature. This particular assumption reflects an intellectual construction of similarity between strangers. It could cause a sense of crisis otherwise (Lee 2014). This kind of belief in mutual resemblance, however monotonous, constructs relational selves. Belonging is the collective name of these threads of resemblance. In other words, the individualist approach relies, in all senses, on a relational assumption, albeit a monotonous one, in order to succeed.

By being relational, actors cannot help but practise and strategize their lives based on mutual understandings that are constituted by expectations and an assessment of how others respond. These expectations reflect the imagined resemblance of all with regard to subscribing to some shared pattern of interaction, including rivalry. Imagined resemblance defines a relation and the concomitant consequence of belonging, without which an autocrat cannot possibly anticipate whether a group of silent followers will remain or depart, or whether their guards, be they physical or institutional, hate or patronize the autocrat. A relational methodology thus conceives of autocracy as a culturally prepared relation that guides the ruler and their population to interact with a minimum level of imagined resemblance in terms of role, entitlement, gods, and so on, to enable their joint reproduction of autocracy. Autocratic governmentality is, therefore, at the same time, embedded in the relation of autocracy.

The attitude of the population toward the autocrat within a Confucian autocracy is unlikely to feel the same anxiety as a liberal democrat would feel in the same situation. Encountering the strangeness of cosmological beliefs of Confucianism induces such anxiety in a liberal democrat (Overing 1993; Heinö 2009). Relying on the relational approach, with a pluriversal sensibility, this book explains how, under Confucian autocracy, the actors belong, behave, perceive each other, and marginalize aspects of their identities that are simultaneously constituted by several alternative relations. In short, the autocrat cannot merely be someone who controls from an external position, as assumed in the recent literature on autocracy (Ong 2022; Levitsky 2022; Guriev & Treisman 2022) and, more specifically, the autocracy of the Chinese Communist Party (Truex 2016; Roberts 2018; Hsu, Tsai & Chang 2021). Autocracy necessarily relies on knowledge about the prior relation, that breeds both autocrats and their population from childhood (Chan 2022). Accordingly, autocratic governmentality simultaneously conceives both the autocrat and the population.

Specifically, the relational methodology, informed by Confucianism and socialism, incurs the interrogation of 1) autocratic governmentality constituted by ritual and benevolence, that ensure that the autocrat simultaneously cares for and fears the people, 2) autocratic governing cycles, constituted by involution and recovery, made plausible by the deeply rooted anticipation that bad autocrats ultimately fall, 3) autocratic love, constituted by differential role reciprocation, to ensure inclusiveness and unity at the expense of entitlement claims and universal solidarity between autonomous individuals, 4) autocratic nationalism, constituted by a certain extent of bottom-up spontaneity, that invites both alert and appropriation by the autocrat and survives for only a short span each time it rises, 5) an autocratic personality, constituted by Confucian and socialist ideas, that the people whom the autocrat rules share, 6) autocratic governability, constituted by self-restraint, that pre-empts the extremity of control or resistance from destroying belonging, and 7) autocratic cosmology, constituted by the encountering and accommodation of strangers, that cannot help but un/learn to achieve coexistence in a pluriversal world.

Chapter snapshots

Chapter 1, adopting a Confucian lens, connects the respective literature on state-in-society and Foucauldian governmentality by extending their application to autocratic resilience. First, the chapter points out that the state/society dichotomy is inapplicable where there exists no tradition of the rights of nature. The naturalness of the autocrat as part of society calls for an explanation of not only how and why people should accept the autocrat but also how and why the autocrat should care for or fear the people. The chapter uses narrative analysis to show that all references to the autocrat in the Chinese premodern texts imply a readiness among the people to alienate abusive autocracy and cause it to fear isolation. The people's hearts constitute the ultimate regime of all regimes, which connotes the counter-governmentality of an autocracy to yield. The chapter thus suggests that, in addition to the autocrat preparing the people to cooperate in certain ways, the imagined agency of the people to disengage likewise prepares the autocrat to cooperate. Counter-governmentality explains how autocracy is state-in-society, or state-*as*-society.

Chapter 2 presents the critical logic that social science's methodological individualism restrains liberal democracy from recovering from involution. It also explains why socialist and Confucian autocracy might recover. Two features of liberalism and Confucianism distinguish the ways in which they cope with involution. First, regarding their imagined origin being a transcendental norm or law-like inevitability, liberal democracy and contemporary socialist/Confucian autocracy cope with involution in different ways. Second, the Confucian norms mainly prepare the autocrats to practice (counter-)governmentality, but liberalism must preach to all individuals. Deliberative democracy and the mass line are compared as the remedies to involution for each system. After all, liberalism's normative governmentality is not binding. The democratic transition to new leadership costs no one their life or property as a result. Moreover, the losers can rally at the next election and might win. Recovery is unnecessary for liberal leadership to consider a survival strategy. Put succinctly, liberal leaders do not care.

Chapter 3 elaborates on the autocratic governmentality that is challenged by the culture of solidarity. Comparing Western and Chinese political thought, the chapter pays particular attention to differential love for relational others, as opposed to universal love for humanity. Specifically, it will employ Confucianism to illustrate this kind of differential love – benevolent love between the autocrat and their claimed population. Benevolent love is, therefore, hierarchical rather than equal and yet potentially universal, because all necessarily play a role in the Confucian hierarchy, and yet are peculiarly equal nonetheless, to the extent that different identities outside these roles do not invite discrimination or even matter. It will also employ the concept of 'One Country, Two Systems' (OCTS), which is Beijing's policy for arranging Hong Kong's way of belonging to China, to illustrate how the belief in benevolent love has caused a sense of repulsion toward the OCTS and critiques of it among those subscribing to a belief in universal love. Ironically, benevolent love, which aims to inspire everyone's selflessness through the familial metaphor, discourages the expression of any imagined intrinsic self-worth. According to this view, legitimate claims to self-worth instead exist exclusively in one's contribution to the reunion with the motherland, as opposed to one's own humanity, which is partially constituted by the colonial past. Among activists who insist on Hong Kong's autonomy, a sense of solidarity develops and challenges Beijing's pursuit of national unity. As a result, the incongruent emotions of Hong Kong's belonging to China have yet to be reconciled.

Drawing on the case of the Wuhan pandemic in 2019, Chapter 4 considers how nationalist discourses, informed by the culture of unity, took root and were transformed within China's autocratic context during the period of quarantine. Following this, it adopts a relational perspective to argue that, just as the COVID-19 pandemic spotlighted countries' vulnerability to all forms of nationalism and the danger that this represented, it also revealed an irony: that, despite being treated as a 'solution' to the pandemic, nationalism could only exist and thrive insofar as its 'alter' – represented by the novel coronavirus itself and, for some countries, the 'China threat' – also thrived. Given that nationalism rarely lasts long or enjoys much stability, Chapter 4 contends that, empirically as well as philosophically, nationalism is no solution to crises and that new thinking on coexistence is the vaccine needed to stabilize the post-COVID-19 world order.

Chapter 5 fills a lacuna in the literature, that is preoccupied with how a ruler's personality, embedded in Confucian and collectivist breeding, can give rise to the ideas that shape their attitude toward the world and other people. This chapter studies Chinese President Xi Jinping's political ideas as his references to the self-in-relation, rather than his schema to assess and treat alters-in-relation. In addition to facilitating the assessment of the world and policy making, personality may cause the political actors to use ideas conversely, in order to engage in self-preparation for acceptance and welcome by their perceived constituencies. In terms of Xi Jinping's evolving personality, his initial need to overcome a sense of vulnerability due to a failure to belong was satisfied through coalescence into the masses. Xi's personality has grown into a quest for popularity through the mass line, informed by 1) a Buddhist thread of transcendence in terms of anti-corruption purges while practising the Party self, 2) a Confucian thread of unity to produce self-disciplining cadres and an affluent society while practising the national self, and 3) a socialist thread of materialism to meet the needs of the world while practising the international self. The illustrative programmes include anti-corruption, the Chinese dream of anti-poverty, and the shared future of humankind. This chapter likewise discusses how an autocracy can suffer involution.

Chapter 6 attempts to create a theory of relations and balances (R&B) to clarify the systemic stability of democracy. It draws on Confucianism and compares Confucian self-restraint with liberal self-restraint. The empirical evidence suggests that, on the one hand, a Confucian constituency dislikes challenges being issued to the authorities for the sake of systemic stability yet, on the other, disapproves of unlimited authoritarian control on the pretext of maintaining a harmonious system. The evidence additionally suggests that, if the systemic identity is weak, the constituency of R&B shows greater support for inclusive, rather than enforcive, autocracy to restore governability. The R&B support for systemic inclusiveness may be mistaken for liberalism. Coupled with the idea of civic nationalism, the contemporary constitutionalism of checks and balances neglects systemic stability and fails to explain the spread of illiberal democracy due to the loss of systemic belonging. The R&B explanation of how a democracy can maintain or lose stability belongs to a systemic level.

Chapter 7 seeks to bring the relational concepts of southern African Ubuntu and Chinese Tianxia into a dialog. It compares the ontological and epistemological positions of Tianxia and Ubuntu and elaborates on the implications of the encounters between these two lenses. They similarly treat the self and the universe as mutually constituted relations. As both inspire the spontaneous pursuit of multiple relations, they can serve as either a resource or a constraint to preach autocratic governmentality. Ubuntu is closer to the micro-universe, while Tianxia lies at the macro end of the spectrum. Ubuntu is often criticized for being used/idealized as a macro theory. As this chapter argues, however, the pluriverse is co-constituted by both the micro and the macro. The chapter likewise translates the Western notion of the state of nature as well as both Ubuntu and Tianxia into a universal language in order to adapt them to suit an audience who lie outside each other's familiar cultural zones. Such communication reveals how the coexistence of different cosmological relations is plausible, unilateral assimilation is unlikely, and pluriversalism is always an ongoing process.

Advance arguments

Only those who feel safely belonging cooperate over governance. Belonging and governmentality form the mutual foundation for each other. Even in the cosmologically imagined state of nature qua anarchy, the law of nature allegedly enables all like individuals – separate, equal, and endowed with desires and capacities for judgment – readily to subscribe to liberalism in return for protection from infringement by the governing power. The culture of liberal governmentality prepares individuals to cooperate over protecting the rights of nature of all until the colonized people of colour emerge en masse, migrate back and forth, and mingle on multiple fronts to reveal they still do not safely belong. Liberal governmentality breaks down when leaders or individuals mutually segregate each other's belonging and concomitant entitlements. Divided groups expediently depend on the leaders to protect their rights from the perceived stranger group's infringement. Democratic leaders thus have an incentive to strategize mutual estrangement in order to contrive dependency on their governing power. Continuously expanding governing power with a shrinking sense of belonging reveals the involution of contemporary liberalism.

In comparison, Confucian cosmology posits that heaven and earth – another version of the state of nature – give birth to ten thousand living things. All varieties are likewise related, but only when viewed together as opposed to individually. The individuality indicated by the desire or judgment of the individuals in aggregate estranges them from each other, and no universal rule can plausibly align such a multitude. The maintenance of order alternatively relies on creating mutually accepting roles. These roles adopt the metaphor of kinship to claim spontaneity. With the Confucian role sensibilities, the key to autocratic governmentality under contemporary socialism is an autocrat who performs a selfless role by arranging collective benevolence. Adopting a role is not about rule-binding behaviour but about improvising, practicality, and reciprocity. Without the imagined law of nature as guidance, role-taking must be repetitive in order to be affirmative. Autocracy that fails selfless performance suffers isolation from people, who soundlessly await its demise.

When the leadership becomes corrupt or suppressive, it violates the regime of regimes, which is embedded in people's trustworthiness. Estrangement threatens all. Arbitrariness substitutes for governmentality. Belonging typically fails when people see strangers rather than universal humanity in one another. People practise neither unity nor solidarity when the community suffers social regression. Liberalism that rotates corrupt or populist leaders through ostensibly free but inconsequential elections cannot recover. However, a Confucian autocracy, under this circumstance, can be removed or punished, ritually or materialistically, in order to restore selfless leadership. Both methods are violent because removal alludes to revolution, political purges, or even massive disruptions, while punishing requires a significant number of scapegoats. Both point to the adoption of some kind of mass line. As a result, political cycles are considered natural within a Confucian autocracy, as the cosmological order is composed of regular cycles of seasons, tides, or lives. Imagined linear progression toward a destiny, such as the end of history, communism, and great harmony, culminates in irrelevance in practice, in the long run.

1

People's Hearts as the Regime of Regimes

Introduction

This book begins by connecting Confucianism with the Foucauldian notion of governmentality through a theory of counter-governmentality. The latter tackles how the contemporary Chinese autocracy is culturally prepared to think about and relate to the people in its entirety, parallel to an aggregate of autonomous individuals in the liberal making of civil society. With the Foucauldian intervention, Confucianism can urge a fresh, critical reflection on the state and society, as liberalism's analytical frame, and thus offer an alternative for interrogating both autocracy and liberal democracy through the adoption of a pluriversal lens.

Studies of Chinese authoritarianism and autocracy have consistently rejected the relevance of the people from their analysis, as if the autocrat were external to or above the people, and governed them from the top down for the regime's own purposes (Gao 2022; Wang 2022). Such a theoretical lacuna echoes an understanding of state and society in mainstream comparative politics, with the society composed of autonomous individuals pursuing their interests by participating in and limiting the state. Autocracy, in contrast, suppresses participation. This chapter aims to bring back the people as a discursive entity into the analysis of Chinese autocracy. The theorization of people in this chapter has significant consequences for comparative politics in general and the frame of state and society in particular. The realization that the people are an intrinsic element of autocracy calls for an explanation regarding why the autocrat, who wields the monopoly of governing power over their subjects, can pre-empt their subjects' needs without their political participation (McDermott 2007; Lauchlan 2013). Such a realization complicates the meaning of democracy and the people, obscures the binary of democracy and autocracy, and invites the literature on democracy to reconsider the duality of state and society.

Preparing the autocrat to govern so that they and their people can anticipate and maintain minimum cooperation is a matter of governmentality. Governmentality refers to 'the problem of government', as Michel Foucault asked: 'How to govern oneself, how to be governed, by whom should we accept to be governed, how to be the best possible governor?' (Foucault 1978: 127). Governmentality necessarily involves a scope that is greater and deeper than that of state and society, because the mutual constitution of the autocrat and their subjects does not begin afresh with each generation and each autocrat. Being both democratic and autocratic, governmentality relies on prior relations to socialize all members of subsequent generations, including the autocrat, into their mutual constitution (Doyle 2013; Salvatore 2013). Although governmentality primarily targets the population (Foucault 2009a: 144), its leaders must also internalize the purposes of the state and surrender to a certain self-/discipline to ensure that they constantly heed the relevance of the people; hence, counter-governmentality prepares the autocrat to attend to the people's welfare and affluence. According to Michel Foucault, the happiness of individuals pertains to the state's survival (Foucault 1988: 155). This chapter accepts that this survival sensibility transcends both the democracy/autocracy and modernity/premodernity binaries.

The following discussion will critically reflect upon the insufficiency of the state-and-society analysis as applied to China and reveal the relevance of the people to autocratic governmentality through a rarely noticed thread of classic (Chinese) discourse on democracy. It will first link the notion of governmentality to the literature on the state-in-society in general and the Chinese state-in-society in particular. It will then interrogate the term *minzhu* (民主), the Chinese translation for the English word 'democracy'. The same term is used to convey the seemingly contradictory meaning of 'the autocrat' in classic Chinese texts. A narrative analysis of the classic texts demonstrates how governmentality can rest upon a particular mode of counter-governmentality, meaning 'an autocrat adapting the self to suit the people's conditions'. The last part elaborates on the caveats of counter-governmentality regarding cultural continuity and its relevance in postmodern times, but ultimately reconfirms the autocratic regime.

Applying governmentality in the Chinese context

This book applies the Foucauldian notion of governmentality (Foucault 1979), and theorizes autocratic governmentality (Tsourapas 2021; Chakawata 2022). As applied to Chinese autocratic politics, this book interrogates how and why, within autocracy, the autocrat can both fear and care for their people. It advances the notion of governmentality in two ways. First, it proposes the notion of counter-governmentality, which does not concern resistance to governmentality, since resistance is often inscribed within power relations as dominated subjectivity (Foucault 1978: 96). Rather, it concerns the constitution of autocrats' self-identities based on the idea of 'the people'. The consideration of the people as a discursive idea extends the Foucauldian methodology of pain as 'the idea' of pain vis-à-vis actual pain (Foucault 1995: 94), which alludes to discursive or abstract people vis-à-vis living people. Autocrats and their, usually silent, people cannot interact cooperatively without constructing discursive people, that is, what the people in a collective *should* look like. The contrast between the discursive and living people reifies the discussion on the 'non-coincidence' of philosophy and politics by Foucault (2008a). On the one hand, such discursive people can philosophically render irrelevant the living people's experiences, that are incongruent unless sufficiently self-disciplined. Politically, incongruence can be too revealing to hide or too dreadful to allow to happen for autocrats, on the other hand. Counter-governmentality speaks to the dreadful autocrat, while governmentality to the self-disciplining people.

Discursive people's construction provides each autocrat, in their epoch, with a reference through which to assess the relations between autocrats and living people, which prompts the autocrat to detect and adapt to living people's conditions. Counter-governmentality, as such, makes autocrats a disciplined kind of subject, as governmentality usually makes their people. Having escaped 'laziness and cowardice', the autocrat can move beyond passive nobility and achieve government of the self (Foucault 2008b: 33). A kind of autocratic enlightenment emerges. Counter-governmentality is thus further conducive to the government of others by autocrats, by actively convincing the population of the autocrats' self-restraint and benevolence. Clues to the incongruence between discursive and living people, when the latter act unpredictably due to unsubstantiated benevolence, enable all who can allegedly settle the incongruence to claim legitimacy to replace the incumbent. Therefore, aborted counter-governmentality threatens autocrats' existential security, despite living people's allegedly limited agency to resist or revolt. The threat is a component of autocrats' self-identity, however. An autocrat must constantly strategize discursive people in order to pre-empt incongruence within their self-identity.

Second, the chapter uses the Chinese classics to inform what Foucault calls a 'completely archaic' form of surveillance within Confucian governmentality (Foucault 2009b: 93–4). This archaic form is necessary in those non-European contexts where the Age of Enlightenment did not occur. It empirically demonstrates how Confucianism has distinctively constructed counter-governmentality to preach to autocrats about (abstract) people, as in Europe before the 16th century (Foucault 2009c: 126), in terms of winning the people's hearts. In premodern times, discursive people were mainly considered to include thoughtless peasants. In modern times, the notion of 'the people' is becoming increasingly discursive, represented by the romantic masses in the Leninist states, for example. The counter-governmentality agenda can contribute to the current literature on Chinese governmentality because the scholarship mainly attends to the state-manufactured, self-controlling bodies of Chinese citizens, which are sometimes constituted by liberal governmentality and at other times by nationalism. With counter-governmentality, the People's War, democratic centrism, the mass line, and so on, are reconstituted by the people's hearts, albeit differently with regard to how the people should look. These modern versions of discursive people adapt accordingly to the effect that, for example, Leninist scientific pioneers could retain a dependent, expectant rather than revolutionary image.

The power of discursive people can discipline an enlightened autocrat; in other words, when people lose the capacity to continue cooperating and become impossible to predict, the incongruence that justifies the demise of autocracy emerges spontaneously. As the Confucian advice on governance mainly preached to autocrats rather than the people, the later discussion of Chapter 1 collects a distinct set of discourses on how autocrats lose their self-discipline, to illustrate Confucian counter-governmentality inductively. Such a discussion calls for a reinterpretation of the contemporary Chinese Communist Party autocracy, which appears to be in total control of its citizenry but continuously and consciously relies on the discourse of the people's hearts, which is the Confucian trace of the 'regime of truth' in which Foucault found power (Foucault 2011: 28). This long existence attests to 'the regime of regimes', a relation of self-dominance beneath the sovereign power at its interior limit (as opposed to dominance beyond sovereignty power 'at its outer limits' in Foucault 1997: 27), which, in our case, is ironically the mind of an autocrat who presumably possesses a dominant rather than a submissive subjectivity. As Foucault noted: 'the Prince's soul must be able to govern itself truly according to true philosophy for the Prince to be able to govern others' (Foucault 2008c: 295).

The notion of counter-governmentality contributes to the literature on state-in-society and governmentality in two ways. First, it demonstrates the insufficiency of liberal governmentality for explaining the state action when its Confucian people are unprepared to see a separate state being limited in power, as in the European liberal thought tradition. In other words, a kind of governmentality condition arises despite the lack of any cultural preparation for democratic participation by the people as an aggregate of individuals, who are conceived of as autonomous, albeit cooperative. Second, it shows why the people can nonetheless await the demise of an abusive autocrat and cooperate, despite having neither a democratic institution nor liberal governmentality.

Foucault's discussion on governmentality attends mainly to the needs and desires of liberal society, that are readily directed to enable governance. It refers to 'the conduct of conduct' (Foucault 1991: 48), which regulates and disciplines the subjects of the governance from within and facilitates the evolving modern (liberal) state based upon the aggregative pursuit of security, liberty, and well-being. The lens of governmentality offers a critique of the romanticized freedom of society under neoliberalism and reduces the rationality of the members of society to an unwittingly collective practice (Foucault 1991; 1988). The analysis can certainly be extended to incorporate the study of the governmentality of an authoritarian or socialist state that publicly promotes collectivism but appropriates neoliberal subjectivity (Vasilache 2019). In fact, China has been one of the sites that have been selected for such an extension (Hoffman 2006; Sigley 2006; Jeffrey 2011; Palmer & Winiger 2019). However, the literature on Chinese governmentality consistently points to the People's Republic of China (PRC) government or Chinese Communist Party (CCP) as a relatively exogenous crafter of governmentality (Hacking and Flynn 2018; Pow 2018; Zhang 2020a; Han 2021; Jiang 2021; Fanoulis and Song 2022; Li et al 2022; Ong 2022; Pang 2022). In the name of sovereignty, the autocrat who heads the sovereign domain is ostensibly free from governmentality's cultivation, according to these lines of analysis.

Instrumental governmentality contradicts liberal governmentality's spontaneity, which is enabled by the prior cultural preparation that is embedded in the capitalist relations of production. The idea that the CCP is above governmentality is also incompatible with the state-and-society lens (Dean 1999; 2019). Such a research design creates a puzzle: how has the exogenous crafter established its (changing) governance goals over time to devise the respective governmentality exclusively for the people? In other words, what does the crafter want, and why? The literature's solution to this puzzle is to invoke the state as a subject to substitute for the autocrat or Party and, by considering all as belonging to the state and all making sacrifices for the state's security (Pang 2022), presumably one's identity as a citizen, cadre, or leader is not crucial, in governmentality terms, to all being cooperative bodies. Nevertheless, the story remains incomplete until the counter-governmentality that attends to autocrats' concerns with the Chinese people's happiness joins forces with governmentality. To that extent, the autocrat, the elite circle, and the autocracy qua the state, that subscribe to counter-governmentality, must believe in and desire their duty to maintain the people's minimum level of happiness.

Let us consider the ruling elite within a capitalist democracy, who share with the people the same liberal governmentality. All take heed of the benefit of capitalism (Barry, Osborne & Rose 1996; Neumann and Sending 2010; Joseph 2012; Buu-Sao 2021; Fanoulis & Song 2022). No one is above governmentality. Allowing only platforms conducive to capitalism, society limits the state's power, which is ostensibly a separate, neutral entity that has actually created the neoliberal society, on behalf of capitalism. Likewise, let us remember that no one is above governmentality in an autocracy. Following Foucault, the agenda of Chinese governmentality ought to interrogate the state and society in a single relational entity. They likewise 'co-determine each other's emergence', as in liberal governmentality (Foucault 1982: 220–1). Without the issue of the separation of church and state in Chinese historiography, it is unnecessary and irrelevant to limit the state's power. Then, 'the conduct of conduct' to assimilate the CCP qua the autocrat into acting responsively and caring for anything apart from its prerogatives, and the people into leaving its well-being up to the CCP's discretion, must rest upon an autocratic governmentality, which is constituted by the people (Chen, Pan & Xu 2016; Heurlin 2016; Qiaoan & Teets 2020).

The effort to 'bring the people back in' takes seriously the concepts of governmentality and state-in-society by adding a discursive dimension to Chinese autocracy. The notion of discursive people, informed by the people's hearts, has linguistically constituted autocratic governance since the beginning of Chinese written history, through its reiteration, adaption, restoration, and even abuse.

That is why the classic texts that stress the 'people's' autocrats remain essential for understanding today's Chinese autocratic governmentality. The counter-governmentality theory, accordingly, disregards the suspicion regarding the relative insignificance of rights consciousness among the Chinese people (Chung 1982; Perry 2008; Pils 2018), 'as inherently passive and in need of tutelage' (Valdez 2016). It rejects the assumption that the CCP is exogenous to governmentality in order to appropriate it merely instrumentally.

Reconsidering the perspectives of the state and society

The perspective of state-and-society in general

The view that the state and society are separate entities persists in both the literature and the practitioners' world (Wang 2021). However, this literature is inadequate regarding its conception of the state. It is always challenging to define the state. Nevertheless, in the majority of the literature on Chinese democracy/democratization and political economy, the notion of 'the people' does not belong to 'the state'. That is why Foucauldian governmentality can serve as a critique. The 'state,' in this literature, can refer to a governing apparatus, which is an arena in which social forces compete, a system for allocating resources, a regime with self-interests, and so on (Skocpol 1979). Granted these multiple understandings, from society's perspective, a common theme that emerges throughout the liberal traditions is the necessity to prevent state power from being monopolized: that would jeopardize society's rights, with society existing and evolving naturally and spontaneously among autonomous individuals.

Civil society, which is arguably parallel to the notion of 'the people' under Confucianism, and yet embodies the participatory rigor and engages the state, is expected to rise wherever economic development flourishes (White 1987; Goldman 2005; O'Brien & Li 2006; Rowan 2007). Capitalism is considered conducive to establishing a robust civil society. The traditional wisdom is that democracy only succeeds under capitalism, and never vice versa (Merkel 2014). The globalization of capitalism reinforces the dichotomy of states mainly into liberal and illiberal types, depending on the level and effect of the people's political participation and alluding to and reproducing the state/society binary. Capitalism that is not democratic but a one-party-ruled, fascist, or military (for example, socialist) state poses an existential threat to the people qua liberal democracy.

Solidarity with the people who should have enjoyed the same rights of nature but who suffered in silence in an illiberal state is the moral implication of the analysis of state and society. The autocratic states that are perceived to benefit from capitalist growth without democratization appear to enjoy a growing power and exclusionary prerogatives, that enable them to deprive social groups and individuals of their rights. Their thriving defies liberal governmentality and calls for a diagnosis, which increasingly points to their problematic statality as the US-China rivalry brings international power politics into perspective. The charge of autocratic power abuse also serves as a foundational legitimacy for lining up liberal allies, singling out the transnational characteristic of state and society.

For three decades, the literature has strived to explain the normalcy of the weak society within an authoritarian system and detect the signs and conditions regarding its thriving (Van Klinken & Barker 2009; Hadded 2010; Lorch & Bunk 2017; Calu 2018; Onwuegbuchulam 2022). This weakness is particularly acute in the PRC's context due to information blocking (Chung 1982), nationalism (Friedman 1995), or the stage of development (Rowan 2007). Alongside this runs the agenda of authoritarian resilience, which attempts to make sense of the effective marginalization of the people and the suppression of civil society. One such research thread focuses on the autocratic state's capacity to enhance its legitimacy through professionalization, the leaders' fixed terms, invited participation, and meritocracy (Nathan 2003; Fewsmith 2019). This assessment appears to be aligned with liberal governmentality, apart from the lack of competitive elections (Zhang 2018; Palmer & Winiger 2019; Habich-Sobiegalla & Rousseau 2020). Another thread stresses the state's capacity to deliver service and welfare, insinuating a like-minded, interest-oriented, albeit illiberal, society (Jacques 2009; Fukuyama 2014; Bell 2016). Yet another thread is alert to manipulating the national dignity in various forms, for example, anti-Japanese, anti-US, the Olympic games, the China dream, the pandemic, and so on, thus perceiving the state's instrumental governmentality (Mayer

2018; Laurent 2020; Fukuyama 2020a; Jiang 2021; Zhang & Chow 2021). In short, an autocrat is hidden behind a deceitful instrument of liberal and nationalist governmentality.

'State-in-society' and 'state-as-society'

The various literature on 'state-in-society' nonetheless makes more sophisticated sense of the seemingly failing civil society in China or elsewhere, compared with the mere two-entity lens. There are likewise different ways of conceptualizing the state in society. Basically, state-in-society suggests that the state is one of the social groups that rely on their connections in order to operate, and the state is composed of levels, regions, and sectors as social groups that are entangled in complex sets of relationships.

Even so, the implicit theme that no such autocracy is above society but interacts with the people is shared. Establishing the earliest sensibilities toward the state-in-society, Joel Migdal (1988) was accustomed to separating the two but recognized that the state operates between all kinds of social groups. Later, Migdal (2001) stressed the mutual constitution of state and society. Another approach examined the local communities, whose leaders negotiate and strategize their positions between state and society. Thus, Vivienne Shue (1988) examines how the state initiates contacts in order to reach out to society. For Philip Huang (1993), those in-between create an entire third realm rather than merely constituting the leaders of discrete communities. According to this view, state and society overlap in the third realm. For Xiangxin Li et al (2022) and Chih-yu Shih (1995), such overlapping is comprehensive, as all of the actors at all levels can play double roles in the state and society dialectically. Several works illustrate how the state has deliberately merged with society in order to achieve its goals. This process occurs mainly during reforms. In this literature strand, Elizabeth Perry (2011) and Dorothy Solinger (2009) examine the workers' participation in or exclusion from governance, abiding by the state's ideology and the need for stability; Catherine Owen (2020), Yuhua Wang (2017), and Baogang He and Mark Warren (2011) respectively explore the incentives of the state to accept the binding of the rule of law or deliberative communication. At the same time, Yang, Wang, and Zhang (2022) analyze the spread of volunteerism, due to the state's encouragement.

This literature thread fails to anticipate the increasingly frequently adopted practices (particularly by Washington, followed by Beijing) that treat the autocrat or an official as one of the people, rather than an entity of a different nature, who interacts with them all. Peculiar clues to the retreat of liberal governmentality have recently challenged the image of the autocratic state as an entity that is exogenous to society. As a noticeable example in the practitioners' world, the adoption of personal sanctions against autocrats and their associates by the US and the retaliatory PRC governments during the recent decade suggests that the state's agents must be socially embedded. Imposing sanctions on individuals, such as the President of Russia, the Executive Head of Hong Kong, and the US Secretary of State, who have led autocratic, liberal regimes, likewise reflects the belief that depriving them of presumably inalienable rights might intimidate them, other officials, and private businesses from further cooperating with the respective states. In these examples, the autocrats have interest calculi as social persons, on the one hand, while all of the state officials are simultaneously people in society, on the other. As another recent clue to autocracy-in-society, the higher degree of satisfaction with the CCP among the Chinese pollees reveals that, although PRC President Xi Jinping recently rendered his fixed terms obsolete, they are quite ready to assess the autocrat positively (Huang, Intawan & Nicholson 2023). Insensitivity to his fixed terms indicates the insignificance of the autocratic monopoly of power as an issue for the people, arguably because the autocrat is not considered external to the people in the first place.

Another thread of literature, albeit sporadic in nature, attends to the composite of the modern state and society. Such a composite disallows a distinguishable state and society at all, thus connoting a further revised version of state-as-society. The initiatives for policy change under this mode of analysis spring from an undivided relational entity, thus serving as a harbinger of how the people can constitute an autocracy, either classic or modern. The issue is why the actors do what they do to cause consequences to the entire entity (Moore 1966). According to Yuzo Mizoguchi (1989), rather than being the target of revolutionary change, the landed classes were the first to initiate capitalist accumulation during the late Qing period. It is unnecessary first to build or take over a state apparatus to initiate capitalism or, for the same purpose, nationalism. The feudal and civil societies were synchronic and could act on behalf of the (at that time non-existent) state. Migdal's (2021) most recent reflections likewise suggest that the state is far more complex than decision-making, as all policies necessarily undergo implementation through society in order to become fragmented, inconsistent, and changeable.

From a history of thought perspective, Mizoguchi (2001) further argued that the public versus private dichotomy (that is, the metaphoric state and society) is discursively spurious in the Chinese context. His criticism reveals an ironic belief that autocracy and the people lie inside each other. Each can expand in order to swallow the other, contingent upon the necessities of the time. In his narrative, the public refers to the nation rather than the state or society. This Chinese public-private symbiosis contrasts with Japan's private sphere. The latter is impermeable, even though the public is usually politically correct. Andrew Walder's (2019) research resonates with his observation of the volatility of the Chinese private and public spheres in various ways, albeit indirectly. Echoing the dystocia of civil society, for example, Lucien Pye (1988) interrogated the PRC's political culture, in which revolutionary modernity carries a Mandarin psychology that reproduces the innate dependency of the masses on their leaders.

State-as-society and autocratic governmentality

Where modernity was imposed by intruding imperialism or colonialism, the defence in the name of an emerging local state was necessarily discursive and abstract. (Abstract) state leaders were indistinguishable from the existing group of leaders, who had no citizens per se to lead, apart from the theoretical – that is, abstract – masses. Under the state-as-society circumstance, how does the state (that is, the autocrat and their apparatus) ensure its people's cooperation and compliance, where the people are accustomed to waiting for the state to take action first? This puzzle points to the discursive, relational governmentality that enables the autocrat to empathize with their people by reflecting upon their own desire and needs as they understand them, while themselves being one of the people. The same group of people and their leaders attain two identities. Living people's trust in and dependence on the state concerns their leader, rather than the abstract state; this contrasts with the distrust of civil society toward an expanding state in liberal governmentality.

The state-as-society can appear socially, for scholars including Yuhua Wang (2022a), Lucien Pye (1981), and Thomas Gottlieb (1977) interrogate the Chinese state as a social network, rather than an apparatus or arena, and the factions as the seekers of embedding. It can likewise appear institutionally, for both Yuenyuen Ang (2016) and Raoul Bunskoek and Shih (2021) notice a style of 'directed improvisation', one domestic and the other international, whereby the demarcation of the centre, the local, and the community merges into a single continuum. It can certainly appear discursively, for scholars such as Kevin O'Brien and Lianjiang Li (O'Brien & Li 2006), as well as Greg Disteihorst and Diana Fu (2019), detect a shared moral logic between the citizens and officials. The former can oblige the latter to tend to their concerns, reminding the latter of the living people.

Entering modernity, the discursive state and people were shadows of society. Nevertheless, the state-as-society and governmentality approaches agree on the mutual constitution of state and society. On the one hand, the literature on Chinese governmentality is concerned with the crafting of governmentality by the central government, the CCP, or simply the governing apparatus, to nurture self-regulating, cooperative subjects. These Chinese governmentalities apply to the environmental (Gilley 2012; Pow 2018), health (Hacking and Flynn 2018; Jiang 2021), educational (Han 2021), social (Gleiss 2016; Wang 2022b), residential (Zhang 2018; Huang, Xue &

Wang 2019), international (Fanoulis & Song 2022; Li et al 2022), economic (Sigley 2006; Pang 2022), and other regimes (Hacking & Flynn 2018; Pow 2018; Han 2021; Jiang 2021; Li et al 2022; Pang 2022). On the other hand, the state-in/as-society literature seeks incentives, mechanisms, necessities, and spontaneity that embed the state in society but has yet to approach systematically their shared prior discursive cultivation (McIlvenny, Klausen & Lindegaard 2016; Derous & De Roeck 2019). If liberal governmentality patronizes and directs the conduct of the participating individuals, the literature on Chinese governmentality requires a mode of autocratic governmentality that patronizes and directs the conduct of the autocrat. Under liberal governmentality, individuals who are cultivated to be self-regulated are ostensibly free. Presumably, under autocratic governmentality, the seemingly dominant autocrat is cultivated to be self-restrained.

A discursive foundation for them to connect and coexist ensures that an autocracy can confidently desire and need what the people desire and need. The key term is *the people's hearts*. In this regard, the idea of the people is necessarily discursive. They are supposedly docile and affluent. Skilful autocrats handle the incongruence between discursive and living people, desiring counter-governmentality as self-disciplining, while living people desire to belong to an affluent, kinship network after the modern state has transformed them into individual citizens. In the past, even if people had views about the autocrat, they had no discourse. In modern times, views can be articulated. The discursive site of incongruence shifts from the autocrat's soul to media of various kinds. In any case, the discourse of the people's hearts never disappears, constituting the regime of regimes over a span of five thousand years. The messages of the people's hearts, via relational networks – be they social/kinship networks, the third realm, dialectical roles, shared morals, policy improvisation, or political psychology – pave the way for ready compliance on the part of both the autocrat and the people.

In an autocracy, the readiness of the people to follow the autocrat, the person, indicates governmentality. Thus, the people are more cooperative with the autocrat's present-day, on-site instructions than with any consensual norms and institutions. The pressure to coordinate the people remains challenging, since the living people, ready to learn, unlearn, and relearn, are hardly synchronic, homogeneous, or self-consistent (Palmer and Winiger 2019; Wang 2022b). Policy processes unavoidably suffer from ambiguities and uncertainties in practice (Migdal 2021). Autocratic governmentality can enable the survival of the regime by focusing on the body politic, with the autocrat-in-person being the reification of society. Given that the autocrat embodies society, their people are ready to transcend specific governmentalities, which change in line with the sequential policy agendas. The autocrat, constituted by the people, yields the autocrat-as-society and is the quintessential form of the state-as-society, the higher form of governmentality and the reification of the regime of regimes.

However, under the prior relationship of the autocrat-as-society, the autocrat would lose their natural embodiment of society should they fail to cope with the non-coincidence of the two versions of the people. Since the people are inarticulate, the autocrat must exercise self-restraint in particular in order for the people to feel secure about following them. Even the autocrat cannot abuse the readiness of their people to comply (Kostka & Zhang 2018; Bo, Böhm & Reynolds 2019; Jessen & von Eggers 2020). In the case of abuse, society collapses due to the division between the discursive and living people. The indicator of this split is the people's incapacity to follow. Indeed, an incapacity to follow the autocrat or, to a lesser extent, a pretence to follow them (Wang 2022b), on the part of their subjects, would be disastrous for the autocrat. Confucius told his students that disengagement would be his precise conscious action during a time of abuse (Chapter Tai Bo of *The Analects*), and it was widely considered in the Chinese classic texts, even before Confucianism achieved its prominent status, as a spontaneous consequence (Valdez 2016), collectively and a posteriori realized by the entire people.

Disengagement appears counterproductive from the state-and-society perspective, to the extent that alienation reinforces the monopoly of the state. This challenge is amorphous and weak. Disengagement is powerful, though, when the incentive is not merely to challenge the legitimacy of the electoral system or a particular incumbent party. In an autocracy, disengagement is an indirect but targeted call for a substitute for the incumbent autocrat. It is an acute accusation of the immoral autocrat, who knows their increasing isolation but has no clue to predict their people's next moves. The people do not know, either, since they disengage. Realization of regime collapse only takes place a posteriori through unpredictable events.

Counter-governmentality
The people's hearts (民心)
In the classics, winning the people's hearts concerns welfare, security, and trust in the autocrat to protect them (Chapter Yanyuan of *The Analects*). Confucius was not alone during his time in warning kings that their typically acquiescent subjects might choose to migrate upon abusive governance, which referred mainly to the over-extraction of labour and crops. Confucius justified his normative advice by invoking the law-like inevitability that bad autocrats fall. Cosmologically, all lives are like gifts, granted by heaven and earth (Chapter Xici of *Zhou Yi* or *The Book of Changes*). Therefore, the king has 'the mandate of heaven' (天命) to care for the people as a father for his children. Note the reiteration in the classics that Heaven sees and hears

the world through the eyes and ears of the people (originally from Chapter Taishi II of the *Book of Documents*). The loss of a mandate would leave a king without troops or crops because the compliant, submissive people do not know how to follow those who impose high levies or resort to killing in order to rule.

Without the protected affluence that the people can enjoy, they would cease to respect the autocrat. Their common heavenly father was represented by the king, to whom the people's disengagement would seem horrifying. Cosmologically, the king would be considered to have been abandoned by Heaven. Indeed, a prevalent topic in the classics is how rulers might keep the people on side. This mandate may be a metaphor for 'the natural contract' between heaven and the king, in contrast to the social contract between each individual and Leviathan (more about this in Chapter 2). A useful reminder is that Heaven and the people in the collective represent each other. Heaven is not transcendental. As individuals, people are entitled to neither rights nor power, but their migration and disengagement in the quest for living one by one indicate the collective retrieval of the mandate. That's why someone dying of starvation at the roadside is considered the most extreme disengagement and, therefore, the strongest accusation.

An analysis of autocratic governmentality must interrogate how Confucianism cultivates the consciousness of the autocrat as the agent of heaven to desire and cooperate under the mandate of heaven. In this sense, the readiness of the people to migrate or disengage collectively conveys counter-governmentality's breakdown, as indicated a posteriori by discursive people's revealed falsehood. Counter-governmentality distinguishes Confucianism from the benign colonialism of modern times (Arneil 2021), because kings who subscribed to counter-governmentality would refrain from engaging in over-extraction in order to ward off the aforementioned falsehood, with the effect that claiming 'the people's hearts' was the king's most significant mission.

To win their hearts, Confucius listed four agendas: the people's trust, food, funerals, and ancestor worship (Chapter Yaoyue of *The Analects*). All four combined ensure an autocrat-as-society, with the first two conducting benevolent governance and the latter two reinforcing the cosmological relation that exists between them. Consider the following Confucian lessons regarding whether or not an autocrat wishes to care for their people:

- Providing people with a secure source for an affluent life – 'those without stable land lack a stable heart' (Chapter Duke Wen of Ten I of *Mengzi*);
- Displaying benevolence toward enemy peoples, preserving animals as the people's reproductive resource, and respecting all ancestors as sharing the same heaven, respectively – three narratives about relatively weak kings

winning the people's hearts, including by abolishing the sentence of burning to death, restraining overhunting, and preserving the graves of the enemy's ancestors (Chapter Respecting Talent of *Garden of Stories*);
- Prioritizing the cultivation of the king's virtue over his efficiency in extraction – good administration leads only to good treasure, whereas good exemplification further ensures that the people's hearts will be won (Chapter Jinxin I of *Mengzi*);
- Sustaining the people as part of the king – 'the king guides the people's mind, and the people are the king's body', so the king lives and dies with the people (Chapter Ziyi of *Book of Rites*); and
- Detecting and enabling people's wishes – 'winning all under heaven means winning the people's hearts', which requires satisfying their desires and avoiding what they dislike (Chapter Lilou I of *Mengzi*).

Among many similar others, these references to the people's hearts unanimously concern the king's benevolence toward the people.

For the purpose of emancipating the contemporary use of democracy and incorporating the notion of the people's hearts, it is critical to review further the classic Chinese narratives on the term *minzhu*. As *min* denotes the people and *zhu* the master, *minzhu* means 'the people's master'. In the ancient narrative, *minzhu* consistently refers to those premodern kings, dukes, and princes, who possess feudal entitlements and the power to extract. The term in itself fails to explain how to differentiate this title from the word 'king'. Rarely noticed, however, is the fact that the term has served as a double entendre since early modern times. The same term has been employed to translate the English term 'democracy' since the late Qing period and was popularized by Japanese modern thinkers, for *min* and *zhu* together can also connote 'the people as the master'. As a result, both the people's master in the classic texts and the people as the master today are expressed using the same characters in modern times. The following narrative analysis may indirectly demonstrate that the discourse on the people's master may atavistically pre-empt the evolution of 'the people as the master' into autonomous individuals.

Given that the narratives regarding the people's hearts persist in modern times, this sort of intellectual exercise continues to have practical implications. In a nutshell, 'the people as the master' refers to the collective people rather than the aggregate of individuals. Recently, with his frequent references to the people's hearts, the Chinese President and CCP Chair, Xi Jinping, left his own mark on what constitutes discursive people. He coined the notion of a 'whole-process people's democracy' to declare that (his discursive) people are involved in every step of deciding and overseeing the personnel and policies. The term 'whole-process' should mean a collective style of democracy, where their 'master', as an obligation, constantly investigates and cares for the people collectively (Ben-Eliezer 1993; Shih 1999; He 2006). Anyone, out of distrust or dissidence, would stress living people's practices and conditions to reveal the incongruence with discursive people in whole-process democracy, thus unconsciously reproducing the Confucian inevitability of resorting to the people's hearts in theory and disengagement in practice.

Counter-governmentality by induction

An in-depth reading of the classic narratives on 'the people's master' reveals a linkage to the modern notion of 'the people as the master'. According to the ensuing induction, the term 'the people's master' stresses 'the people' far more than 'the master' in the sense that the people have an a priori existence, to which any master must likewise belong. Compared to the references to kings, dukes, princes, and gentlemen, the term 'the people's master' is invoked as a relegated description. As for the formal titles (that is, kings, dukes, or princes) that are used widely in the classics, these typically refer to superior roles and positions that require rituals of respect. In contrast, the term 'the people's master' describes a person who faces the people without being either superior or mandated. Past studies of the Chinese classics, and Confucianism in particular, have yet to notice such usage, not to mention the distinctive warning and the alluded counter-governmentality it carries.

The references to the people's master in the classic texts reveal the consequences of losing the people's hearts, a metaphoric expression of trust in today's liberal democracy (Li 2010). Three possible consequences ensue: discursive people will disappear upon people's unpredictability; they will leave for another master; or they will either slay the master or welcome another who can. Under modern conditions, unpredictability can be broadly defined as 'uncertainty in the force and direction of arousal, what triggers it, and when triggered'. Unpredictability is tantamount to a charge that the autocracy is isolated rather than loved. The incongruence between the discursive and living people breeds unpredictability.

The following narrative analyses empirically collect all of the available warnings in the records in the 'Chinese Text Project' (available at https://ctext.org/) that the people's master should consider when the term *minzhu* is used explicitly in the classic texts. Such confusion related to the word 'master' across three millennia implies that it has never been discursively separate from the people, as a distinct entity. The same must be true regarding the contemporary use of the term *minzhu* as democracy, which likewise contains these two terms. As such, governmentality is necessarily an embedded relation, constituting both the autocrat and their subjects. Reading each of the ten narratives currently available yields ten ways to falsify the benevolence of the people's master, although implicit overlapping between them is inevitable.

1. Holding an unreliable attitude toward crops

The three earliest references to *minzhu* include the following two references in *The Chronicle of Zuo* (4th–3rd century BC). A report by a Lu official attending a rite of crops in the Qi Kingdom noted the rumour that the Qi people were to be fed using Lu's crops. This led to the impression that the prince of Qi, as 'the people's master', uttered erratic words that were incompatible with his most important duty; hence, the comment that he was destined to demise.

2. Spreading erratic words that were incompatible with the king's role

Shusun Bao, a Lu official, delivered a report to his king concerning his meeting with the head of the Zhaos, one of the three most prominent families of the Jin kingdom. Shusun believed that his host's days were numbered, for his erratic words were incompatible with the role of 'the people's master'. Shushun advised his king to establish a relation with his most plausible successor. However, the Duke of Lu considered occasional erratic words as normal for all. Shushun thus regretted that his king's days were probably likewise numbered. Both kings passed away shortly afterward.

3. Being unforgiving to the losing subjects

Both *The Discourses of the Kingdoms* (5th century BCE) and *The Chronicle of Zuo* recorded the story of Pi, a eunuch, who persuaded Chong Er, the new prince of Jin, to accept Pi's allegiance. Pi used to serve two rival princes, each of whom ordered him to kill Chong Er before the latter became Prince of Jin. Chong Er thus refused to meet Pi, due to his past enmity. Pi reminded Chong Er that Pi had only been playing a role in fulfilling his duty. He warned Chong Er that, unless he were allowed to show loyalty to the new 'people's master' but forced to leave instead, many others like him would also leave. Chong Er would lose all of these talented officials. Pi thus successfully gained acceptance by Chong Er. He later thwarted an assassination attempt against his new master.

4. Failing integrity

In the *Lost Book of Zhou* (3rd century BCE), 'the people's master' was advised to be clear about right and wrong so that his children could learn respect and even the birds and animals could demonstrate the virtue of benevolence. This connotes an ecological harmony, presumably because of the king's restraint from excessive killing and consuming natural living things.

5. *Committing extravagance and arrogance*

In Jia Yi's *New Book* (2nd century BCE), he noted that Zhou, the last Emperor of the Shang Dynasty, became 'the people's master' due to circumstances, but was avoided by his people, eventually abandoned by his troops, and abused by onlookers even after fighting alone to his death, all because he had disdained his role and propriety, failed to display gratitude and vigilance, and indulged in unrestrained arrogance. Although the onlookers were unconnected, Jia Yi found that they could desert Zhou simultaneously, as if a 'prior contract' had existed between them. According to Jia Yi, Zhou's decline began with his love for ivory chopsticks, indicating hubris. The master was guilty of his unalerted evil. A small sin and a great evil were of the same nature.

6. *Executing those who committed misdemeanours heartlessly*

In *The Records of the Three Kingdoms* (3rd–4th century), a local official was recorded as being 'the people's master'; he tried to appease an invited immigrant, Mu, by abiding by the law and executing a countryman who seized crops that Mu had grown. Mu, by contrast, disapproved of the execution and departed, despite the official soliciting his return. Mu built his reputation due to his tolerant nature.

7. *Being indifferent to the people's hardship*

The Record of the Three Kingdoms (280s) also records a conversation between Xia Houdun and the King of Wei. Xia advised the king that "since ancient times, anyone who can relieve the people from hardship and gain their trust is the 'people's master'". The king accordingly reiterated that the aim of politics is to gain the people's trust.

8. *Defecting to rebels*

In *The Collection of Literature Arranged by Categories* (624), anyone following a betrayer was hardly qualified to be 'the people's master'.

9. *Committing self-involvement*

In *The Principles of Governing from Many Books* (631), 'the people's master' would fail if he were too self-obsessed or self-glorifying, and insufficiently accessible to allow the people to perform their best or reveal their feelings fully to him.

10. Setting a bad example to the people

In *The Book of Zhou* (636), Heaven bestowed the mandate on the Emperor of the Shang to adopt the role of the people's master after the Emperor of Xia and his people all lost the mandate of Heaven.

Discussion: cultural continuity in postmodern times

The idea of the people in the degrading title 'the people's master' refers to discursive people, as in the upgrading norm 'the people as master'. The discursive people's thread has continued to constitute Chinese autocracy through into the 21st century, albeit in the name of democracy. The idea of people is more relevant than the specific discourses of people in different epochs and contexts in motivating autocrats to care for them. Discursive people, embedded in the competition for the people's hearts, ensure that the state and society are discursive. Autocracy must be a democracy at the same time, provided that counter-governmentality defines the autocrat's self-identity. Even when the autocrat betrays themselves by failing to amend the incongruence between discursive and living people, incurs unpredictable disengaging behaviour, and finally ruins their regime, their demise will reproduce the idea of the people's hearts in subsequent regimes, which informs the regime of regimes. Under counter-governmentality, no romanticized society requires defending, nor does a separate state need expanding, as the autocrat must belong to the people.

On the other hand, the rise of mass society in modern times still makes a significant difference. Foucault recorded the classic debate about 'the meeting point between philosophical truth-telling and political practice [that] found two points of insertion: the public arena or the Prince's soul'. In a modern, mass society, the incongruence and non-coincidence between discursive (philosophical truth) and living (political practice) people challenges not only the autocrat's soul but also the enlightened masses, for the theme 'the people's hearts' constitutes the public discourse in addition to the autocrat's enlightenment (Foucault 2008c: 292). In other words, living people not only know discursive people in the form of 'vulgar Confucianism' but also grow through an indoctrination pedagogy to surrender their hearts (Berger 1983; also see Cheek 1997). Given that the autocrat grows through the same self-/indoctrination, people's loss, failure, and stupidity synchronically allude to those of the autocrat.

Even in premodern times, Confucians predicted that things that prompt incongruence with discursive people would occur. They mentioned many possible instances of this. One typical sign was migration to a place where a benevolent autocrat might be found. Rightfully, an appeal to a higher-level governor is another alternative, if the abuse occurs at a lower level (O'Brien and Li 2006). Protest is yet a third alternative, one that is becoming popular in the current century (Perry 2009). Further, Mencius mentioned revolution and slaying the autocrat, as indicated in the fifth narrative scenario listed previously. These are neither Confucian advice nor norms. Rather, these are predictions that connote inevitable uncertainty, unpredictability, or volatility. The discursive idea of the people has a weaker influence on the identities of living people than their leader. These possibilities remind the autocrat of a dissolving autocracy to which they might no longer belong. Under this circumstance, the meme is that anyone can slay the autocrat legitimately, even today. This is the source of an existential threat to them. Parallel to Foucault's ironic title 'society must be defended', counter-governmentality suggests 'the people must be loved'.

In addition, modern autocracy differs from premodern or classic autocracy with regard to the former's need to belong to the territorial state with borders and acquire citizenship, that keeps people from crossing borders. Postmodern autocracy consists of multiple, nuanced identities that align individuals who can invoke their peculiar sensibilities to join forces with others coming from other sensibilities to execute a common project, a shared relation, or simply a collective action at a site. Even postmodern autocracy investigate people's need as an abstract duty. The power of counter-governmentality is unrelated to the number of people in a union of resistance, which could quickly crash in the CCP's case, but from the incongruence with abstract people, for example, from an image of the starving body instantly invoking the emergence of a thousand others, which rocks the autocrat's self-identity and stirs their anxiety about unpredictable events occurring around them physically.

Manoeuvres of counter-governmentality in modern times strategize alienation, sabotage, idleness, misinformation, cynicism, over-flattery, West-worshiping, and so on, in the present day. Counter-governmentality allows the people to be generally perceptive about the estranging messages of these disengaging tactics; any insinuated lack of benevolence could spread and shame the leadership (Schoenhals 1993). The degree of unpredictability is far higher, with the people's hearts attaining a strategic dimension, but one could never predict the series of surprises during the very unpopular third year of quarantine since the outbreak of the COVID-19 pandemic: first 'lying flat' to give up fighting the pandemic (Lin & Gullotta 2022), then 'collective crawling' on college campuses to abort interrogating the meaning of life (Mistreanu & Pan 2022), finally culminating in 'White Paper Protests', a silent protest (Thornton 2023: 75; Wu & Acharya 2023) which ended the three-year quarantine in three days. Being politically weak, incidents of revealed incongruence seriously threatened autocracy's legitimacy by methods of targeting that everyone understood, anticipated, and instantly emulated and, therefore, invoked the reversion of quarantine. Hearing criticism, for the people, is more exciting than its contents. The autocrat would certainly adjust but hardly continue on the liberalization track (Fukuyama 2020b).

Modern autocracy can create disciplined citizens, who can desire strong autocracy and mould themselves into discursive people according to autocratic indoctrination. This is well-researched in the aforementioned literature on the PRC's governmental conditionality. Self-governing citizens may remain consciously and willingly passive and submissive in the premodern sense (Cheek 1998), to the extent that the citizens are prepared (through indoctrination, embedded relationships, and economic dependence) to look mainly to autocracy to provide security and affluence for the system, the people, and the autocrat. Consequently, counter-governmentality creates a deep source of, often mysterious, authoritarian responsiveness (Heurlin 2016; Kornreich 2019; Wei, Yao and Zhang 2021). For a society that relies on the individual citizen's efforts to engage in self-defence, against state intrusion, this responsiveness makes little sense. However, if liberal governmentality, invoked by the state, enlightens the discursively self-defending society, counter-governmentality enables Chinese autocrats to care for discursive people. On the other hand, the Confucian ontology understands people as the autocrat's body; therefore the autocrat caring for their people (their body) is likewise a self-defence measure.

A counter-governmentality definition of democracy is due. Consider defining democracy under liberalism as 'exercising the natural right to government by consent' and democracy within Confucian autocracy as 'the spontaneous following of benevolent leadership'. Therefore, in the PRC or CCP autocracy, democracy is denoted by pursuing benevolence embedded in well-being and security in the eyes of the people rather than the depth and breadth of their participatory autonomy. Counter-governmentality compels the autocratic CCP constantly to adapt to the incongruence between the discursive and living people. Combined, liberalism and Confucianism point to a common desire for a style of policy making that is *exempt from a monopoly*. Liberal governmentality and counter-governmentality are respective measures for reversing the monopolizing tendency of those in power, regardless of governmentality. The sharing of governmentality by the state and society testifies to the state-as-society. Parallel governmentalities enable a pluriversal agenda of governmentalities and the state-as-society.

Under this composite definition of democracy, Confucian governmentality transcends the binary of liberalism versus socialism (Gan 2019; Tseng 2023). To the extent that Confucianism values the people's spontaneity, in line with John Locke and Adam Smith, and the welfare of the subaltern population/classes, in line with Karl Marx, Confucian autocracy preaches the people's autocracy. Liberalism and socialism collide in the institutionally desired level of state intervention, depending on whether the targets of this protection are each individual citizen or a collective class. For Confucianism, in contrast, the desired level of intervention cannot be institutionalized because the state is not separate from society. The level of intervention must be a practical decision, adapting to the conditions. That is why Confucianism shares common ground with both socialism and liberalism while being neither. For liberalism and socialism, democracy becomes a monopoly when the state seizes and allocates the people's property without their prior consent. Confucianism becomes a monopoly when the state fails to detect and adapt to the people's hearts.

Counter-governmentality periodically involutes because the autocrat takes for granted the people's submission and ceases to care for or be alert to the people's needs, that have been familiar to them since childhood. Living people lose their relevance. Counter-governmentality does not guide the people to revolt. Since the autocracy owns all of the resources for controlling information, deferring reform, and promoting the cult of autocracy, alienation, in its various forms, is the sensible way of recalling counter-governmentality. Restoration necessarily relies on those autocrats who were cultivated with counter-governmentality to proceed. Therefore, counter-governmentality is always cyclical, but by no means elegant. The long game of counter-governmentality means that the autocracy can retrieve its forgotten duties, either with a different regime resorting to, or the same regime surviving on, timely reform. In these cycles, the unpredictable strategizing of the people's hearts for a tentative victory over the government (such as the White Paper Protests that overturned the quarantine earlier than the autocracy would have wished) reproduces an adaptive autocracy that is in line with the regime of regimes.

Two caveats regarding counter-governmentality can plague the people's well-being. Consider Confucius' advice to win the people's hearts by feeding and protecting them. It alludes to the relative insignificance of corruption, inequality, and abuse in the conducting of counter-governmentality (Hsu 2001; Harding 2014). In other words, the autocrat can survive if they allow sufficient resources for their people to live minimally. The literature on authoritarian resilience focuses on this. Only during economic hardship would corruption, inequality, and the abuse of power cause unpredictability for living people, because submissive, compliant consciousness is insufficient for survival, not to mention happiness. That said, the autocrat would not tolerate corrupt officialdom to be publicized, as their (relatively affluent) people might read corruption as aborted selflessness. In addition, officials who embezzle public property might jeopardize the people's sense of security and trust in the autocracy (Zeng 2014; Li & Xiao 2016). Nevertheless, corruption is not an urgent threat to the people, especially when associated with those of high status, as if they were entitled to engage in it.

The other caveat regarding counter-governmentality is the rise of modern nationalism (Downs & Saunders 1999). Nationalism has a parallel in Chinese, although it is classically termed 'cultural or dynastic revival' rather than 'nationalism'. In modern times, the nation-building by the PRC and its predecessor, the Republic of China (1911–49), has relied heavily on anti-imperialism. Throughout these historical periods, having been fixed to bounded space (Dumm 1996), the people, together with the autocracy, desired revival (Krolikowski 2018). Nationalism can justify distraction from the people's well-being by providing security and dignity. As a counter-governmentality pressure on the autocrat, nationalism simultaneously imposes a mode of 'counter-counter-governmentality' – conduct that prepares all to cooperate over the substitution of nationalist mobilization/extraction for the promotion of well-being. On the one hand, rivalry within international relations is intrinsic to counter-counter-governmentality. On the other, autocracy is subject to a few higher modes of governmentality, for example, sovereignty, NGOs, modernity, and postcolonialism (Smart & Smart 2017; Meinhof 2018; Liu & Palmer 2021); Fanoulis & Song 2022), forces either promoting or suppressing nationalism. These many possibilities will result in a cycle of liberal governmentality, Confucian counter-governmentality, and nationalist counter-counter-governmentality for an autocracy-as-society.

Conclusion

Past studies of the state and society within China's autocracy are short of an engagement with how the autocrat and society discursively subscribe to shared conduct to make them mutually cooperative with regard to understanding and desiring a governance idea that is anchored in the people's hearts. Past studies of Chinese governmentality have attended to the autocratic appropriation of neoliberal governmentality to achieve the autocrat's purpose of governance. The notion of counter-governmentality supplements the state-in-society approach to the study of autocracy by providing its discursive constitution, which prepares both the autocrat and their people to focus on the latter's well-being in governance. It adds the autocrat to the list of objects of governmentality to explain how they care and fear. Counter-governmentality within Chinese autocracy sensitizes the signs of disengagement, to the detriment of trust in the autocrat. The autocrat understands and dreads the implications of failing to care for their people's well-being. While their subjects lack the right to vote out an abusive, omniscient autocrat, the unpredictable behaviour of the people, bureaucrats, factions, and international rivals threatens to expose any incongruence between the discursive and living people and compels the autocrat back onto the track of benevolence. Counter-governmentality testifies that the people are part of an autocracy and that an autocracy is part of society.

Given the change and continuity of all regimes and their practices, counter-governmentality – with its cosmological roots and cultural embeddedness – belongs to the continuity realm, which is incompatible with the postmodern sensibilities toward discontinuity, deconstruction, or instability. The regime of regimes is discursive and even linguistic, as the utterance of the people's hearts has become an unavoidable political grammar, that recurs in the historical records and is repeated during important rituals. As such, counter-governmentality, informed by the people's hearts, has been necessarily recorded as collective, in-depth, patient, inarticulate, spontaneous, intermittent, and versatile for almost three thousand years, since Confucius' time.

Counter-governmentality conveys a consistent message that the people spontaneously follow the most benevolent leader. This message resonates with the dictum of government by consent of liberal governmentality, since both types of governmentality seek to reduce the monopoly over policy making. However, counter-governmentality is additionally exempt from a majoritarian monopoly over issues concerning minorities (Abizadeh 2021). To avoid an involution period, liberal governmentality relies on the people to vote out the incumbent. By doing so, the people strengthen their desires and cooperation to compliment liberal governmentality. Still, counter-governmentality ultimately reveals the level of cultivation of the (abstract) people's hearts with the incumbent autocracy, while the (living) people's readiness to alienate themselves from the regime and enact solidarity with each other determines this level.

2

Restoring Normalcy during Involution

Introduction

This chapter proceeds to compare democracy and autocracy in terms of the people's hearts and crosses the stereotypical binaries between the two concepts. It purports to explain why liberal democracy cannot recover from involution but that socialist and Confucian autocracy might. The logic likewise concerns governmentality. If governmentality is primarily about cultivating norms, involution occurs when enforcing and practising norms paradoxically harms the norms. As bad money drives out good, those benefiting from breaking norms will be emulated. In comparison, if governmentality is about law-like inevitability, subscribers may have incentives to avoid defying the inevitable and endeavour to restore norms as their coping strategy. Liberal democracy is a norm rather than a law-like inevitability. Its philosophical foundation is Christianity, which informs equality and individualism. By adopting methodological individualism, however, social science mistakenly studies liberal democracy as if it were inevitable. On the other hand, Confucianism appears to be a normative school yet, along with all other Chinese schools of thought, premodern and contemporary, it subscribes to a consensual, law-like inevitability about the power of 'people's hearts'.

The confusion created by the misconceived norm-driven science and law-driven norm distracts attention from their different epistemologies of involution. Discussing this hitherto neglected epistemology contributes to a deeper, more comprehensive understanding of democracy vis-à-vis autocracy.

The purpose of this chapter is to provide a theoretical logic, as opposed to empirical evidence, concerning why liberal democracy cannot restore normalcy from the institutional and moral recession, while autocracy might. It begins by discussing governmentality's nature, as a norm or law-like inevitability. A theoretical comparison regarding leaders' accountability and involution follows. Without abandoning the relevance of socialism, the rest of the chapter mainly attends to its constitution by Confucian governmentality. Then, deliberative democracy and the mass line are compared as remedies to involution for each system, with an additional note on the original sin. In a nutshell, liberalism's normative governmentality is not binding, even though leaders subscribe to it. Recovery is unnecessary for liberal leadership to think about a survival strategy.

Democratic recession and studies of democracy

As Arthur Schlesinger Jr once remarked, 'republics lived and died by virtue – and that in the fullness of time power and luxury inexorably brought corruption and decay' (Schlesinger 1986: 6) However, the literature has not compared how democracy and autocracy cope with such institutional involution, either empirically or theoretically (Wahman et al 2013; Hadenius & Teorell 2007). The existing points of comparison concern accountability, efficiency, stability, international power, and so on (Chang et al 2013; Hyde & Saunders 2020; Kroenig 2020; Mauk 2020). However, democracy is facing a recession in the 21st century (Crouch 2004; 2020). All kinds of social cleavages, as well as the exacerbating class stratification and populism, are rampant in almost every leading democracy. Internally, trust in democratic leadership and institutions yields to that in authoritarian leaders (Rosta & Tóth 2021). The rising political alienation reflects the loss of participatory efficacy among the electoral constituencies. Externally, an autocratic alternative, that is, the People's Republic of China (PRC), threatens to represent a plausible substitute – a role model for development and non-intervention that allows the Global South postcolonies to reconsider alternatives to liberal democracy. Therefore, recovering governmentality during involution deserves a place on the comparison list.

It is a cliché to say that (liberal) democracy is not perfect but, to date, the best available political system and definitely better than autocracy (Kennedy 1963). The invincible advantage of democracy is, to say the least, that: 'it peacefully holds accountable leaders who don't fulfill their promises' (Stavridis 2018: 39; Helms 2020). In contrast, autocratic forms of transition swing between arranged heir apparent, negotiation, revolution, coup d'état, systemic collapse, and foreign intervention, or a combination of these, which causes uncertainty and sometimes violence (Jason 2007; Barbara et al 2014; Erica & Elizabeth 2017; Andrej & Anders 2020). The feature of leadership transition presumably demonstrates that people who live in liberal democracies place a limit on the government's power. Despite the nuances and technicalities, liberal democracy is considered, in principle, long-lasting, rational, and relatively just.

The moral binary of democracy and autocracy appears so logical that even a widely considered autocratic leadership would wish to claim democracy in order to pretend legitimacy (Kailitz 2013). So, it is necessary to restrict the reference to liberal democracy in the following discussion to only those regimes that rule with the consent of the ruled, obtained via regular, competitive elections for government officials. However, there exists more than one kind of liberal democracy. Deliberative democracy, for example, is presumably a remedy for the populist involution of liberal democracy worldwide, including the use of ideological, ethnic, religious, and indigenous correctness by political parties, that inflicts serious discrimination, stratification, and social cleavages upon democratic regimes.

Democratic recession challenges the political science research that has mainly engaged in two related, politically correct agendas since the end of WWII. The first agenda is the democratization of the Global South nations (Riedl et al 2020; Skaaning 2020; Boese et al 2021). This agenda adapts to the evolving democratic conditions of these postcolonies. It began with their alleged need for liberal values and institutions to execute democratization. Then, it proceeds to democratic transition and consolidation, as well as authoritarian resilience 'precisely when they most want to hear it' (Morefield 2022: 781). The other agenda monitors and explains the vicissitude within voters' democratic attitudes under different national systems. A representative example is the Global Barometer Survey (see https://www.globalbarometer.net/). Despite periodical retreats, both agendas take for granted that any reasonable person, who is entitled to a governing regime that achieves the consent of the ruled and operates peacefully and stably, would accept the necessity and inevitability of becoming democratic. These agendas are no longer sufficient, given the democratic recession everywhere. Illiberal democracy does not seem to move from autocracy to liberal democracy. Reflecting 'the flaws and failings of democratic systems' (Mounk 2021: 163), the trend appears to be in the opposite direction.

More importantly, democratic recession challenges the very consensually held assumptions about the advantages of democracy over autocracy, granting that the latter has as many kinds as democracy (Wright 2021). In other words, democratic regimes are neither peaceful, given the expanding extent of domestic violence and frequency of external war associated with them, nor more accountable, since, arguably, the level of the people's satisfaction with the governance situation can seem higher within China's socialist autocracy (Chu 2013), for example, than in the US's liberal democracy. Such an irony calls for a revisiting of the core assumptions concerning the advantages of liberal democracy over autocracy and a critique regarding why the former is incapable of recovery.

Normative liberalism versus law-like Confucianism

Against the widespread impression that Chinese political theory is idealistic while modern political theory is scientific (Holbig 2013), a law-like sensibility regarding the demise of bad autocracy already existed five thousand years ago in Chinese historiography. It is simultaneously about 'the people's hearts', that attest to the quality of an autocrat. During the Spring and Autumn period (771–476 BCE), it prompted various versions of what we can call autocratic governmentality today, with Confucius being only one of them, to be differentiated from other schools, such as Daoism, Legalism, Mohism, Agriculturalism, the School of Nomenclature, and so on. It is unclear which rigorous procedures undergirded the historical enlightenment – that bad autocrats ultimately fall – that all of these ancient schools shared. 'Winning the people's hearts' ('得民心') and 'soothing the people's hearts' ('顺民心') are phrases that appear repeatedly in the classics. During the 21st century, the same term continues to engross the top leaders of the Chinese Communist Party (CCP) (Wu 2022). Xi Jingpin's utterance in January 2016, "the greatest politics is about the people's hearts" ("民心是最大的政治"), has been reiterated from time to time thereafter (Xu 2022). Xi's many critics likewise accuse him of losing the people's hearts. A span of much longer than five thousand years was a powerful test in itself for any consensual governmentality that emerged. Empirical research on modern 'inclusionary' autocracy confirms similar success with the people's 'minds and hearts' (Neundorf et al 2020). In this regard, stable governmentality refers to 'all practicing mutually conducive governing normalcy' that facilitates governing.

Accordingly, all premodern thinkers agreed that the people's hearts could determine the life and death of a regime. The consensus connoted the reality that these schools believed they faced, rather than the norms that they used to judge right from wrong. They embraced the law-like sensibility as the starting point for crafting the political norms and preached to princes how to compete for the people's hearts. Daoism taught that the best way to avoid losing the people's hearts was to remove their expectations by doing nothing (Sun & Sun 2023: 18), thus challenging the Confucian promise to feed, protect, and educate the people. For another example, due to its doubt regarding the regime's capacity to retain the people's hearts, Legalism suggested simultaneously cultivating petty incentives and punishing wrongdoing in order to co-opt their hearts (King 2020). Mohism advocated a peace-loving troop that would indiscriminately defend against invasion anywhere in order to inspire the people's hearts (Chapter 'Zashou' of *Mozi*). The School of Nomenclature's wishful regime was so nuanced that every policy or law was to be distinctively amended to fit every differing person (Yang 1990: 99–102; Shih & Yu 2015: 26–35). Xu Xing's (roughly 372–289 BCE) School of Agriculturalism endeavoured to convince princes that they should personally cultivate the fields, like a peasant, to convince everyone of absolute equality (Chapter Tengwengong I of *Mengzi*).

All thinkers prior to the Han Dynasty and all Confucians after it felt compelled to cope with this governing normalcy as self-restraining enlightenment. For Confucians, benevolence toward the people was the answer, but its contents were intensely debated. Even Confucianism was, in itself, a belated missionary label, posthumously applied to premodern history. Even so, generations of Confucians employ the unfailing theme of 'the people's hearts' to discuss politics, regardless of their variety and incompatibility regarding how, philosophically, to read the classics and practise moral teaching. The factual nature of the theme, in their eyes, as in the eyes of almost every other pre-Han political philosopher, was firm and beyond their influence. Confucianism was merely 'an art of governance' (Lee 2020: 82), and one among many. Despite many points of contention, the contending schools did not question the key wisdom of several centennials, that is, no people, no regime, and vice versa, as Confucius was quoted in Chapter Ziyi of the *Book of Rites*: 'To the people, the ruler is as their heart; to the ruler, the people are as his body.'

Note that, as with the other schools, except for the School of Nomenclature, their references to people did not allow any individuality. It was exclusively down to the autocrats' performance to determine how *collectively* the people could feel secure or insecure. The collective nature of the people's hearts regarding a particular regime would not be easily subjected to preference manipulation, as in the situation where each individual articulated preferences and, as an aggregate, could be subjected to division and rule. Given that the collective could not become an owner of preference, the autocracy could neither anticipate nor control it. They would thus resort to pre-emption instead. In the Chinese classics, the second-ordered inevitability, reality, objectivity, and restraint for all autocracies to heed was that *the people's hearts were volatile*. There are numerous references in the Chinese Text Project (https://ctext.org/) of various schools of thought to the people's hearts being easily lost (失), offended (逆), disintegrated (不一), unstable (不定), turned away (外), unpredictable (无常), confused (惑), betrayed (违), shaken (摇动), rocked (摇荡), shallow (靡薄), drifting (无所法循), or altered (变). The people's hearts formed the foundation of Chinese autocratic governmentality across the board. All learned persons viewed them as the ultimate yet unownable power source, crafted norms for autocrats to remember to honour them constantly, and created policies to pre-empt their estrangement.

There was no guarantee that autocrats, despite their knowledge of the law-like warning, would practice benevolence, however. The majority probably did not. Mencius (372–289 BCE) commented that history before him could witness a kingly ruler, who could win the people's hearts literally, every 500 years, on average (Chapter Gongsun Chou I of *Mengzi*). After all, benevolence is a role that maintains the credit of autocratic governmentality so that the people remain integrated by belonging to an imagined benevolent regime. The advisors and dutiful officials who performed benevolent love heeded the people's hearts on behalf of the autocrat, who would be deposed otherwise, according to the law of demise. In short, the regime, rather than its people, is responsible for stabilizing potentially volatile hearts. To my knowledge, the law-like objectivity that the regime causes its own fate has not been interrogated previously in the records.

This flow of Chinese history of thought, from this shared enlightenment, based on a long history – that is, a premodern version of social science – to the contending normative interpretations to cope with it, continues to evolve today. Despite the diverging versions of Confucianism, the law-driven normative interrogation of benevolence contrasts with the evolution of modern Western political knowledge. The latter crafted a progressive modernist historiography to invoke a normative solution to the endless wars between different kingdoms and churches. Philip Schaff (2022: 140), for example, notes that 'church has made herself almost more offensive in the eyes of the world and of modern civilization than by her peculiar doctrines and usages'. The solution then emerged from the prolonged embedding of the Renaissance, the Reformation, and the Industrial Revolution, with a transcendent, albeit intensely disputed, image of God as the sole common thread (Zafirovski 2021; Gregory 2022). The modernist interpretation of this image that all human beings were created equal became the normative foundation of modern social science, whose methodology was individualistic and whose core subject consistently pertained to the limitation of governing power by the ruled (diZerega 2020), and hence reifications and the reproduction of individualism qua liberalism.

Ironically, this normatively driven science acquires an objective appearance. On the other hand, however, normative hybridity in contemporary Confucian/socialist China, prompted by the law of autocratic governmentality, attains an idealist image in the eyes of social scientists. For scientists, God is transcendent, rather than historical, empirical, or apparent in terms of His will. Liberalism, as well as Christianity, takes individuals as the motor of politics and history for granted and explains the fate of a regime by giving credit to the choices of individual members (Iorio & Chen 2019; Neck 2021), but not explaining. However, liberalism-informed social science fails to explain why (for example, by or against the Heavenly Mandate), or how (for example, through benevolence or extraction), regimes – the autocracy and the autocrat – satisfy or fail the people's hearts collectively, as Confucianism does. The individual-oriented lens was a normative critique aimed at transforming medieval politics composed of churches and kingdoms. For liberalism, no social science can be morally acceptable unless initiatives for actions and their consequences begin with individuals.

To substantiate individuality, individuals' innate capacity to form opinions and preferences are the ultimate factor in determining and explaining behaviour (Mauk 2020: 17), only behind the Creator, who enables 'all modern revolutions' (Arendt 1977: 16). For a noticeable example, Almond and Verba's system theory begins with how the citizens articulate their interests regarding the political parties to aggregate them into platforms: the citizens vote for a ruling party; the constitution checks the government's power wielded by the ruling party; and the citizens assess the government's policy (Almond & Verba 1963; Almond et al 1996). This is an awkward theory for understanding regime-centred governmentality. The latter is by no means exclusively Chinese or Confucian.

The intellectual history of US political science thus suggests a quest for law-like explanations that are informed by liberal norms, contrasting with the intellectual history of Confucianism. The former considers individuals' innate capacity to choose, which is essential to scientific research even though misinformation can seriously influence individuals' preferences. The latter strategizes norms for the regime to survive the law-like inevitability: bad autocrats ultimately fall (despite individuals possessing no recognized roles to coordinate for the falling to happen).

Christianity, liberalism, and individualism are closely connected. Even so, every normative stance evolves into different versions and schools of thought as under Confucianism. In the US case, the behaviouralist offensive in the 1940s and 50s was a noticeable example. Amid the fascist and communist challenges of the time, the debate was simultaneously focused on the fate of liberalism (not least due to its individualist relativism that allegedly tolerated fascism) within political science (Greenstein 1968; Gunnell 1988). During this brief period of confusion, David Easton, an ardent supporter of scientific study, manifestly revealed, as a snapshot of the disciplinary future, that his system theory was founded on sustaining and advancing liberal democratic values (Easton 1950; Easton 1953; Gunnell 1988: 80). The system theory has dominated the subsequent comparative politics agenda. Combined with neo-institutionalism, which is informed by a higher statist and collective sensibility, since the 1980s, the same liberal premise has undergirded the curiosity regarding the state-and-society relation well into the current century (Immergut 1998). This relationship is likewise normatively individualist in nature.

People not caring versus people not cared for

Liberalism is a normative claim. Ideally, no one will face any inevitable outcome due to practising the norm. All individuals are entitled to distinctive preferences and are responsible for their choices. Why would anyone, people or leaders, yield unless they wish to? To yield is a virtue of solidarity for communitarians and philanthropy for individualists (Illingworth et al 2011; Laville & Eynaud 2019; Harvey et al 2021). Either way, the choice nevertheless lies in the hands of individuals. Therefore, the outcomes for each individual will always be conceived as uncertain to some extent. Subscription to liberalism offers no sure clue regarding the outcome. Theoretically, the outcome ought to be uncertain. After all, the inspiration for individuals to achieve upward mobility and self-fulfilment must appear plausible, in the eyes of the subaltern population above all, in order for liberalism to remain normatively convincing. This population refers to those who suffer a low fixed living standard due to insensitive governance, and its scope is increasing. Under Confucianism, uncertainty among the subaltern people can shake their volatile hearts and indicate the existence of a bad autocrat.

The social sciences research echoes democratic elections, since a common epistemological lens, embedded in individual preference, reproduces the incumbent norm of accountability. Through aggregation, based on the currently available statistics, the social sciences can analyze the distribution of individual preferences across all governance issues and normatively equalize all of them (Vaccaro 2021). There exist a multitude of these. Comparing democracy statistics is, in itself, a research agenda. Paradoxically, the social sciences thus release policy makers, together with the relatively well-to-do who support them, from feeling responsible for governance problems, provided that they can manage to attract sufficient votes. Even losing elections harms them very little. After all, the democratic transition to new leadership costs no one their life or property as a result. Moreover, the losers can rally at the next election and stand to win. Allegedly, with the governing power under democratic control and individual rights under protection, leaders by no means need to be morally conscious, although they can acknowledge their policy mistakes. There is nothing lethal that need concern the incumbent.

Nevertheless, all democracies suffer involution. Social democrats, for example, are alarmed at unequal distribution and welfare/poverty; environmentalists at over-extraction and pollution; and liberals at authoritarianism and/or populism. Other issues, such as economic dependency, national debt, the military-industrial complex, corruption, social, ethnic, and religious cleavages, the mafia and violence, and so on, are being exacerbated continuously (Harvey 2006; McAdam & Kloos 2014; Dougherty 2019; Karl 2019; Achiume 2021; Nyberg 2021). Retaining liberal governmentality by restoring a minimum of equal capacity of individual members is crucial in order to reverse the involution. However, beneath these exacerbating trends lies the increasing irrelevance of liberal values and popular voting with regard to coping with these points of involution. While, epistemologically, Confucianism regards the alienation or following of the people as a dependent variable that is contingent on the level of the autocrat's benevolence, individuals' capacity to form preferences and choices is the ultimate, independent variable in explaining policy making within a liberal democracy.

As a result, liberalism and social science reinforce each other in the opposite direction to Robert Putnam's foresight, which explored 'what are the conditions for creating strong, responsible, effective representative institutions' (Putnam 1993: 6, 8). Note the firm lens of liberalism in his conception of the model of governance: 'social demands → political interaction → government → policy choice → implementation'. Liberalism can do nothing when the voters have no alternative to candidates who are drawn mainly from a rich, elitist circle, seeking to protect their own, their associates' or their patrons' interests by assuming office repeatedly. All liberal democracies are composed of political families and partisans. Ironically, their winning or losing enables social sciences to claim the relevance of the voters' preferences, as if they could make a difference to governance issues, thus reinforcing and justifying liberalism. So, the political leaders do not need to care whenever they can get by with political correctness, the exchange of favours, and scapegoating. Accountability collapses to the extent that individual freedom is 'easily appropriated … for the most cynical and unemancipatory political ends' (Brown 1995: 5).

Granting that liberal governmentality cannot recover normalcy, restoration can still occur, however, in the aftermath of a war. The breakdown of the Taishao Democracy and the Weimar Republic witnessed a resurgence of democratic rigour respectively in Japan and Germany, for example, following their total defeat at the end of WWII. Jimmy Carter's human rights policy recovered the liberal rigour from the plague of Watergate and the loss of the Vietnam War, as another example. These were ironic, for they defied the myth that liberal democracy promises a peaceful leadership transition rather than the loss of an imperial war. Nevertheless, those who voted for the Nazis, however unfortunate that might be, could not be committing moral wrongdoing by choosing who they voted for. Liberalism as the norm has remained correct. After all, a normative value can do no wrong. In any case, those in power who master but escape accountability will launch the involution, sooner or later. Consequently, arguably, involution could only be ended by war. It would be perpetuated and exacerbated otherwise.

Confucian governmentality similarly suffers involution. At the societal level, the expanding population or merging of arable land led to pressure on resources (Elvin 1973; Hartwell 1982; Skinner 1985). At the court and policy levels, factions competed for the emperor's attention in order either to survive or triumph (Johnson 1966). The ruling group thus lost its focus on the people's welfare. Then, as bad money drives out good, the imperial officials worked only to benefit their own small circles. External wars, as well as other extravagant projects (such as canals, walls, and palaces), also unduly squeezed the imperial finances. At the personality level, autocrats were generally self-involved due to their supreme status (Zhao 2022). Bad autocrats were known for being incompetent, oppressive, lusty, lavish, and narrow-minded. The personal and national styles of governance are allegedly intertwined (Wang 2017). This personality tendency was an increasingly acute problem if, surrounded by eunuchs who accompanied their growing up, they had encountered no commoners outside the court before assuming the emperorship.

This unsystematic historiography reveals a consistent message about losing touch with the people, overlooking their conditions or wishes, and failing to gather feedback (note the 9th narrative cited in Chapter 1). For Confucianism, however, none of these involutions would matter to the virtual emperor as a role until they damaged the people's welfare and then blocked information about this. From its beginning, Confucianism was intended to represent a lesson for autocrats. It preached that, provided that the autocrats behaved correctly, people would fall into their roles (Chapter Yanyuan, *The Analects*). The indoctrination of the people would be redundant. Therefore, the indoctrination of advisors since the Han Dynasty and even people at the present time under the CCP rule would indicate involution because indoctrination would silence feedback but also excuse the emperor from caring for the people.

Opposite to the liberal myth that society controls the leadership, the Confucian view has autocrats on top, for society to emulate. The autocracy achieved peace by being selfless; in other words, it allowed an affluent society rather than an affluent court. An affluent society would be unachievable, according to Confucianism, if autocrats strove for power. They endangered the safety of their regimes if they extracted more than was strictly necessary to satisfy their thirst for more. As with the Christian practice, Confucius accepted 10% of the harvest as tax as a rule of thumb. This should be sufficient to cover the prince's needs, without needing to impose any further tax (Chapter Wangyanjie, *The Analects*). In a sense, Confucianism and liberalism share the same ideal of people living spontaneously and freely, but the duty to achieve such a positive state should fall differently on the shoulders of the autocrat and the people, respectively. Confucian autocracy is extremely cautious about coping with the volatility of the people's hearts. In comparison, liberal voters, who are responsible for ending involution, cannot invoke politicians' care beyond their revealed but shallow preferences. The voters may not care, either.

Liberalism as a norm gives people the moral power to restore normalcy but can do nothing if the people in aggregate fail to act. After all, liberalism is constituted by individualized taste (Wolf 2022). Adherents of Confucianism only wish to follow but cannot if their leaders remove their capacity to do so. They do not know when or how they will collectively lose the capacity to follow, that is, the capacity to earn a minimal living by staying rather than running away. Such collective volatility and unpredictability pose a threat to the security and stability of autocracy, because they allude to the loss of mutual belonging between the autocrat and the people. Conversely, uncertainty alludes to an opportunity for liberal individuals, contingent on the level of their efforts, as restrained by others' choices. Collective volatility compels autocrats constantly to bear in mind the people's capacity to stay with autocracy. Such volatility grows when the people are more deeply indoctrinated, because they endure and conceal their aggravating conditions. This is why an autocracy either detects a problem before it is too late and adapts, or awaits its demise. A common thread emerges between Confucians and liberals to cope with involution: getting as many people involved as possible (Pei 1991). Liberal governmentality must restore equity to open up a political monopoly by the elite; Confucian governmentality requires the people's practical conditions to arrange a survival strategy to pre-empt people's volatile hearts.

The mass line versus deliberative democracy

The mass line

When autocrats failed with regard to governance, indicated or caused directly by over-extraction and worsening distribution, they faced the pressure of autocratic counter-governmentality. In Chinese history, some recovered while others fell. Ending autocratic involution often called for violence. Accordingly, revolutions appeared inevitable throughout the cycles of Chinese history. Through revolution, future leaders recovered the people's hearts. According to Xunzi, 'pursuing self-interests without worry and releasing unlimited desires prompt impetuous, disaffected hearts of peoples' (Chapter Fuguo of *Xunzi*). Alternatively, out of disrespect for bad autocrats, high officials could split and end the autocracy from within through civil war. The violent uprisings at the margins, with the aim of breaking away from the empire, foretold the coming demise of an autocracy, too. On the other hand, however, ending involution could be renovative rather than violent. Advisors could convince emperors to launch reforms. Successful reforms released the people from levies and public labour. Reforms could fail if loyal officials, concerned with people's hearts, were purged during these intense periods.

In his reading of the Leninist notion of democratic centralism (Ball & Dagger 2008), while inspired simultaneously by Confucian governmentality, Mao Zedong and subsequent Communist Party autocrats crafted the 'mass line' approach. Lenin meant maintaining control by the proletarian leadership while leaving room for discussion and criticism. In comparison, Mao's mass line is, succinctly, 'for leaders to learn from the people about reality and the ways to improve it'. (This definition is in line with Hauck 2020; Newman & Zhang 2021.) This was adapted in various ways in Communist China, including being bifurcated into top-down mobilization campaigns and bottom-up policy adaptation (Holbig 2022). In this sense, learning from the masses to cope with the perceived problem does not allude to the destiny of either the learning cadres or the learned masses (Luo 2021). Mao's two most notorious applications were the Great Leap Forward, which aimed to decentralize policy making but consequently ruined economic production (Chen & Xiao 2020; Newman & Zhang 2021), and the Cultural Revolution, which aimed to destroy the Party's command system (Blecher 1983; Hauck 2020). Mao intended the mass line to end the involution of over-centralization but it suffered its own involution during these two campaigns. In sum, gathering information about reality to improve governance and organizing the people into common actions in the name of improvement constitute the mass line simultaneously (Frenkiel 2019; Toepfl 2020; Tsang & Cheung 2022). Only the former recovers governmentality. The latter defeats the purpose of investigating reality.

While the practices of the mass line evolve over time, the CCP consistently resorts to the cliché whenever autocratic legitimacy fades; for example, it was believed to be successful in winning the peasants' hearts during the ruthless Chinese Civil War (Chan 1980: 11; Wang & Klein 2021). Another example was a mass line style of presumably institutionalizing reform in terms of decentralization and reallocation ('fangquan rangli') to break down the ministerial and regional barriers at the end of the Cultural Revolution (Unger 1987: 20, 35). Yet another example was a call to strengthen the mass line, according to 'the CCP Center's Decision on Strengthening the Connection of the Party with the Masses' on 12 March 1990 (http://dangxiao.ruc.edu.cn/llxx/llqy/hygb/42a2471f48d040aeba9cf9bdc1f2798a.htm) in order to restore the people's trust in the Party following the crackdown on the pro-democracy movement in the previous year. The most recent example was the immediate reversal of a three-year anti-pandemic quarantine in the face of spontaneous protests – the White Paper Protests – in 2022 (Thornton 2023). The quarantine policy had ruined people's means of earning a living so that even loyal supporters were unable to make ends meet. The mass line, incurred as a remedy to involution, typically displayed a low degree of violence. However, its top-down style was identical to the more violent mass line in terms of improving political correctness (Cheek 2021). The protests proved effective in ending the intensively involuted quarantine policy. On the other hand, many protesters received varying degrees of harassment in the aftermath.

The mass line can be institutional, administrative, and policy. The most important formal institution of the mass line is political consultation conferences, which recruit leaders from various sectors and locations, at all levels, to inform the people's reality (Lee & Schuler 2019). At times, officials are sent down to engage in welfare-related activities, such as environmental protection, school recruitment, poverty relief, medical services, and so on. The mass line characterizes the top-down style of decentralization. It pre-empts the perpetuation of political correctness, which impedes the political consultation processes at the basic level, hence leading to 1) 'directed improvisation', meaning 'the paradoxical combination of a top-down direction and bottom-up improvisation' (Ang 2016b), 2) 'interactive authoritarianism', meaning 'a discriminative approach that limits the costs of repression by targeting specific individuals under specific circumstances through frequent interactions, while continuing to facilitate opportunities for free expression for the vast majority of the nonthreatening public' (Sun & Zhao 2021), or 3) 'evolutionary governance', meaning cycles of 'hard state/hard society, hard state/soft society, soft state/hard society, and soft state/soft society' (Tsai 2021). The latter concept is particularly ironic, as it appears to contradict the revolutionary message of the classic mass line, but all are, in fact, related dialectically (Perry 2021: 393).

A romantic notion of 'whole-process democracy' emerged in 2019, allegedly to involve the entire population in every step of every policy cycle, thus combining information-gathering with organizing common actions (Backer 2022; Boer 2023: 165–90). A failure to link the people becomes a threat to legitimacy. The White Paper Protest testifies to the plausibility of the politically silenced masses exerting legitimacy pressure a posteriori, with unpredictable creativity, on the autocrat to listen and adapt. The balance between these two functions can reveal how confident and ready the Party is to face and handle the reality of the people's hearts. Provided that the mass line retains the Confucian governmentality of the people's hearts as a component that informs the autocratic demise, periodical enlightenment will remain possible during involution.

Deliberative democracy

In the *US Declaration of Independence*, Thomas Jefferson wrote that all humans are 'created equal'. He was inspired by the European and Christian traditions (Cooper & Dyer 2017). The same applies to the *Declaration of Universal Human Rights* (The Carter Center 2018). The quest for equal rights, the foundation of modern democracy, is both Qur'anic and Christian in nature, but not true in practice:

> [W]hile human beings are born equal in rights and share the same intrinsic dignity, they are not equal in terms of capacities and have different skills and intellectual levels. Therefore, human beings are equal by nature and unique by potential, which creates a problem in fully applying the concept of equality in a fair and comprehensive way. (Halabi 2022: 705)

The reason for being born equal still appealed to a transcendental God, the same source that justified the previously unruly churches prior to secularization (Arendt 1977: 16). It is unsurprising that the current democratic recession primarily promoted efforts to restore true equality, paralleling the spirit of the Protestant reform of the church. It continues to carry a hidden thread of Christianity, but humans had no clue what to make of equal rights within a liberal democracy without referring to their incompatible, mundane, and personal needs. Consequently, caring is reduced simply to preferences, and the unequal capacity determines the balance of preferences.

Deliberative democracy has represented a noticeable effort to restore equality and policy quality during serial crises (Curato et al 2022). Deliberative democracy is a discursive practice that centres the legitimacy of policy making on the consensual choices of members who attain public stances through mutual consultation without being restrained by uneven capacity (Bohman & Rehg 1997; Gutmann & Thompson 2004: 3–5). Therefore, neither political correctness, which supports popularism, nor the misdistribution of wealth, which perpetuates a monopoly and corruption, nor other qualities such as education, religion, gender, race, and age, which incur discrimination, can affect the quality of deliberative democracy. Rather, deliberation encourages publicity, reciprocity, and inclusiveness (O'Flynn 2007). It tackles the increasing irrelevance of individuals in the current democratic recession. It posits a communicative solution that targets the recovery of the mutuality of individuals and a resulting public spirit that can regroup individuals as the equal agents of democracy. Implicitly, nevertheless, this agency is entirely religious in nature (Laffin 2020).

Deliberation has the same nuanced sensibility, embedded in a sincere appreciation for otherness, as in the School of Nomenclature, that is, to recognize everyone's distinction. In addition, deliberate democracy's epistemological lens of absolute equality is similar to the advocacy of Agriculturalism. According to the latter, princes should cultivate crops in the field in the same way as typical peasants do. However, these premodern Chinese schools of thought provided practical methods for pre-empting the situation where bad autocrats ruin governance and fall. They craft heart-winning measures on behalf of autocrats rather than rejuvenating the aggregate of individuals. The adherents of Confucianism wait for the autocrats to initiate solutions to their life difficulties, unlike liberal individuals, who are prepared to articulate their complaints and vote out the incumbent, albeit with little chance for improvement.

On the other hand, liberal democracy, that protects property rights, intrinsically contradicts the equality that prioritizes an equal capacity (to own property). Recently, a refocus on the democratic system de-centres the deliberative model to consider the achieved 'connectivity' of those practices that are not typically considered deliberative (Hendriks et al 2020). Equal property, or other qualities, is less of a binding condition, provided that the systemic deliberation benefits from the democratic morale of these practices (Warren 2017), as if, to say the least, all could enjoy ontological or existential equality at the systemic level. The contribution of instances of 'democratic mending', initiated by average people, can gain recognition (Scudder 2023: 252). Even so, non-deliberative deliberation is likewise related to how individuals should prefer to 'retain the critical and normative insights of deliberative systems thinking' (Scudder 2023: 253). Therefore, individualization and normativity are indispensable components of both deliberative and liberal democracy.

Given these two components, at any point in time when certain politicians, due to their peculiar rationality, resort to political correctness in the emerging public, which subverts the public sphere (Sharon 2019: 368–9), others within the ruling circle can only follow suit in order to counterbalance this. Since individual citizens cannot cope with the complexity (Somin 2010), the ruling circle can dispense with deliberation. The problem is that deliberate democracy lacks a reason, apart from 'this is how it should be' (Hammond 2019), why humans are born equal, or the ruling circle must resume and protect equality. If the involution of liberal democracy into populism, authoritarianism, or exploitative capitalism renders equality impossible, methods for establishing mutual respect for one another's differences and equality could make little progress, to the extent that they remain contingent on the mercy of almighty God, which is incomprehensible to humans. The deliberative solution continues to rely on and even deepen the individual's capacity to reason and prefer, which has already failed.

Original sin: in lieu of a solution

Christianity has noted a well-established inevitability, similar to the premodern Chinese consciousness, according to which all bad autocrats fall. That is related to original sin or the natural capacity for 'hurtful desire' (Pane 2019: 2072). Christianity provided a transcendent solution to those who claimed to believe in God and Jesus Christ. The Church was the medium through which the sinful person could access the transcendental world. The law-like belief, or guilt, compelled all to reflect critically upon their endeavours in a mundane world. Believers needed to contemplate this sinful character of humankind and cope with it institutionally, psychologically, and practically. As a result, the Church was able to challenge the authority of kings who could similarly contest religious power, testifying to the significance of determining the identity of the one who held God's mandate to establish a heavenly city on earth. Both the constitutional principle of check and balance and the international political logic of balance of power reveal a deep-rooted distrust toward human nature. The politico-religious premise consistently connoted the need to rescue humankind from its original sin.

With the protracted but ultimate arrival of a secular age (Taylor 2007), both humanism and the separation of the state from the church interrogate the emerging relation between the state and society. The social contract theory stuck out as the sanction of modernity that transferred the responsibility for guarding the rights of nature of the people into the people's own hands. Desiring, as a secular indicator of humanity, defines the essence of human rights, leaving its religious characteristic (original sin) in oblivion. One plausible cause of the failure of constitutional democracy and deliberate democracy is their common privileging of rights over sin, in the sense that solidarity remains a cultivated (that is, unnecessary) norm rather than an insufficiency of the relational self to overcome or transcend. To the extent that this insufficiency reflects a law-like inevitability of fallibility, recovery from social regression, cleavages, delusions, and similar symptoms can occur as a human necessity. In that case, deliberate democracy might restore liberal governmentality upon the drive for solidarity.

Furthermore, original sin rings a Confucian bell of 'nature is evil' in the texts of *Xunzi*. In later generations, tempering evil nature is a forgotten message about how Confucianism means more than simply breeding and maintaining selflessness. Given that Confucianism is an attempt to curb abusive autocracy, it serves as a reminder of both how benevolent autocrats can tame the people and how the people can become wild in the face of abusive autocrats. The question of whether or not they are evil (that is, able to desire and self-centred) by nature is a semantic issue, however. Original sin is a theme of not wanting to belong but pursuing desires, a silenced theme that ubiquitously haunts Confucianism. Original sin serves as a plausible point of connection between classic liberalism and Confucianism, as well as a reminder of the inevitability that autocracy is destined to fall if the desires of the people are frustrated.

A third possible solution – civic nationalism – will be discussed in Chapter 6.

Conclusion

Two features of liberalism and Confucianism distinguish the ways in which they cope with involution. First, regarding their imagined origin being a law-like (allegedly) known reality or a yet-to-be-fulfilled transcendental norm, contemporary socialist/Confucian autocracy and liberal democracy cope with involution in different ways. A law-like reality is not subject to change, so Confucians can only prescribe benevolence for tender autocrats to win the people's hearts and avoid their own demise, along with other thinkers who propose other autocratic norms for the same purpose. From the social science point of view, Confucianism and its rivals merely appeared to be competing norms. Second, the Confucian norms prepare mainly the autocrats to practise governmentality skilfully, but liberalism must preach to all individuals. Confucianism focuses on deterring one autocrat at a time. In contrast, the capacity, incentive, and perseverance of all individuals to adopt liberalism necessarily fluctuate and diverge. That is why Confucian autocrats, engrossed in the governmentality of the people's hearts, are ready to care, but the elected rulers of liberal democracy are ultimately evasive.

The obsession of social science with individual preferences tends to prompt agendas that explain the changing realities that are contingent upon the aggregate of individual choices. The equality of individuals, each with a capacity to express preferences and opinions, is an unwavering assumption. This assumption guides research designs of democratic transition and consolidation, as well as authoritarian resilience, regarding how to make government power subject to a society that is composed of autonomous, equal individuals. This chapter then presents the provocative logic that social science restrains liberal democracy from recovering from the situation in which individuals are practically unequal. There is no guarantee that an electoral system makes a government more accountable to the voters or more capable of recovering from corruption than a failed state. Losing a major war could prove a destructively effective route to recovery.

Being an example of a remedy to involuted liberal democracy, deliberative democracy fails as a remedy because reiterating normative equality can only reproduce rather than alleviate the falling of normative equality. Confucianism appears to have a greater potential for recovery. Consider Confucian governmentality as a meme of reality or fact, rather than a normative statement. Autocrats' incentive to regain the people's hearts is thus to protect their own security. They do not have to listen, and may also develop new skills besides benevolence to attain the people's hearts, including faking success by blocking information about alienation. Even so, fakery will not sustain alienation, as even isolated individuals can hide information and destroy productivity collectively. Five thousand years have passed, reinforcing the governmentality belief that autocrats either adapt to suit the people's hearts or fall.

In the contemporary world, both modes of governmentality endeavour to involve more people to restore normalcy during involution, with a deliberative process for liberal democracy and the mass line for socialist autocracy. A difference exists in their discursive logic of reliance on the people. For deliberative democracy to restore liberal governance by bringing the people back into the direct deliberation and equalizing their decision positions, the solution is essentially normative in nature. The people must be taught, which hinges on equal eloquence, time, patience, and so on. In comparison, Confucians think in an ostensibly objective manner, which leads them to believe that the spontaneous disengagement of the people from politics will eventually prevail over bad autocrats, without any normative intervention by either deliberative or Confucian theorists.

3

Governing Hong Kong by Loving the Nation

Introduction

This chapter continues the discussion presented in Chapters 1 and 2 regarding the impacts of the national and nationalist discourses on autocratic governmentality, with a particular focus on how the discourses of unity and solidarity, as two contrasting public duties to love one's fellow citizens, are mutually challenging. On the emotional side of autocracy, Chapter 3 employs Confucianism to illustrate a kind of differential or benevolent love, which people offer in accordance with their relations and roles. In this sense, Confucian benevolent love is more of a duty to create a sense of mutual belonging than an emotion of solidarity as in communitarianism (Koschut 2018; Lynch & Kalaitazke 2018; Koschut 2019).

This benevolent love contrasts with the universal love of liberalism and the resultant solidarity that those who express this form of love feel for one another – these people sometimes being distant and unacquainted – whose presence would puzzle Confucian leaders in terms of their roles and duties. Confucian roles are, in comparison, contextual, evolving, and reciprocal, in order to cope with a variety of encountered strangeness. The liberal belief that all are ontologically equal and free deemphasizes the effect of silencing the other's strangeness. As a result of this, a Confucian and liberal's love for one another may ironically cause, in both, a moral outrage qua a sense of deprived belonging (Knab & Steffens 2021; Tava 2023).

My case study will be the institution of 'One Country, Two Systems' (OCTS), on which Beijing relied to arrange Hong Kong's return and belonging to China. This case has become one of the focal points in the US-China rivalry during the 2020s and illustrates how benevolent love and universal love have yet to be reconciled. In Hong Kong, the quest for the direct election of the Chief Executive and political autonomy led to two mass demonstrations (in 2015 and 2019), which were accompanied by months of bloodshed on the streets. Although these demonstrations were suppressed by the Hong Kong police, with the support of the central authorities in Beijing, this suppression was followed by a series of welfare programmes that aimed to improve social, as opposed to political, justice. My discussion will show how Confucian benevolent love is philosophically illuminative in such policy thinking, while also committing an apparent assault on universal love.

During and after the second rally, the US Congress passed the Hong Kong Human Rights and Democracy Act (2019) and Hong Kong Autonomy Act (2020). These two laws reveal in what terms intervention is a laudable, correct narrative within the liberal discourse of the endorsing members of the US Congress, despite the fact that they may have incongruent motives that are both relevant as well as irrelevant to the liberal democracy of Hong Kong. These laws presumably inspire people – and therefore reflect a prior (at times tacit) consensual solidarity – to join forces in order to resist Beijing's conceived suppression of Hong Kong through the imposition of its political will in the form of claiming a love for it.

The chapter will begin by problematizing 'universal love', then introducing 'benevolent love'. Given the Anglosphere's unfamiliarity with the latter, the chapter invokes the aforementioned notions of natural contracts and unity to elaborate on benevolent love's contrast with the liberal ideas of social contract and solidarity. The chapter will then present the policy thinking and practices of OCTS, as informed by their Confucian underpinnings. Based on an understanding of these two philosophies of love, the conclusion will interrogate the sense of mutual belonging under the OCTS circumstances.

Problematizing love as emancipation

As the horrors of the Holocaust came to light following WWII, political culture and psychology became almost exclusively concerned with studying the totalitarian personality, which loathes, dehumanizes, and seeks to annihilate certain 'others', that is, 'absolute strangers' in my terminology. How and why democracy failed during the Nazi rule was the main puzzle, and questions about how to prevent a similar horror from happening in the future took centre stage. *Escape from Freedom* by Eric Fromm (1941), *Power and Personality* by Harold Lasswell (1948), and *The Authoritarian Personality* by Theodor Adorno et al (1950) offer the most prominent theories regarding the spread of societal as well as personal disorder. During and after the Chinese Cultural Revolution, psychoanalysts offered similar theories to explain the psychology of Mao Zedong and his followers. These can be found in *The Spirit of Chinese Politics* by Lucian Pye (1968), *Revolutionary Immortality* by Robert Lifton (1968), *Mao's Revolution and the Chinese Political Culture* by Richard Solomon (1971), and *The Revolutionary Aesthetic* by Bruce Mazlish (1976).

The disintegration of communities, as indicated by the slaughter of humans, challenges readers to ask how a person can determine whether or not someone is entitled to belong to a certain community, and execute their exclusion accordingly. In response to this, Erich Fromm (1956) offered a diagnosis, arguing that modern capitalism engendered alienation. Dependence alleviates alienation, and radical dependence rescues those under the circumstance of severe alienation. Radical dependence calls for a clear binary of the self and its other and the reproduction, securitization, and victimization of the latter to affirm the binary. Fromm offered a romantic therapy, informed by a rational kind of love, which would overcome the individualization of society under capitalism (Fromm 1957). Expressing this form of love would enable individuals to achieve emancipation by relating to one another, so that they would not seek a therapeutic reliance on a totalitarianism that sanctions exclusionary binaries.

Half a century after the end of WWII, amid occurrences of genocide in Rwanda, the Balkans, and East Timor, political theorists and psychologists continued to ask the same questions. One notable example was James Glass (1989; 1993; 1995), who revisited the Holocaust but instead asked how and why someone can feel fragmented and come to dread the im/possibility of belonging to a community. Glass (1993) expressed his disapproval of the critical scholarship of his predecessors half a century before him, as well as the postmodern deconstruction of his time. He proceeded to detect within the postmodern personality a delusional split that was also present within the Nazi psychology. In contrast to his predecessors, Glass (1995) prescribed a liberal 'illusion' for those who suffered paranoid delusion. His solution was to restore the integrity of the democratic community, which was composed of members who were secure in their own 'illusionary' boundary, undergirded by liberalism. Together, these members would be ready to embrace and calm those suffering the horror of self-disintegration and thus rescue democracy from the instinct of annihilation. Glass (1995) believed that the survival of the community relied on strong personalities who could 'hold' others, especially those suffering fragmentation, in order to enable them to regain (the liberal illusion of) an integral self. Regarding this notion of 'holding', Glass relied on the metaphor of a mother holding a hysterical infant to denote a democratic environment that caters to the patient's aggression until she learns to cope with it independently.

Fromm treated regression as etiology, and advocated love to facilitate an internal recovery from this regression. Glass, in contrast, regarded regression as a symptom, and prescribes an external 'holding' of the patient by other secure members of the community. In other words, both of these conceptions of regression brought with them the idea of an integral self. Fromm and Glass both recognized the contagious nature of regression, and the capacity of infected patients of a higher status to weave and spread laudable narratives that trigger and escalate collective dependence and aggression. Both researchers would agree that an integral self with a secure boundary is essential in order to avoid the desire to dominate and oppress, with Fromm prescribing self-fulfilment, and Glass, self-security. Despite this difference, both approaches subscribe to the following assumptions:

- therapy at the individual level;
- a community conception in which all of the individual members are equal;
- emancipation from dominance or oppression for all;
- a desire to correct diagnosed psychotics; and
- the intellectual capacity to demonstrate solidarity toward strangers/aliens, and hence embrace universal love.

These assumptions conceive universal love as a vehicle for social solidarity within as well as between communities (Walzer 1992; Etzioni 2004). Equality between loved ones must be something that exists before members of a community acquire a sense of social belonging and local identity. Otherwise, these identity productions would call for self-other binaries and discrimination in order to reproduce them (Cooper-Cunningham 2020). Accordingly, this prior equality between the members must rely on a belief in certain natural rights to which all loved ones are entitled, regardless of other, later aspects of their identities. Together, relying on Europe's own political thought resources, both Fromm's and Glass' critical reflections elevate European civilization to another level and emancipate the totalitarian personality from its WWII nightmare.

Ironically, such quests to understand the totalitarian personality leave contemporary critical thinkers unprepared to make sense of communities that fail to share those same sensibilities, including countries that Europe formerly colonized. Therefore, the dominance, exploitation, and division of colonies did not prompt any critical self-reflection among the European colonizers: the ways in which the colonized populations belonged to their communities was of little concern. Issues of colonialism and colonial division, by contrast, sank into oblivion. At best, Europe's colonial past remains a memory – fleeting and redundant – amid the aforementioned critical reflections. This therapeutic lens, provided by the concept of universal love, can be used to contemplate the contemporary suppression and dipartition within the postcolonial world and forget about its roots in colonial legacies. Employing this lens can additionally suggest how problematic it would be to restore or appeal to the primordial belonging, such as dharma, ayllu, Ubuntu, Tianxia, zen, or Sikhi (Trownsell et al 2021), that existed long before colonialism.

In this regard, postcolonial Hong Kong problematizes universal love and raises two critiques. One is that Hong Kong never belonged to the scope of universal solidarity under colonialism. The other is that Confucian benevolent love remains a viable cultural component in Hong Kong society (Lo 2020). Through the process of decolonization, the revival of China's benevolent love toward Hong Kong could cause the citizens of Hong Kong to become ambivalent toward Hong Kong's identities because Hong Kong would occupy a lower status in the national hierarchy. Alternatively, the spirit of universal love might emancipate Hong Kong: positioning it as equal to the colonizing world and balancing the national hierarchy by acting as a separate, higher civilization in the face of China. On the other hand, solidarity in support of Hong Kong (in the form of universal love) could equally help the former colonizers-turned-liberals to leave historical colonialism behind.

Beijing's use of a Confucian lens would find liberal solidarity-love for either strangers or former colonies incomprehensible. Within the Confucian framework, it is only natural to love one's kin. Expressing love beyond one's close circles would be considered suspiciously corrupt and detrimental to kin love, especially in the absence of a selfless leader, who can metaphorically play a parental role and engage in acts of reciprocal benevolence with their subjects in order for encourage them to accept each other as belonging to an imagined national family. In the same vein, refusing to give or accept metaphorical kin benevolence would not only be considered shameful, but also threaten to reduce all onlookers to strangers (Goodman 2021). Confucianism instead discusses a seemingly contrary focus, where:

- the therapy is at the group level;
- a communitarian conception is composed of hierarchical rather than equal relations between the members;
- a quest for security is equivalent to the enforcement of self-discipline rather than the pursuit of self-fulfilment or self-security;
- the first desire is to camouflage as opposed to remedy; and
- the intellectual appreciation is for differential love toward relational others as contextual individuals, *rather than* indiscriminate, universal love for all.

Confucianism and benevolent love

The Book of Changes, as one of the major sources of Confucianism, contains a statement pertaining to the state of nature: 'the superb benevolence of Heaven and earth is giving and maintaining life' (Chapter Xi Ci II, *The Book of Changes*). However, individual human beings are considered incapable of securing an order of life; Confucius himself believed that women and commoners struggle to reciprocate properly (Chapter Yang Huo, *The Analects*, or Dawson 2008). *The Analects* explains how a king of virtue, with the Mandate of Heaven, may guide amoral people to become benevolent subjects, but warns that they all have the potential to fall back into being strangers to one another if the person of virtue aborts the Mandate of Heaven and stops loving (for example, by levying, conscripting, killing, or indulging). Accordingly, top-down exemplification and hierarchical role-play are the ways to proliferate benevolent love.

In contrast, in European political thought, individuals recognize the laws of nature in a social contract whereby they consent to the rule of Leviathan, according to Thomas Hobbes, or the general will, according to Jean-Jacques Rousseau, in exchange for the protection of their rights of nature (Friend 2020). Their ex ante consent, embedded in rights and solidarity, rather than the ex post desertion to another prince, constitutes a key contrast to Confucianism, according to which the population and the followed prince as a father are always endowed with one other. While all oppose all others within a Hobbesian anarchy and individuals are autonomous, rational, and competent under the Lockean scenario, Confucian benevolence remains simultaneously spontaneous, natural, and allegorically relational (Wang 2018). The Confucian agenda rejects the idea of governing as a power based on the necessity to ensure maximum freedom.

Then, consider the family within liberalism (Chapman 1975; Munoz-Dardé 1998; Bilba 2011; Chambers 2013). According to Hobbes, a child's submission to their father's authority is intrinsically rational for the sake of the child's own survival. This implies, however, that it is not relational (Hobbes 2019: chs 20–24). John Rawls likewise deliberates on the rational characteristics of the family (Kearns 1983). Liberal rationality contrasts with Confucian benevolent love within the family. Mencius (孟子), for example, specifically distinguishes humans from animals in terms of the former's consciousness of kinship (Chapter Tengwengong II, *Mengzi*, or Ivanhoe 2009). Kinship love, especially that for one's parents and offspring, is natural, intuitive love, which requires neither deliberation nor the consent of the loved ones; nor is this benevolence concerned with the solidarity that grows through an implicit social contract.

That being said, Hobbes also adopts the analogy of the father through the Leviathan. However, unlike the Leviathan, who is motivated by power, Confucian princes are obliged to rule with love. Under Confucianism, the prince relies on the Mandate of Heaven, which echoes the voices of those over whom he rules. The notion of the Mandate of Heaven amounts to a kind of 'natural contract', through which Confucianism reminds us that the commoners' entitlement to metaphorical parental love is the ultimate guarantee of harmony. Commoners would otherwise abandon reciprocity and might even, in the worst case scenario, regress to cannibalism (see the 10th classic narrative on the people's master in Chapter 1), thus engulfing any prince-hood. In other words, Confucius' commoners do not surrender to a Leviathan. Instead, they follow their righteous leaders to reflect their

Heavenly nature. Thus, Confucius (Chapter Yanyuan, *The Analects*) advises that a prince must always provide his people with sufficient food and security for, if they were to migrate, the prince would be left with neither levy nor troops.

There is also an expansive logic in the making of a community during Confucius' time – a return to 'oneness' (*yi*). Oneness refers to the unification of the entire world as well as harmony between all under Heaven. Oneness is, therefore, an alternative expression of the Confucian Way (or Dao). According to Chapter Grand Harmony of the *Book of Rites*, another major source of Confucianism, the metaphorical Way, is presumably so broad that no one can be excluded from walking together. Both oneness and the Way denote the principle of governance – 'all under Heaven belong to all' ('Tianxia wei gong') – and this is, in the contemporary terminology, a reasonable decision made by all, as all are presumably better off than they would be otherwise (Zhao 2019). Oneness is the ultimate form of equality and would lead to a borderless community; for example, before becoming emperor, the legendary Emperor Shun (21st and 22nd centuries BCE) had already attracted voluntary followers who gathered at a place where he grew crops so quickly, that a city-sized community emerged within a year. This is a famous narrative of the 'Annals of the Five Emperors' in *The Book of Historical Documents* (Chinese Text Project, https://ctext.org/shiji).

As with the philosophy of oneness and the Hobbesian rights of nature (that is, the right to life), Mencius advises that 'those who do not enjoy killing can achieve oneness' (Chapter Lianghuiwang I, *Mengzi*). Killing may be justified if the prince is able to call his opponent 'a dictator' (*yi fu*) (Chapter Lianghuiwang II, *Mengzi*). The battle of discourse is, therefore, a critical component regarding the prevailing of the Way. All three kinds of bad friends, whom Confucius specifies, abuse discourse (Chapter Jishi, *The Analects*). The ethics of killing dictators and instigative politicians to achieve oneness reveals an unspoken tendency for expansion (more in Chapter 7). According to this logic, the higher the reputation of the prince for possessing selfless benevolence, the stronger the appeal to the population elsewhere, and the greater his legitimacy to reign over the world of oneness. Presumably, creating the regime of truth and the regime of regimes across all ages (see Chapter 1), commoners are the ultimate judges of legitimacy.

In short, commoners are preoccupied with growing their own food and practising kinship love to the degree that they have no credit with other similar, but unrelated, commoners. They are inevitably compelled to rely on a trustworthy prince to protect them from strangers' encroachment and heavy levies incurred in the name of protecting them. The caveat implied in the anxious quest for a benevolent leader under Confucianism is the commoner's conservative preference for both the relational hierarchy and the status quo: accepting that whoever rules now has the Mandate of Heaven and deserves to play the role of a metaphorical father (Zhang et al 2005). In reality, bad princes are inevitable. As a result, cycles of harmony and disorder are completely natural.

Metaphorical kinship love must be hierarchical. Commoners who have never met each other do not relate to one another through empathy and a shared rationality, that is, any internal quality, prior to encountering each other. The idea of solidarity existing between the members of a community who have never met, due to their being constituted by a universal humanity or God, is unfamiliar, if not absurd. Instead, they indirectly relate to one another and are united by their metaphorical relations with the same prince, relations that are expressed through their various roles as ministers, soldiers, or subjects, as well as scholars, peasants, workers, or merchants. They are unable to address a wider audience because their role relations are discursively restricted to relatives and acquaintances. The relation between unrelated commoners is similar to that which exists between strangers before a metaphor of kinship is reciprocally arranged. Consequently, the natural contract between Heaven and the prince necessarily privileges the collective characteristic of people, not an aggregation of God-made, individual rights owners. The collective people used to be known in the classics as ten thousand people ('wan min') or a hundred clan-names ('bai xing').

If natural rights both testify to the ontological sameness and equality of the members who have agreed to the social contract in the European tradition, and also entitle every individual to claim to be special in terms of the specific needs, opinions, and preferences of each, oneness does the same for Confucianism. This is because its pervasiveness reduces all of the role-hierarchies that exist in the mundane world to ontological irrelevance, if not utter vanity. As such, all are related while being a selfless, benevolent role-player. It is the people's entitlement to belong through role relations, regardless of their ontological beliefs and practices, and dispensing with opinion and values, that enables them to remain ultimately equal outside their role hierarchy.

To love is to relate, but not in the solidarity sense of all being constituted by a prior humanity to hold one another. Rather, role-embedded love is emancipatory in the sense that the differing identities hidden behind the roles are: 1) irrelevant to the unity of the community, provided that the role is played, 2) exempt from dominance or oppression provided that they do not interfere with anyone's role-play, and 3) entitled to security, food, and education. That said, no quest for emancipation is legitimate while playing a role. Unity through reciprocal role relations acts as a substitute for solidarity as the practice of self-fulfilment. Under this circumstance, prior equality between autonomous individuals can be a disturbing premise, as oneness transcends the binary of the self and other, informed by the identities of autonomous individuals.

As such, role-embedded love concerns, not emotion, but obligation. Emotionally indifferent love is more likely to occur in the giving of material benefits, as opposed to passionate holding. An important intersection between Confucianism and Marxism is the materialistic sensibilities, albeit the units of concern differ, being a hundred clans and class respectively. In practice, the issues of tax, welfare, workload, and shelter are essential agendas for Confucian governance. With their materialistic sensibilities, commoners are able to decide relatively objectively to whose reign they wish to belong. Thus, they can deny the benevolent love of the prince as hypocritical and legitimately desert an oppressive prince. However, self-fulfilment is an irrelevant value, as agency lies only in escaping from dictatorship or merely following one's basic, materialist needs.

The practical challenge to Confucianism is that, in reality, no one can determine whether or not the prince has the Mandate of Heaven, not to mention the challenge in a modern cosmopolitan setting (Zhou 2015; Xie 2017). This makes unity a paramount political necessity for the prince to maintain his claim to legitimacy within the politics of belonging. Unity indicates the selflessness of the leaders and their followers, while selflessness embodies the essence of Heavenly reason. The political correctness of unity has the twin effects of silencing and concealing differing desires and identities. Order and freedom are two sides of the same coin. As a result, benevolence and dominance are barely distinguishable in real politics. Both the prince and the revolutionary suffer (or strategize) this ambiguity.

'One Country, Two Systems' as benevolent love

The case study for benevolent love is how the situation in Hong Kong challenges the understandings of its belonging to 'the motherland', China, having been a British colony for 155 years. While 'One Country, Two Systems' (OCTS) is the pragmatic response of the PRC, this chapter interrogates it also as a philosophical issue (Pan 2017; Shen 2017). OCTS is an ironic institution involving both integration and autonomy, aimed at promoting the prosperity and stability of Hong Kong. The primary criticism of OCTS since the 2010s has consistently been that Beijing has encroached on the autonomy of Hong Kong at the expense of its repeated promises. Investment, which has slowed down in competitive cities, especially Shenzhen and Macao, is one example that affects Hong Kong's revenues. Migration affects Hong Kong's stability and human resources (Chen & Kinzelbach 2016). The Hong Kong government's accountability to its population is also affected by the Beijing authorities, who choose Hong Kong's leaders. The choice always involves long negotiations and indirect elections based on a complex consultative process instead of direct election. The most notorious intervention pertains to personal safety, as exemplified by the alleged kidnapping of private citizens for political reasons (Palmer 2018), violence on the part of pro-Beijing gangs, and Hong Kong police abuse.

However, the main purpose of Beijing's OCTS proposal was neither to enhance nor to curb Beijing's influence in Hong Kong after its return. Rather, it was, in principle, a benevolent guarantee of Hong Kong's 'prosperity and stability', so that its return to the motherland would affect the welfare of the Hong Kong people as little as possible (Zhang 1988). As discussed in earlier chapters, 'the people' here refers to the discursive rather than the living people. Beijing's status quo sensibilities were based on a wilful policy of refraining from exploiting the highly developed Hong Kong economy at the critical moment when China joined the world market (Das 1993), in order to soothe the anxiety regarding the involuntary transfer of wealth to the mainland after 1997. Even so, an exodus of Hong Kong migrants and wealth occurred immediately after 1982, the year in which Hong Kong's return in 1997 was sanctioned. Having entered the new century, China's economy overtook that of several major economies. While OCTS continues in a spirit of peaceful coexistence, Beijing, rather than Washington, is the party that appears to be the more generous and strong party, still honouring OCTS.

The only ongoing issue, where no compromise has been possible, is the correct (that is, metaphorically parental) relation between the PRC and Hong Kong. According to Deng Xiaoping's (1984) remark, "only those Hong Kong people composed mainly of *Ai Guo Zhe* (AGZ) are entitled to rule Hong Kong". Answering his own rhetorical question, "What makes an AGZ?" (literally, in Chinese, 'a person who (role-)loves her country', but often expediently translated as 'patriot'), Deng Xiaoping mentions that an AGZ "respects her nation", "supports the motherland to extend sovereignty over Hong Kong", and "will not harm Hong Kong's prosperity and stability". These are mainly clues to behavioural propriety, as opposed to constitutive traits that define the identity of a patriot. In short, the term 'AGZ' concerns role-obliged love rather than sincere love for substantive, transcendental value. So, none of the "beliefs in capitalism, or feudalism, or even slavery" disqualifies an AGZ. The role-relationship of an AGZ is registered in the belonging of Hong Kong to the motherland, that comes with no levy of any kind. The AGZ's success is demonstrated more by Hong Kong's stability and prosperity as a collective good, than by the fulfilled preferences of individuals in aggregation.

With the distinction between socialism and capitalism becoming more obscure, the integrity of OCTS is increasingly referenced with regard to democratization (Ortmann 2015; Bush 2016; Lo 2016). An early debate regarding the ownership of the residual power foretold the challenge to the relations between Beijing and Hong Kong today. The residual power concerns those governing powers that are not mentioned in the *Joint Declaration on the Question of Hong Kong* (https://treaties.un.org/Pages/showDetails.aspx?objid=08000002800d4d6e). According to the natural law tradition, all of the remaining powers belong to the people, except for those powers that are specifically stated in the constitution (Cheng 1988; Loh 1996). This understanding affirms that the people have ownership over these powers. The dispute over this naturally extends to the interpretation of the law and the judicial review (Allan 1998; Chan, Fu & Ghai 2000). It is also of great relevance regarding the direct election of the Chief Executive and legislators by the people (Lo 1997). Since 2007, the demand for universal suffrage has been mounting, and indeed culminated in two mass movements (in 2014 and 2019).

For Beijing, the central government represents the entire nation, to which Hong Kong belongs. According to this view, the interpretation of the law is exclusively at the discretion of the central authorities, especially the *Basic Law*, which defines the scope of OCTS. Autonomy is not endowed, but contingent upon Beijing's concession (Holliday, Ngok & Yep 2008). Nor is there such thing as a division of power (Rao & Wang 2008); instead, it is only proper for the National People's Congress to approve and delegate powers to the Hong Kong government.

While not necessarily anticipating these movements, Beijing pre-emptively issued a White Paper on *The Practice of the 'One Country, Two Systems' Policy* (https://bit.ly/3l124Gi), which reiterates that the Chief Executive must first be proved to love their country, echoing Deng's advice. However, the duty to love one's country is not legally documented anywhere. It can only make sense in terms of role propriety, that is reciprocally enforced upon a perceived violation. In fact, in 2017, four legislators who refused to read the prepared patriotic wording of the oath at their inauguration were disqualified on the ground of disloyalty, being sanctioned in the interpretation of the National People's Congress (NPC). In addition, the White Paper denies any residual power owed to Hong Kong. It reaffirms that all of the powers that Hong Kong possesses were delegated to it by the National People's Congress. Any power that is not mentioned in the *Joint Declaration* or *Basic Law* can be delegated to Hong Kong only if the National People's Congress so approves. National unity would otherwise be obsolete.

From a liberal point of view, how one belongs to Hong Kong vis-à-vis China is a decision that each individual can only make for themselves, given that all are equal in terms of natural rights and government by consent. Accordingly, critics of China exhibited their solidarity-love for the Hong Kong street demonstrators. The demonstrations revealed the difficult choice between becoming Chinese and remaining transnational (Thomas 2018; Chan 2019); for example, within the National People's Congress' exclusive power to interpret the law, and the common law tradition of colonial Hong Kong, there exist two dilemmas. The first is between the monopoly of the residual power – which is not mentioned in the legal documents – and the consent of the ruled. The second is between the AGZ's role as required by the judge and Chief Executive, and democratic selection by the people.

For concerned onlookers in China, the Hong Kong people appear reluctant to belong to China and are instead using OCTS as a form of leverage against a benefactor community (presumably) of their own. The claim to the residual power which lies in the hands of the Hong Kong people and the resulting anxiety regarding the disintegration of China attest to this assessment. Benevolent love appears to have backfired. The Hong Kong people respond with increasing activism in their quest to become autonomous and eventually, institutionally and socially, distinctive from the mainland (Wasserstrom 2017: 217). This latter desire further amounts to a claim to existential difference (Leung 2019), which was perceived as morally outrageous by China and led to the arrest of the leaders of the two aforementioned mass movements in 2020, due to 'national security concerns'.

Even so, these different attitudes toward the operation of OCTS, embedded respectively in Confucianism and liberalism, do not determine the positions of specific actors, who are capable of shifting sides, for the people of Hong Kong are culturally bilingual and intellectually appreciative of both attitudes. Confucianism and liberalism represent two threads of relational beliefs rather than two mutually exclusive populations, cultures, or religions. Accordingly, OCTS is not about an essentialized Confucian China rivalling a liberal Hong Kong or the liberal West. In other words, benevolent love and universal love, as conceptual types, are practically contingent upon the context and agency for the adaptation of the actors at a site. Communitarian consciousness is composed of both kinds of love. Therefore, Hong Kong protestors are capable of appreciating the efforts of the central government to push for land and rental reform, while a significant number of Chinese bloggers have expressed sympathy for the protestors during the two movements. Implicit in the shifts between or coexistence of the two kinds of love lies a universal clue, suggesting that severe unity can ironically prompt solidarity even among those who subscribe to benevolent love. In contrast, rampant solidarity can enhance the support for benevolent governance, aiming to promote group unity among those members who are accustomed to practising universal love.

'One Country, Two Systems' as a system of belonging contested

Benevolence and solidarity are forms of love that are different both rationally and relationally. While it is untrue that there exists no intersection between them, nor room for creative reconciliation (Angle 2015; Shih 2022), in practice, this intersection would require unlearning and mutual appreciation between the narrow-minded practitioners of the two different philosophies of loving. The greatest challenge lies in the fact that the contrasting epistemological lens of benevolent love is hierarchical in nature, as opposed to egalitarian and universal. Benevolent love obliges its recipients to reciprocate it by honouring the ritual that reflects the hierarchical relations between those expressing this form of love. The argument that Hong Kong possesses the residual power, that is not mentioned in the *Joint Declaration* or *Basic Law*, is not only estranging, but also disgraceful in the eyes of those who celebrate the perceived goodwill of Beijing in seeking to safeguard the prosperity and stability of Hong Kong (Chang 2007; Fong 2017). Stability is something that is granted to Hong Kong, allowing capitalism to continue under the presumably anti-capitalist socialist system of China. In addition, prosperity is promised to Hong Kong, allowing it to take advantage of the resources that the motherland is able to supply. Hong Kong is expected to take advantage of all of these resources and feel grateful for the special relation that has been crafted exclusively for the former colony.

In both 2014 and 2019, however, activists similarly stressed the universality of their rights – the right to political participation in 2014, and to personal security in 2019. According to the ideological positions of these two movements, rights are neither material nor policy privileges granted to the people; rather, rights are considered inherent to humanity. Ironically, in both movements, a pledge to rights applied primarily to Hong Kong residents, excluding Chinese expatriates in Hong Kong. Such discrimination reveals the Confucian sensibilities of the activists toward (Beijing's lack of) role propriety, which magnifies their alarm at the strangeness of the motherland, and contradicts solidarity-love (Dupré 2020).

Consequently, the rights argument forms a boundary between the former colony and the motherland: between those (in Hong Kong) whose humanity their rights naturally constitute, but who never gave their consent to OCTS, and those (on the Chinese mainland) whose humanity the autocratic PRC leaders monopolize. Not only do rights consciousness and the resulting boundary consciousness contrast with the materialist characteristics of benevolent love, but rights consciousness also implies Hong Kong's ultimate belonging to the Anglosphere (that is, to the former colonial world (Vucetic 2011)), rather than to China (Cheung 2017). To that extent, the universalist narrative of belonging to the world's rights community entails a desertion of irresponsible leaders by the people. In fact, this desire for solidarity-love internationally was most apparent in the 2019 movement, where the protesters exhibited the British and US flags. According to Reuters' report on 16 October 2019 (https://reut.rs/3jZ5ok0), Singaporean President Lee Hsien Loong conceived of these flags as a humiliating instrument, indicating as they did that Hong Kong belonged to the Anglosphere rather than to China (Duruz, Luckman & Bishop 2011; Rocha 2014; Yeoh, Acedera & Rootham 2019).

Needless to say, the OCTS-derived role expectations and obligations, once failing, immediately incurred anxiety regarding the loss of oneness qua the legitimacy of the higher leaders in Beijing. Usually, a process of balancing relationships would ensue. This balancing of relationships involves a combination of two strategies (Huang & Shih 2014; Shih et al, 2019). The first prescribes gift-giving by either side – for example, reducing tariffs, bestowing honourable titles, reiterating loyalty, repatriating criminals, or donating to show propriety and forgiveness – in exchange for the continuation of a hierarchical relation. The second recommends imposing sanctions to repair a corrupt relationship in the eyes of the sanctioning party, to allow for the correct one to (re-)emerge. How to combine gift-giving and sanctions depends on the judgment of the Beijing authorities as well as that of mass demonstrators regarding the intention underlying the betrayal of the demonstrated benevolent love. Gift-giving is particularly useful for clarifying an intention by monitoring the subsequent responses. It may also convey pardon and patience to allow the relation to recover.

Cultural resemblance, in terms of Confucian benevolence between Hong Kong and China, reveals the ironic readiness of the protesters to turn toward belonging once those perceived to have aborted the role-propriety within the Beijing authorities were seen to be engaging in providing a remedy. Indeed, the government of Hong Kong launched an unprecedented scale of landing and housing reform following the crackdown on the 2019 rally, illustrating its intention to restore relationality. Of course, such an attempt at remedy does not answer the quest for rights, but it does answer the quest for propriety. It is a gift intended exclusively for the protesters and to attest to mutual belonging.

Even so, for some activists, an additional sense of belonging to a distinctive Hong Kong did not arise from any specific political platform or philosophical school. Rather, it was an unconventional sense of solidarity, defined by mutual sympathy between participants who are strangers to each other, and, to that extent, a universal rather than role-embedded love (Partaken 2017; Tsang 2018; Ku 2019; Lee 2020). Emancipation from concerns about reciprocity, albeit romanticized, facilitates an emergent sense of solidarity, even for teenagers. In the aftermath of the Umbrella Movement, one high school activist Lin Yongyao (at 45 mins, 10 seconds, at https://n.pr/38h2EMv, accessed 10 September 2020) reflected on his new-found self-confidence: "Democracy that I have understood now is to help those who need help. This is what justice means." His implicit reference to solidarity and universal caring addresses the foundation of democracy. Such solidarity-love between strangers is peculiarly embedded in their shared quest to avoid belonging to OCTS, hence a comradeship that combines belonging and humanity. Moreover, his readiness to help strangers within the same movement testifies to a hybrid of universal and Confucian love, informing a cognitive capacity to unlearn a culturally prepared disposition and emancipative practice to transcend Chineseness, that is allegedly embedded in

Confucianism. Thus, neither is Chinese political love necessarily Confucian nor is Confucian political love essential for the Chinese.

In response, Beijing's design of OCTS aims to promote national unity and regards international solidarity-love as an imperialist intervention. However, if activists can perform the role-embedded love or belonging to China – accepting an electoral system, in which only an AGZ can run for election as Chief Executive – autonomy would be followed as a matter of course. The main criticism launched by the central government carried with it appeals to benevolence. These were consistently materialist in nature, and almost entirely irrelevant to the people's rights. The backers of OCTS in Beijing reflect on both what the motherland can do to relieve activists of their life difficulties, and how activists can intellectually appreciate the welfare that has been specially granted to them.

On the first point, abundant analyses have emerged from the benevolent love perspective, that explores the activists' grievances regarding their living conditions and political environment. One widespread narrative focuses on the monopoly that a few groups/tycoons have over real estate in Hong Kong, which has caused intense residential conditions (Feng 2019). For the central authorities, a proper show of benevolence to the common Hong Kong residents is to convince the tycoons to begin to release their properties. This show of benevolence also conveys the political message: Chinese OCTS was not the source of the uprising.

The second point concerns the perceived failure of the activists to understand the rise of China. According to this view, China is able to provide ample opportunities for Hong Kong's youth to prosper. Moreover, the rise of China allegedly enables the motherland to view Hong Kong more patiently and confidently (Hu 2019). No direct interference is attempted. Rather, the People's Liberation Army soldiers took off their uniforms and voluntarily cleared from the streets the barriers that the activists had installed. In addition, noted by the *BBC News* on 4 November 2019 (https://www.bbc.com/news/world-asia-china-50297024), the Beijing authorities several times reiterated their support for, and confidence in, the ability of the Hong Kong government and its police force to handle the uprising. Implicit in this is the idea that the Hong Kong activists simply failed to understand the exact extent to which the motherland cares about their welfare.

In addition, critics of the two campaigns identified two major sources that caused an aversion to role propriety among the activists. One is the colonial and postcolonial education, which defies patriotism (Fifield 2019). As a result, there has been no opportunity for the nascent generations since 1982 and 1997, the two turning points in Hong Kong's return to China, to reflect critically upon the legacies of colonialism. Chinese cultural cultivation is believed to be extremely lacking and biased. The current teachers were either trained during the British colonial rule, or are younger teachers, who were trained by this group after the colonial period ended. According to this view, colonized pedagogy acts as an obstacle to the former colony's return to the motherland. As a result, the solidarity that emerged among the activists during the movements does not contribute to Hong Kong's stability and prosperity. Rather, by defying the role-embedded love for the country, it contributes to the reproduction of British colonization, camouflaged pedagogically within its liberalistic solidarity-love values.

The second alleged source points to the practices of solidarity-love primarily by Washington, Taipei, and London, all of which represent Beijing's strategic rivals (Brennan 2019; Bureau 2019). These forces help the activists to organize uprisings, enlist international opinion leaders to support them and fund their training (including their logistics, travel, and meetings), harbour activists when they need a break, and ship their logistical supplies from overseas. In other words, from the perspective of benevolence relations, the solidarity between the activists during the two movements was based upon strategic relations without any kin or metaphorical role propriety to support it: it was, by necessity, calculative and short-lived.

Conclusion

Universal love is both a passion and an anxiety that emerges from, and sinks into, every individual. Even so, universal love establishes relations between individuals by providing them with mutual holding when they suffer social regression. It emancipates individuals from an estranging modernity through solidarity. Universal love presumably constitutes self-identity and self-worth when a sufficient number of like-minded individuals engage in it. In contrast, benevolent love is not based upon such an intellectual and rationalist construction. Benevolent love would rather embrace natural and metaphorical kin relations, with the latter obliging mainly a social role-embedded love. Being a role-embedded love, benevolence is by no means a choice between whether or not to practise it, as it is in the case of universal love. Rather, it is an intersubjective judgment on reciprocal propriety in accordance with the context and relationships involved. Both kinds of love explain why belonging to a community is plausible, despite occasional interruptions.

OCTS sits between these two kinds of love, but illustrates the dilemma of belonging. By design, OCTS is intended to guarantee benevolent love for Hong Kong, being a former colony that is returning to the motherland. The utmost benevolence for Hong Kong is, according to this perception, that it is not obliged to supply the motherland with anything while also enjoying exemption from administration and intervention by the central authorities. With no need to reciprocate by displaying benevolent love for the motherland, nor any political room to develop its autonomous identity for recognition, Hong Kong's unfulfilled relational identity is becoming increasingly disempowering. Compared with Britain's colonial rule, under which the Hong Kong people felt superior to the motherland, OCTS positions Hong Kong below China. Hong Kong's colonial identity can ironically provide compensation in this sense. International intervention in the name of solidarity-love, embedded in humanity and rights, provides Hong Kong with the holding that is unavailable in the motherland.

However, universal love cares for neither stability nor prosperity, a principle that defines the role-propriety of the Beijing authorities. Faced with the Hong Kong activists, who were concerned about autonomy and rights, such as the unrestricted election of the Chief Executive by the people, Beijing could not help but see the activists' liberal pedagogy, judicial independence, and discriminatory treatment of Chinese migrants to indicate non-Chineseness as colonial legacies, and ones which they watch with apprehension. Consequently, autonomy is no longer a role relation of OCTS, but an entitlement that constitutes Hong Kong's self-identity and self-worth. From its benevolent love tradition, Beijing then appeals to a balance of relationships, indicated by both concessions and sanctions, aiming at ever more material benevolence and ever less room for political autonomy. This led to the two Hong Kong Acts that were passed by the US Congress. All parties ostensibly claim to love Hong Kong, but this love backfires. It will continue to backfire until the day when both of the philosophies of love are able to appreciate and recognize each other intellectually. Given that both practices of love are familiar and agreeable to the people in their daily lives, Hong Kong remains the most plausible site where such intellectual unlearning will occur.

4

Pandemic Nationalism from Wuhan to across China

(Co-authored with Pichamon Yeophantong)

Introduction

It seems logical that autocrats are accustomed to instrumentalizing nationalism and nationalists to embracing autocracy (Posen 2020; Simon 2020; Huang 2021; Bieber 2022). Nationalism can engender discursive binaries, which serve to unify or silence those people who may be losing their belonging sensibilities within a failing or challenged autocracy. However, nationalism risks defying Confucian benevolence because unity informed by binaries inevitably incurs fear, pressure, and duty, which parallel levy and labour during Confucius' time. To pre-empt the curse whereby all bad autocrats fall (see Chapter 2), the autocracy can exert caution and keep nationalism minimal in terms of its duration and intensity. In other words, nationalism, if over-stretched, simultaneously jeopardizes the credit of the autocrat as a benevolent leader and is not politically free (Han 2019). After a while, nationalism usually falls back into different forms of coexistence that restore relationality. In this regard, pandemic nationalism is a particularly apt topic. The rise and fall of pandemic nationalism reveal the symbiosis of the autocracy and its people and the irony of being nationalist in terms of governmentality and counter-governmentality.

In the absence of a common understanding of the concept of nationalism, the attempt to exploit it nevertheless continues, with apparent irony; for example, while competitive nationalism may be observed between the US and China (Jaworsky & Qiaoan 2020; Yan 2020; Yang & Chen 2020; Boylan, McBeath & Wang 2021), there simultaneously exist internal distrust and xenophobia against citizens of different ethnicity within each nation-state (Bieber 2022). Consider nationalism loosely as 'the practice of caring for the national group to which one claims to belong'. This chapter will consider how governmentality, that was embedded in nationalism during the COVID-19 pandemic, has been manufactured by the state through both top-down and bottom-up processes as well as by different 'relational communities': that is, communities that are defined by solidarity informed by the common leadership, crisis experiences, needs, or values of their members, in addition to merely an obliged belonging to a particular national category. In the case of Wuhan city, a localized form of solidarity emerged among its population in response to the discrimination by other parts of China of the city and its citizenry as a diseased 'other'. This, however, changed as the nationalist framing shifted to one that emphasized unity against the pandemic.

The Chinese experience of the COVID-19 pandemic demonstrates the unpredictable dynamics of solidarity and unity in cycles within the rise and fall of pandemic nationalism (see Chapter 1 for a definition of unpredictability). Solidarity emerged, unpredictably, among Chinese citizens with Dr Li Wenliang, the whistle-blower who issued a warning at the very start of the pandemic but was punished by the local CCP. His death shortly afterward discredited the autocratic leadership, for displaying unpredictable solidarity among otherwise stranger citizens under a culture of unity, that was alluded to an isolated – that is, unapproachable – leader. The alert CCP effectively turned Li into a national martyr to bring forth counter-governmentality. The Party reinforced nationalism by securitizing the criticism of the Party as being internationally connected. The CCP regained and retained its selfless leadership reputation by mobilizing the people to fight coronavirus. Alongside, a national quarantine policy allegedly protected the old and weak members of every family. The people internalized severe quarantine governmentality until they finally became exhausted socially as well as economically, three years later. At this point, nationwide solidarity with the predominantly Uyghur casualties of a Xinjiang blaze, arguably caused by an abusive quarantine practice, again unpredictably spread nationwide in the name of the White (or Blank) Paper Protest. For an autocracy composed mainly of docile supporters, the incapacity of the latter to remain docile poses a far greater danger than deliberate rebellion. The once-again discredited autocracy immediately resorted to counter-governmentality by relaxing the quarantine measures to reclaim its siding with the masses.

Ultimately, this chapter argues that practices of nationalism have multiple facets that reach beyond autocracy, the abuse of which leads to alternative solidarity. Indeed, the national mobilization of medical staff nationwide, each of whom bore their municipal, provincial, or regional team name, led to an unprecedented surge in national morale and the concomitant governmentality of readiness for self-sacrifice. Self-sacrifice could not last forever, though, and involution followed. As the cycles continue, pride and anger on multiple fronts for those engrossed in the Chinese nationalist sensibilities represent the means of constructing a relational network of decentred (that is, CCP-neutral) nationalism as well as a reconstituted autocracy. Eventually, such de-national threads of unpredictability helped to spread disillusionment in the hearts of the people, which culminated in the termination of the anti-pandemic quarantine policy. The regime of regimes was informed by the people's hearts, manifested in the unpredictable open aversion to leadership, and rocked the quarantine regime, which yielded accordingly. Pandemic nationalism disappeared overnight, testifying that it was neither a value nor a suppression but a belonging discourse of the autocracy, which was designed to solidify the people's hearts. The success of this was limited.

Surveying the literature on Chinese pandemic nationalism

Using the case of Chinese 'pandemic nationalism' as a basis, it becomes apparent that the existing literature in English tends to internalize the problem of rising nationalism, in the name of China, as an autocratic governmentality. Critics analyze how the disease was primarily managed by an autocracy, in order both to bring the entire citizenry under its control and also to expand China's influence in the rest of the world. Together, such critiques reveal four assumptions that it is important to discuss:

1. Chinese people tend to be accepting; for example, regarding the use of the nationalist ideology to reframe the Wuhan outbreak and subsequent developments, Fei Yan (2020: 640) argues that 'the new government narratives resonated easily with the Chinese people, who had long been subjected to political indoctrination through the state-controlled media and schooling system'. Moreover, Ming Mu's statistics-based evidence suggests that Chinese people display a particular type of dark-triad personality – narcissism, Machiavellianism, and psychopathy – that is driven by subconsciousness rather than prudence (Mu 2020).
2. Nationalism is primarily politically engineered. It is both a strategic and emotional response to the external accusation that the coronavirus originated in China or Wuhan. In fact, as Zhang and Savage (2020: 6) assert, '[t]he Chinese government is thus upset with the US and its allies (Australia, Germany, European countries), who are insisting on a thorough investigation on the origins of the virus'. Or, as Hughes observes, bans on travel from China led to a charge of racism by the Chinese government (Woods et al 2020: 814). Hugues further suggests that the political motive of the Chinese government was 'to propagate the superiority of the "China Model" of politics, after the legitimacy of the Chinese Communist Party (CCP) was badly dented by the early

mismanagement of the crisis'. Greenfeld sees Chinese nationalism as amounting to a challenge to 'the United States to a single combat, so to speak. Could you match us, President Xi essentially offered, in containing a pandemic?' (Woods et al 2020: 811).

3. It is a chronic phenomenon. This appears deeply rooted in Chinese modern history and the ensuing psychology that still prevails today. As Jaworsky and Qiaoan (2020: 298) observe: 'The glorious memory of Imperial China and the bitter memory of a "century of humiliation" serve as unifying factors for these nationalists and motivate them to exert pressure on Chinese foreign policy. Such pressure from nationalists has become one of the major reasons China has difficulties adopting more moderate foreign policy, especially in its interaction with the US' (also see Bieber 2022).

4. It is basically a Chinese problem. Nationalism is believed to serve the purpose of enhancing the CCP's legitimacy. Liu Jiacheng (2021: 486) argues that '[i]t also prioritized the national over the personal. People's personal suffering was not to be totally forgotten but was only invoked to affirm collective loss and national resilience'. Consequently, Liu (2020: 487) continues, '[t]he overwhelming performance of national triumph and repression of personal narratives marked a turn in the state's cultural governance'.

Viewed individually, these appear to be valid but nonetheless insufficient or even misleading critiques, unless we also note the emergence of voluntarism in Wuhan, the city where the first noticeable COVID-19 outbreak occurred; this has contributed to the growing sense of solidarity among and beyond the city's residents. It likewise ignores the fact that Tokyo and Taipei, both having been rivals of Beijing for different nationalist reasons prior to the outbreak, acted completely differently in order to effect changes in their relationships. Finally, it overestimates the power of an allegedly autocratic government, for Breslin (2010) observes, 'we should not imbue the Chinese leadership with total power, authority, and capacity. Even in a state as strong as this, state power has clear limitations – and crucially is much more limited than some of the official words of Chinese government seem designed to have us believe.'

Even so, as the literature suggests, nationalism is widely believed to have been a common tactic that the Chinese autocracy employed in order to galvanize the public and reorient the focus away from the state's alleged culpability regarding its crisis response (Richburg 2020; Verma 2020; Zhao 2020). The literature is indeterminate regarding whether the target of nationalism was the virus, the West, or both. For example, Kloet, Lin and Chow (2020) observed that Beijing's COVID-19 containment measures were stirring up what they coined as 'biopolitical nationalism', especially vis-à-vis the 'inefficient West'. Constructed narratives that focus on the heroic sacrifice of individuals and national unity were allegedly responsible for the rise of disaster nationalism, plus a sense of national pride and belonging, that subsumed the dissatisfaction with the government (Zhang, C. 2020b).

According to the literature in English, nationalism mainly targets the West rather than the virus. Wong (2020) noted an inward pivot of the Chinese nationalistic rhetoric that appeals to domestic audiences, to the extent that it is a by-product of the increasingly bellicose rhetoric against Chinese communities and businesses. Such 'a binary opposition between a homogeneous China and a homogeneous "West"' reinforces the view that any criticism of the government promotes the enemy's cause (Zhang, C. 2020b: 164). The discursive strategy ironically undermined the autocracy's international reputation and undercut Beijing's efforts to attract global support (Richburg 2020; Weiss 2020).

Limited discussion has been circulating on the Chinese-language platforms. Xijin Hu (2020) was among those who condemned the nationalist 'netizens' who mocked the Western countries' struggle to contain the pandemic. One rare publication that directly addresses COVID-19 and nationalism in China points out the risks associated with the irrational development and expression of nationalism during a pandemic, that might backfire regarding Xi's call for a 'Shared Future for Humankind' (Peng 2020). In the same vein, another critic equates the growing nationalism in this context with anti-Westernism that is, in essence, 'anti-human, anti-science and a wholesale rejection of our shared humanity' (Zi 2020). On the whole, though, the Chinese public played a more significant role than is generally perceived in promulgating the nationalist rhetoric and fending off dissent (Kim 2020). Before people began to act unpredictably in late 2022, following a protracted period of harsh quarantine, it was unclear how extensively the scope of this dissent might grow. On the one hand, nationalism might put pressure on the government to placate domestic audiences, thus increasing the costs of constraining it (Weiss 2020). On the other hand, the autocracy may lose sight of living people's suffering of scarcity, and so misconceive the continuing quarantine as benevolence.

Wuhan and pandemic nationalism

In the early stages of the COVID-19 crisis, the public fury that grew over the authorities' slow response to inform the public and contain the epidemic was merely intensified by the former's rush to silence the public's mourning of Li Wenliang, who was seen not only as a whistle-blower but also a martyr who died of the disease. Negative sentiments toward the government, fuelled by a sense of solidarity toward Li, rose to an unprecedented degree but proved relatively short-lived. This might be attributed to the Party's strict censorship, propaganda, and efficient counter-governmentality in redressing a spontaneous, alternative solidarity toward Wuhan in substitution for Li, as well as a genuine (regained) confidence in the government that resulted from the domestic success in curbing the virus' spread. Notably, the media content in Chinese cyberspace is marked by sentiments of national solidarity as well as a more muted nationalistic tone. What this points to, in effect, is how the formation of public opinion must be understood from both the top-down and bottom-up perspectives (Modongal 2016).

Certainly, 'positive energy' has gradually become the prominent governmentality discourse in China (see, for example, http://www.court.gov.cn/zixun-xiangqing-220051.html); Roberts (2018) especially accentuated this amid the COVID-19 crisis as serving to 'veil the harsh realities' and, as others noted, 'aim more at creating rally-around-the-flag effects' (Bandurski 2020a; Chen & Wang 2020: 213). Amid the crisis caused by the pandemic, the phrase 'Wuhan jiayou' may have sparked the most 'positive energy'. 'Jiayou', meaning literally 'add oil', is a common Chinese expression that is used to encourage people to persevere and remain strong. On the sixth day of the city's lockdown, the residents of Wuhan responded to an initiative circulated on social media to open their windows at 8pm and shout 'Wuhan jiayou', as an act of solidarity (Su 2020). This collective action lightened the mood and boosted the morale of the isolated residents. More significantly, it demonstrated the human face of the city to national audiences. Video clips of Wuhan residents shouting 'jiayou' and chanting patriotic songs on their balconies captured touching moments, that allowed people to see the city as a victim and comrade in the battle against the common enemy of coronavirus, rather than as the origin of the epidemic. As these clips went viral online, 'Wuhan jiayou' started to trend on Weibo, and Chinese netizens pledged their support for and solidarity with Wuhan during its lockdown.

'Wuhan jiayou' is a unifying slogan that prompted many spontaneous, individual initiatives that subsequently gained great traction; for instance, widely circulated on Weibo was a cartoon depicting a personified bowl of Wuhan's signature dish, hot dry noodles ('reganmian'), as a quarantined patient, while Chinese snacks from other regions were shown pressed up against the ward window, cheering him on with placards that read 'Be strong, hot dry noodles' ('reganmian, jiayou'). Within 24 hours, this post had attracted tens of thousands of reposts, including on several state official accounts such as Xinhua News (see, for example, http://www.xinhuanet.com/english/2020-02/01/c_138747797.htm). 'Reganmian' soon became an endearing term through which to refer to the city, and a symbol of national solidarity, which has since prompted many initiatives among the media and individuals, including the trend to display solidarity with Wuhan by pairing photos of reganmian with one's own hometown signature noodle dish. The mainstream narratives of community resilience and solidarity enlivened the complying autocracy. They consequently shifted the focus away from criticism of the authorities and toward the message that the government and people were fighting together (Su 2020).

In addition to the unifying power of empathy, national pride is also an element of governmentality that has engendered a greater sense of positive solidarity. Examples include the widely circulated screenshot of a COVID-19 patient's medical expenses that totalled over one million Chinese yuan. The caption read, 'perhaps only in China can the government cover all your medical expenses for coronavirus' (Wang 2020). A notable example that demonstrated 'China's power' was the construction of Huoshenshan and Leishenshan hospitals. With more than 30,000 workers working around the clock, these two makeshift hospitals were built in just over a week, in response to the strained resources in Wuhan. The international recognition of this achievement was welcomed by the Chinese public (Xue, Gao & Ma 2020). During the construction, Beijing's state broadcaster hosted real-time live-streams of the construction progress, which instantly went viral and attracted millions of netizens to join the 'online supervision' ('yunjiangong'). Nicknames were given to the hoists, forklifts, and cement mixers, and viewers could vote for their favourite (Allen 2020).

China's aid began to develop a new profile, as a result. Neil Thomas tracked the references to 'assuming the role of a great power' ('daguo dandang') in the *People's Daily*, and found that the phrase had taken off since Xi Jinping assumed leadership and surged in the first quarter of 2020 (Albert 2020). Serbian President Aleksandar Vucic stated, "the only country that can help us is China" (Hu 2020). His comments were widely cited by news outlets and public accounts on WeChat, in posts celebrating the close relationship, not only between the two countries, but also with others to whom China had been 'selflessly' sending both material assistance and medical experts. The goodwill toward and support of China were subjects of national pride, as they reflected how the country is shouldering a great responsibility and echoing the discourse of building a 'community of shared future for humankind'.

There was also arrogance. An emerging narrative on social media that compared the exceptional performance of China with that of the unenlightened West with regard to containing coronavirus stated that other countries should 'copy the homework' ('chaozuoye') that China has completed when facing the test of COVID-19, even though this metaphor was disavowed by the Chinese Ministry of Foreign Affairs (Yu & Li 2020; Zeng 2020). The arrogance of one party incurs anxiety among another. On WeChat (see, for example, https://finance.sina.com.cn/wm/2020-02-29/doc-iimxyqvz6762015.shtml), many pointed out the difficulties associated with implementing the best practices and immorality of engaging in schadenfreude. Some, moreover, pointed out how the idea had homogenized the responses of different Chinese provinces and sidestepped issues such as the mishandling of the epidemic by Hubei's provincial authorities (Jin 2020).

Public opinion in China is not homogenous. Many express a lower appreciation of the waves of positive energy and emotional tropes that are designed to stir public sentiment, with questions still being raised about government transparency and accountability (Bandurski 2020b). Although the online discussions were heavily monitored and suppressed by the ongoing censorship, Chinese netizens devised innovative ways to evade censorship and spread critical messages (Bandurski 2020c). In many cases, the propagandist messages overreached themselves and backfired publicly (Zhang, P. 2020). According to *BBC News* on 21 February 2020, (https://www.bbc.com/news/world-asia-china-51583186; also see Jane Li 2020) certain events also led to the increased public discussion of social issues, such as the gendered stories in the state media, which lauded nurses for returning to work only days after having an abortion, treating COVID-19 patients while being pregnant, or shaving their heads before joining the frontline. Many people were similarly irritated by the exploitation of people's suffering for propaganda purposes, comparing these stories to eating 'blood-soaked steamed buns' ('renxie mantou'), a well-known metaphor in Chinese that critiques profit-making at the immoral expense of others (Tian 2020).

Chinese nationalisms compared and reconsidered

Each type of nationalism is unique in the sense that solidarity and feelings for others are basically discursively or ideologically prepared in context, often mediated by a centralized being or concept – such as a legend, God, leadership, sovereignty, ideology, or race – as opposed to practical life experiences. Only after nationalism can persuade its believers to offer sacrifices to this conceptual being will it become a materialized relation and believers will collectively feel that they belong to something real. Wars are, therefore, a familiar measure in this regard. Pandemics are another. During the days of nationalist correctness, confronting a perceived nationalist regime by an inversely perceived counterforce merely serves to substantiate its imagined collective paranoia. The autocracy and its people's ability to sympathize with each other's pain and struggle testifies to the existence of nationalist counter-/governmentality.

While the binary seems conceptually indispensable, it has always been fluid in daily life. The political aspect of nationalism is doomed to lose steam after a while. This is because the social roles of real persons are malleable, as their social and cultural relations constantly evolve. There were always coexisting relations that cut across the binaries prior to or parallel with the rise of nationalist sensibilities (Bieber 2022). In fact, in the US, Woods et al (2020; also Su & Shen 2021) identify a challenge to the 'nation-state': the relation that the people will be searching for in this time of crisis is 'ideological validation', rather than 'national identification'. This further and directly relates to their support of the nation-state: if the state's policies identify with their ideology, they will support them; if they do not, they will not support them (Perry, Whitehead & Grubbs 2020). Once incurred, nevertheless, nationalism can unite as well as divide people in the short run, so politicians tend to employ it in order to manipulate the relational lens to inspire practices that silence alternative lenses for the time being.

Historically, Chinese nationalism has been defined by binaries of insiders and outsiders, patriots and betrayers, or simply you and me, as was the case elsewhere. Modern Chinese nationalism can become xenophobia, too (Liao 1990). Granted that the need to draw a boundary in order to protect an imagined nation has been the result of governmentality, it requires sacrifice, such as a memorized war or massacre, as shared prior experiences to make and reproduce the sense of political community. This is certainly not unique to either China or the Xi regime. To the extent that the binary is politically obliged and lacks shared sacrifice, there will be no sincere attempt to define or sustain it.

Indeed, various (non-nationalist) binaries are not conceived of as existing between 'the Chinese' and 'the alien'. Whether or not a person is treated as an 'other' depends not on citizenship, language, skin colour or religion, which are stable phenomena, but on the relations embedded within the context of interaction. Therefore, an alien may be exempt from the exclusion that is allegedly applied to aliens, provided that she meets the role expectation of her Chinese friends. This can usually be achieved by arranging a proper ritual or gift-giving (Shih & Huang 2020). Noticeable historical examples of individuals who have crossed the racial binaries include Anson Burlingame, Pearl Buck, Edgar Snow, and Henry Kissinger. Inversely, a Chinese person may be subjected to discriminatory treatment if she abandons her expected social role as a Chinese person. The binary of nationalism, accordingly, does not enforce a self/other frame strictly. The scope of the self is both contextual and processual; it is discursive as well as behavioural. This is likely to be true of all types of nationalism, albeit to varying degrees.

Nor is nationalism always binary, within China's COVID-19 experience. Wuhan's nationalism illustrates this point. Prior experiences of sacrifice, such as during the COVID-19 outbreak, nurture a conducive atmosphere for site-centred nationalism, unless sacrifice continues to cause exhaustion. Peculiarly, the shutting down of Wuhan proved to be such an unconventional turn of nationalism. There is no clear human target or binary. The passion for togetherness is less a matter of performing political roles than an intuitive response to the participatory sense of human struggle and strength. The binary is subjective. Those who have experienced the sacrifices of, and for, Wuhan resent anyone who appears to disrespect such solidarity, including the unresponsive CCP-led autocracy during the pandemic's early stages. That said, ostensibly the literature outside China has been alarmed by the potential capacity of the autocracy to take advantage of the Wuhan-bred nationalism, but analyses will remain superficial if they ignore how China's nationalist sentiments toward Wuhan have evolved.

The efforts to curb Chinese nationalism during the period leading up to the Beijing Olympics in 2008 are a case in point. It was argued that Beijing would use the Olympics to boost Chinese nationalism (reminiscent of what Adolf Hitler did for Nazi Germany). This seemed to make sense, given that the members of the international community had used the Olympics as an opportunity to level a global critique at China due to various issues, including Tibetans' human rights. The result was an upsurge in Chinese nationalism throughout the Olympic Games. However, this proved relatively short-lived, with Beijing spending the whole of 2010 preparing for Hu Jintao's state visit to the welcoming US in January 2011. This cycle resembled the upsurge in nationalism that occurred immediately following the bombing of the Chinese embassy in Belgrade by the US in 1999. It was anticipated that the incident would give rise to a new May 4th Movement, a nationalist movement that arose following the Paris Conference in 1919, which was considered the origin of the Communist revolution. Yet this failed to transpire, as the world accepted China into the World Trade Organization in a timely manner, in 2001.

Wuhan's absence from the nationalist literature is unsurprising. After all, Wuhan is neither a familiar nor sufficient site for the construction of a self–other binary – that is usually defined by imagined racial, statist, or civilizational differences – that would receive international or national representation. Consider the dominance of the statist discourse at the international level, which was embedded in a colonial kind of worldview. Note, for example, in hindsight, how the World Health Organization (WHO) officially announced the pandemic only after it had already hit Europe and the US. In fact, the WHO's official announcement triggered 17 countries to adopt lockdown measures of varying degrees in a matter of days (15 were European countries, with the addition of the US and Australia). The immediate implication of the timing of this judgment reflects that the Global South, including the postcolonial world of Asian countries in general – noticeably China and Iran specifically – regardless of the size of its population and territory, is not sufficiently 'the world'. In fact, according to Aso Taro (https://snjpn.net/archives/187001), Japan's vice-minister, his Italian counterpart at the G7 teleconference had responded in a lukewarm manner to his suggestion of further cooperation to control the spread of the virus because, for the latter, it was a disease of 'yellow skinned people'. Infamously, and similarly, President Trump insisted on the racializing narrative of the 'Chinese virus' rather than employing the official name of the disease.

Relationally embedded nationalism

Rightly or wrongly, observers adopted several relational themes to explain away other cases where the pandemic had been handled relatively successfully. These themes allude to the relevance of a much longer trajectory of the conditions of how people who consciously belong to the same communities have been related and, indirectly, how the Wuhan experience might evolve into wider support for CCP-led nationalism. In particular, this concerns cultural and colonial relationalities.

To begin with, colonial legacies engender psychological pressure among the postcolonial population to adopt the standard of civilization acquired from past colonial governmentality. Although such pressure breeds a sense of inferiority, it simultaneously creates an agency for adaptation, according to the perceived power matrix in context. After all, conformity is the major theme of the literature on postcoloniality (Nandy 1983; Brissett 2013; Davies 2016). Postcoloniality thus implies a thread of governmentality that leads former colonies readily to accept their vulnerability in the face of any imagined alien force, including COVID-19. It is noticeable that some commentators attribute a stronger ability to cope with COVID-19 to past colonial experiences. This relates to Korea, Singapore, Taiwan, Mongolia, Vietnam, arguably New Zealand, and, relatively speaking, even Ireland (White 2010). In the words of Fergal Bowers: 'It's the actions of citizens that have brought Ireland to this precious position. This is an astonishing feat, not to be easily squandered' (Bowers 2020).

In addition to postcolonial conformity, the trust of the authorities allegedly has other sources. Others argue, for example, that these systems are prone to illiberal democracy, which enables top-down and mutual monitoring governmentality (Kundnani 2020). Still, others see Confucianism as a contributing factor (Escobar 2020). Regardless of their veracity, these theories allude to the empowering relationalities of conformity and collectivism as necessary, albeit not sufficient, conditions for anti-pandemic performance. During the pandemic, these relationalities are believed to have reflected as well as contributed to greater governmental effectiveness.

In an attempt to save the reputation of democracy, Francis Fukuyama (2020a) accordingly argues that all that matters is the state's capacity and, therefore, the effectiveness of a state's response is completely unrelated to whether or not it is democratic. The alleged failure to anticipate the relevance of the state's capacity can serve to rescue the reputation of democracy because themes of state capacity neutralize relationality. The theme thus silences the postcolonial relationality at the national level and suffering at the subaltern level in democratic societies, as neither dissociates democracy from its performance. In fact, the term 'state's capacity' is a double-edged sword. It embraces an implicit criticism of the use of this capacity beyond disease control (for example, nationalist mobilization) and pre-empts praise for authoritarian effectiveness (Fukuyama 2020b). Instead of winning recognition from the former colonial powers, China in general and Wuhan, in particular, appear to reproduce the image of a failing regime that embraces authoritarianism – an image that has already been popularized by the anti-extradition public demonstrations in postcolonial Hong Kong, whereupon Beijing vehemently defended its right to sovereignty (see Chapter 3). COVID-19 has thus worked to enflame the old divisions, rather than uniting the people of the world (Schertzer & Woods 2020).

At least two sources of Chinese nationalism are present – Wuhan-bred and CCP-led. Wuhan-bred nationalism embraces a binary that is informed by the pandemic regime, that need not include either Hong Kong, Taiwan, or even Chinese citizens abroad, and obliges the presumed members to subscribe to a digital system of control. Such pandemic/digital nationalism breeds a sense of security among those who willingly observe the disease's control – to be controlled is equivalent to being in control (Kloet, Lin, & Chow 2020). Discrimination against unspecified others, who are not under digital control/security, is indeed apparent, but neither required nor fixed in terms of its boundaries. In contrast, CCP-led nationalism includes all of those considered Chinese nationals and obliges them to support the state in order to rival foreign intervention. Even so, the standards for determining 'Chineseness' are always interactive, contextual, and, hence, unstable.

Mutual othering is, therefore, an unnecessary prescription for Chinese nationalism (Diaz & Mountz 2020). In fact, however, discursive othering is prevalent everywhere (Cervinkova 2020) – othering the virus as an alien intrusion, othering Wuhan's residents as the virus, othering China as the invader, all of which are to be excluded/quarantined/discriminated against. All of this indicates the continuation of a deeply rooted governmentality of othering that stereotypes and reproduces a relation between the virus and an imagined alien world (Meinhof 2020). However, this delusional practice of othering has camouflaged the embedded victimization within the structuration of class, gender, and the colonial legacy as well as race (Jerónimo 2020). CCP-led nationalism commits the same camouflaging fallacy, as it adopts an epistemological binary to judge between friends and adversaries. As reported by *Guardian News*, Boris Johnson declared coronavirus to be an 'enemy' against which he went on to lead a 'national battle' (*Guardian News* 2020). This contrasts with his earlier 'herd immunity' approach, which sought to promote the coexistence of humans and the virus. Likewise, Trump's determination to decouple China took advantage of the othering discourse and a sense of exclusion (against China/the virus).

Two cases – Taiwan and Japan – illustrate how democratic relationality can both commit and transcend nationalist othering. As one of the major (allegedly internal) targets of CCP-led nationalism, Taiwan is a key representative case of mutual othering thought. In fact, the state is engaged in a peculiar practice of self-othering, or counter-nationalism. If 'othering' refers to the construction of a self–other binary and, hence, practices of exclusion, demonization, and discrimination against the other (Gover, Harper & Langton 2020), self-othering does the same by further recategorizing those presumably belonging to the scope of the self into the scope of the other due to the imagined danger of the former's relations with the other side. From the very beginning of the pandemic, Taiwan has victimized its own citizens or the PRC Chinese who are most closely related to Taiwan, who chose to cross the border to study, work, or attend family reunions, in order to demonstrate that Taiwan is more Western than Chinese. As the *Taipei Times* reported on 7 August 2020 (https://www.taipeitimes.com/News/front/archives/2020/08/07/2003741257), Taiwan refused to allow Chinese students studying in Taiwan to return to Taiwanese universities along with other international students, even though some of the latter came from areas where the pandemic was far more rife. The more extreme measure was to record the names of all of the Taiwanese people in Wuhan in its immigration data set so that, even if they were able to arrange transit using a third airport or a stopover in a third country, they would still fail to pass through passport control once in Taiwan. This lasted for over six months after the quarantine in Wuhan had been lifted.

Contrary to the Taiwanese authorities' counter-nationalism, civil society in Japan displayed an unexpected solidarity with the Chinese during the pandemic. In practice, it represented almost a copy of the Wuhan spirit with, metaphorically, China equating Wuhan and Japan equating China. Indeed, a cultural way to restore a dented relationship is through gift-giving and ritualized reciprocal role-play. This has been the tributary tradition for several thousand years. While the Taiwanese authorities succeeded in constructing the equivalence of China with the virus and immediately igniting the governmentality of its counter-nationalist platform, Japan has been enmeshed in a rapprochement with China. What, for Taiwan, was a matter of constructing an existential threat from a deadly disease was, for Japan, an issue of solidarity. The level of perceived threat contributed to the de/construction of right-wing nationalism. The mass support for China within Japanese civil society at the beginning of the pandemic is the best metaphor for vaccinating a (political) antibody. Such displays of solidarity immediately 'melted the hearts' of the Chinese people who, generally speaking, feel an intuitive distrust of Japan due to historical animosity. The resulting atmosphere of reconciliation requires neither the signatures of foreign ministers nor the initiation of a 'democratic peace' project. It also transcends national boundaries.

A metaphoric prescription for nationalism

Chinese nationalism has yet to become a long-lasting value rather than an expedient belonging discourse to distract people from their otherwise unbearable suffering. After all, prolonged nationalism defeats the purpose of caring for people's security after exerting pandemic control as a substitute for providing welfare to become the purpose of autocratic governance. What effectively restricts the overstretch of nationalism, in the long run, must be the regime of regimes, that attends to the incongruence between the discursive national people and the suffering living people, and the danger of the latter's unpredictable uprising. Even so, the danger exists within autocracy as well as democracy. The pandemic provided a metaphor for how it might rise or fall.

As Florian Bieber (2022: 22) warns, 'government responses to the pandemic risk turning fragile democracies into competitive authoritarian regimes. Such competitive authoritarian regimes might initially rely on the pandemic to justify repressive policies, but they are likely to turn to exclusionary nationalism as a key legitimizing ideology in order to sustain power.' Even so, national leaders, almost everywhere, tend to call for nationwide support in the name of nation or nationalism. Pandemic nationalism is also implicit in the recruitment of foreign, low-waged nurses and doctors to serve on the dangerous frontline. When brought to consciousness, this could inspire governmentality defined by binary correctness. Solidarity ends where the binary emerges. Even solidarity at the global level implies a binary – the human versus the coronavirus. Whatever the scope, each imagined scope necessarily indicates a self–other binary.

In the longer run, however, as the virus and humans are commonly constituted by the same ecology and related in a prior ontology, quarantine must yield to the antibody/vaccine, through which humans and the virus can restore their coexistence. Let us consider the mutual relationality resulting from the complicated intersections existing between multiple relational communities as a metaphor for a vaccine to immunize them from the othering practices toward 'yellow skin', the former colonies, Wuhan's residents, or China. In fact, such a spontaneous development of political immunity is a registered human capability, regardless of culture (Nordin 2016). Without it, critical reflections on the distribution of the pandemic as sharply disadvantageous to certain classes, races, occupations, and genders cannot emerge, and nor can democratic solidarity.

With concern for the disadvantaged in mind, China's policy of absolute quarantine, after three strict years in a row, finally made the most loyal, docile citizens desperate for an end to it in December 2022. Docile citizens are intrinsic to the governance of autocracy. However, they were unable to live a normal social life or make a living without doing business during the quarantine. The incapacity of these people to continue with usual support recalls one of the Confucian anxieties around the population and the advisors leaving the prince, immediately rocking the ship of state. Solidarity among individual citizens becomes the alternative vehicle to social belonging. According to the Confucian metaphor, the people are seeking a benevolent alternative to substitute for the extracting incumbent autocrat.

A vaccine may be an apt metaphor for a solution. Antibodies rebuild an integral community of both the virus and humankind. From the political science point of view, the people are external to autocratic governance, and electoral/partisan rivals often portray the other side of the divide as the virus: something alien, obnoxious, and contagious. This indicates political science's failure and the rejection of solidarity. The externalization of a political rival always proves a failure eventually. The vaccine, once injected into the body, reinternalizes the virus. A political antibody is not unlike an alienated population that has been reincorporated through deliberate democracy or the mass line. The incurrence of the notions of the people and the people's hearts in the studies of autocracy can deconstruct the divide between autocracy and democracy and reveal, revise, and restore the relations that have already encompassed all polities.

5

Xi Jinping's Quest for Acceptance

Given nationalism's multiple sources, potential to backfire, and unsustainable platforms in the long run, it is not a reliable vehicle for achieving the unity of the people belonging to an autocracy. An autocrat usually acquires other ideas to inform these relations, in which the people willingly centre on the autocrat at the cost of varying degrees of self-interest. These ideas reflect as well as constitute the autocrat's self-understanding. However, each autocrat inevitably experiences a fairly distinctive social preparation before assuming their incumbency. While autocrats of different generations may similarly rely on Confucianism to find their selves-in-relation vis-à-vis the people, the same ideas almost always provide different clues, that encourage them to create self-roles they think will be agreeable to the hearts of the people of their respective generation. This is why autocracy involves intersubjective interactions between the autocrat and their people, on the one hand, and is not independent of the personality of its leaders, on the other. Autocratic governmentality cannot be sufficiently understood without studying how the regime of regimes prepares each specific autocrat, and how these approaches differ or are replicated.

Between ideas and personality, a dispute always exists regarding which is responsible for the consequence of political non-/action (Tetlock 1983; Rathbun 2020; Zmigrod 2020). Well-debated examples include the impacts of Martin Heidegger's philosophy of being on his acquiescence regarding extermination camps (Wolin & Rockmore 1992), Pol Pot's indoctrination by Marxist and Maoist egalitarianism regarding the horror of the Khmer Rouge's killing fields (Ciorciari 2014; Galway 2022), and, for a more contemporary example, the effect of jihad on terrorism (Cherney & Murphy 2019), respectively, at the personal, regime, and global levels. Note the irony whereby these political ideas typically embrace and praise the infinite varieties of natural and social living things yet, at the same time, inspire an autocrat, thinker, or their alleged apologists to claim their entitlement to the infinite power to care for the people. This twist alludes to a personality trait; for example, Harold Lasswell (1948: 37–8) posited that the nature of politics is the practice of private motives displaced upon public objects and rationalized in terms of public purposes. For another example, the literature on authoritarian personality (Adorno et al 1950; Pye 1985; Nilsson & Jost 2020; Zmigrod 2020) furthers the argument to a collective level by revealing the shared need to dominate or depend among the people and its resulting appropriation of a particular ideology.

This book fills a lacuna in the literature – the use of ideas to prepare the self for challenges. The literature is instead preoccupied with how a (Chinese) autocrat's personality can lead to the ideas that shape their attitude toward the world and other people (see, for example, He 2013; Lee 2018; Luttig 2018; Torigian 2018; Gries & Yam 2020; White 2021; Zhao 2022). However, the literature neglects how personality and ideas lead to self-strategizing. Case-sensitive analysis rather than universal theorization is required in order to connect, through the medium of political personality, an idea – broadly defined as including cosmology, religious belief, ethics, and ideology – on the one hand, and policy behaviour, on the other. Accepting that ideas and personality affect the policy consequence jointly is insufficient because, as a case-sensitive agenda demonstrates, they are neither mutually independent nor stable. In addition to enabling the assessment of *the world* and policy making (Gerber et al 2010; Fatke 2017; Weber 2019; Beattie, Chen & Bettache 2022; Ollerenshaw & Johnston 2022), personality may inspire political actors to use ideas conversely to engage in *self*-preparation for being accepted and welcomed by their perceived constituencies.

From the relational perspective, again, Chapter 5 defines personality as 'the felt need of a person to be (or not be) related in certain ways' (Hansson, Jones & Carpenter 1984; Kluwer et al 2020; Kershaw et al 2021), including both the belief-evoked and non-consciously driven needs, and a political idea as 'a belief in how people are and should be related'. Chapter 1 calls this idea about people 'discursive' or 'abstract' people, as distinguished from 'living people'. An autocrat must indicate how they think the people whom they lead are, and should be, related in order for the autocrat to govern and mobilize them. Therefore, instead of a material-based influence, the autocrat's capacity to keep actors related in certain ways through discourse, affect, and rationality informs what constitutes 'power' (Pye 1985; Neustadt 1991; Zhao et al 2016; Jian 2022).

Complicating the mutual constitution of ideas and personality, China's President Xi Jinping's personality affects how he has derived inspiration from a combination of socialism, Confucianism, and Buddhism. Xi Jinping's case can exemplify the uncertain role of ideas. Autocratic governance under Xi – while relying on the ostensibly identical philosophies of Buddhism, socialism, and Confucianism, that have, arguably, albeit indirectly, respectively led to the Greater East Asian Co-Prosperity Sphere (GEACPS) of WWII Japan (Shimizu 2022), the Great Leap Forward (Baum 1964), and the Cultural

Revolution of the Chinese Communist Party (Walder 1994) – displays a different character. For Xi, these ideas do not concern the political struggles to achieve emancipation or transformation of some kind, as they were for his predecessors. Instead, these ideas inspire and guide him to protect and expand his popularity (as will be discussed later) (Schneider 2022).

To the extent that it does not concern aspiration for emancipation, Xi's cult is unlikely to be copied elsewhere, unlike Mao and Maoism, which contributed to the global revolutionary spirit (Chakrabarti 2014; Galway 2022). Xi's substitution of his popularity's protection and expansion for the emancipation of others suggests that the idea is not independent of personality. Accordingly, an idea enables the autocrat to connect specifically with their people, on top of even a spontaneous hierarchical relationship that is allegedly being prompted by the same authoritarian personality that they share (Cheng 2006). The characteristic need of an autocrat for relations explains explicitly why they need and appropriate an idea in a particular way (Smith & Mayorga-Gallo 2017).

This chapter first discusses how a study of Xi's personality may contribute to our understanding of the political consequences caused by ideas both in China and within international relations. There follows a brief review of the formation of Xi's personality during the Cultural Revolution and the implications of this for his later political style. The third part illustrates how he uses ideas to practise autocratic governmentality that simultaneously engrosses the autocrat and their people. Chapter 5 ends with a brief discussion of involution, caveats, and a conclusion.

Political ideas not for emancipation

This chapter studies Xi's ideas as his references to the self-in-relation rather than his schema for assessing and treating alters-in-relation. Implying a stable self, the literature on political personality and attitude mainly focuses on the latter agenda (see, for example, Osborne, Satherley & Sibley 2021; Federico 2022; Bromme, Rothmund & Azevedo 2022). The literature on Xi's personality likewise attends primarily to how this influences his attitude toward the world and his relations with others (He 2013; Lee 2018; Torigian 2018). It thus neglects the aspect of how Xi's relational sensibilities feedback his self-expectation or self-role to affect the use of ideas. The literature fails to address an autocrat's need for self-preparation in order to win the acceptance of the masses in context, especially within an autocracy. To that extent, it is worth noting that Xi's reliance on his ideas to inform how the world evaluates him and yields to his self-assessment precedes his attitude toward the alter masses. Nevertheless, a personality can adapt. Xi's conscious self-preparation does not preclude him from hoping, likewise, to develop (that is, emancipate) his audience into proper alter-roles, thus indicating enhanced self-confidence and changes in the relational functions of his ideas.

Personality and ideas are both attributes of political action. On the one hand, the theory of the authoritarian personality (Adorno et al 1950) explains the spontaneous mutual attraction of authoritarian leaders and their followers (Gandesha 2018; Harms et al 2018; Liu et al 2019; Nilsson and Jost 2020). Even so, the personality factor fails to explain how they interact in reality without a seemingly shared idea to guide them. Intellectually, on the other hand, leaders and their followers may consider it correct to strive for a political idea. However, an idea does not inspire subscribers automatically. An autocrat depends on ideas to conceptualize their desired relations, but maintaining a relation does not necessarily entail adhering to any particular idea (Gandesha 2019; Finchelstein 2022). Personality re/selects and re/combines ideas according to their effects on the need of the autocrat to be related in a particular way, and those successful ideas reconstitute personality (Federico & Malka 2018; Kalmoe 2020; Costello et al 2022). A nuanced understanding of the personality factor reveals that a political actor must acquire specific inspirations from an idea and the motivation to interpret and practise the idea in their own characteristic ways. These considerations illustrate the relevance of a case-sensitive analysis of Xi's personality to the literature.

The literature contains a critical thread that demonstrates how specific ideas have had severe consequences on the alters-in-relation through individual thinkers' reformulation of an idea or political leaders' reappropriation (Kurunmäki & Marjanen 2018; Sanders 2019; Chemouni & Mugiraneza 2020; Congleton 2020). The most relevant ideas here are those that gave rise to Xi's political discourses, including Buddhism, Confucianism, and socialism. All three phenomena have, in some sense, borne the blame for inspiring or justifying suppression in specific contexts or breeding particular personality types that embrace authoritarianism. These political ideas are emancipative in general, in the sense of their common praise for humanity and infinity of origin in the face of modern conditions regarding alienation and suppression. This is why they can support a relatively stable, consistent lens, that allows autocrats to assess and rectify the alter-roles of their people. A few examples will serve to demonstrate the emancipative versus suppressive sensibilities of the literature on these three ideas.

The first example is how the Kyoto School of Philosophy – with a solid Buddhist Zen legacy that facilitated an imagined transcendence over national sensibilities into a 'world history standpoint' and the Greater East Asian Co-Prosperity sphere during WWII – ironically relieved the Japanese troops from any moral restraint in the conquered areas in the name of building a kingly land. This school of thought was in itself suppressive for Kosuke Shimizu (2015: 3–5, 14) since it shuns 'critical epistemology', but 'perpetuate[s] power relations' (Stone 1999a). However, Christopher Goto-Jones sees the use of political theory by the totalitarian state as independent of the choice of the theorists, so that Nishida Kitaro, the Kyoto School's founder, could only accept that 'his ideas effectively formed part of Japan's aggressively imperialist Great East War of ideas' (Goto-Jones 2005: 2). Arguably emancipative theories defied the Kyoto School philosophers, who had to write 'between the lines', according to Kenn Nakata Steffensen (2017: 77) and suffered, in his words, 'the dismissal of the ideas' in the aftermath of Japan's defeat. Alluding to a collective personality type, which is ready to appropriate a broad spectrum of mutually incongruent theories, Tatiana Linkhoeva (2020) discovers a constituting drive of the time for liberation from Western imperialism, shared by the military and activists in the 1920s, from the left and right alike.

The practices of the Kyoto School and controversial 21st-century reassessments suggest that Buddhism can inspire autocrat-believers but not in any fixed manner (Shimizu 2021; Shimizu & Noro 2023). Theorists are not innocent, though, if their reappropriated ideas contain no check on their destructive use, leading to the unpredictable reconstitution of ideas (Shimizu 2015). While the emerging literature on the Kyoto School interrogates the philosophical thinkers' roles, intentions, and choices regarding inspiring the fascist regime, they fail to determine how the regime accepted their ideas (Goto-Jones 2008). The studies of Xi's personality can shift the focus toward the autocrat's personality instead of the philosophers' use of, and deriving of inspiration from, political theory.

For another example, the Confucian stress on education, hierarchy, self-sacrifice/discipline, and loyalty is conducive to modernization and development through the personality characteristic that is incompatible with individualist liberalism (Baumann, Winzar & Viengkham 2020; Tu 2000; Chen, Q. 2022). The literature on Mao Zedong's political personality unfailingly notices its Confucian influence, beginning from his earlier career and culminating in the mass re-education process that unfolded during the Cultural Revolution (Chang 1978; Guo 2019). Studies of the Cultural Revolution raise the analysis to the level of the national character, embedded in a family and educational tradition that is heavily informed by the Confucian institutions and ethics, which, for Lucien Pye (1968), cultivates a collective personality of repressed aggression (Solomon 1971; Chan 1985; Huang 2023). The personality type served the endless rectification campaigns and cycles of learning to unlearn. While Confucianism, in this light, is both emancipative and suppressive in terms of a general personality type (Pye 1988), the question of which phase prevails must depend on the incumbent autocrat's characteristic need for relations or, as Brown and Bērziņa-Čerenkova (2018) put it, 'utility'. This need can sensitize a particular Confucian idea, such as harmony, hard work, filial piety, or literacy.

Since Mao's Confucian influence is understood to illustrate the Chinese personality's revolutionary phase, which parallels its conservative dimension that is likewise embedded in the Confucian legacy, Maoism alerts the contemporary literature to the perceived tendency of the Confucian personality to seek dominance in the world. It refers to the totalitarian personality of the Chinese Communist Party and its leaders (Wang 2019). Nuances are seriously missing in this thread of literature, however (Jay 2022). An individualized treatment of how different leaders appropriate Confucianism to meet their characteristic needs for relationships is required (Kubat 2018). Such individualized needs are consistently overlooked in the aforementioned literature, that attends to either national or party culture. It is otherwise hard to avoid the temptation to normalize the Cultural Revolution, as if Confucian breeding routinely engenders the repetition of such extreme activism and conservatism in Chinese political history (Chien 2016). In this regard, a focused discussion of Xi's personality may provide a remedy. It can explain why he, on top of the harmony ideal, adds the self-discipline components of Confucianism, for example, and why he invites Buddhism to join forces.

For the last example, Pol Pot's obsession with egalitarianism, arguably acquired entirely through his indoctrination by Marxism and Maoism to emancipate the populace from private property, resulted in the 'killing fields' of the Khmer Rouge in the late 1970s (Pina e Cunha, Rego & Clegg, 2011). However, Henri Locard (2004: 194) interrogates the personality factor, wondering if it were 'more about the paranoia of Pol Pot and the leadership group than about … a man who espoused Maoism in his youthful days'. The class struggle has been the Maoist brand and has inspired many revolutions. Whether Maoism instigates revolutions, the revolutionary appropriates Maoism, or both, is debated. In the case of Pol Pot, there is arguably a thread of Buddhist nationalism (Appleby 2000; Salter 2000). Matthew Galway (2010: Abstract) further spots a 'racialist agenda' and 'ultra-nationalist inspiration', which, in his final analysis, was nevertheless Maoist (Galway 2022). Artificially or blindly applying a Maoism that was practically geared toward Chinese conditions to the different Cambodian conditions (Galway 2017), Pol Pot and Maoism constituted and continuously adapted each other, probably like Maoism anywhere.

Once contextualized in different relational needs, Maoism can be reconstituted. Pol Pot's genocidal programme differed sharply from the 'People's Republic of Berkeley' in the 1960s and '70s, whose believers mildly complained that 'China has changed colour' with its economic reform (Shan 2019: 383). Berkeley's group was certainly not in any leadership position but exemplified a conscious belief rather than a non-conscious need. Even Mao himself switched his reading of Maoism, composed of class struggle, command economy, and central planning before the Great Leap Forward in the late 1950s but, conversely, reduced to the Cultural Revolution since the mid-1960s. The mass-line approach was specifically evoked on each occasion to guide a political/policy turn toward emancipation or rehabilitation (Meyskens 2021), depending on what productive relations the CCP judged appropriate in the context (Solinger 1984; Emerton 2018; Hauck 2020). Xi Jinping enters the picture meaningfully because his mass line reflects his personal learning during the Cultural Revolution and, therefore, informs his belief system, which alerts him to his relation with the concrete masses. Unlike Pol Pot, who allegedly operated under the influence of paranoia, or Mao, who used the mass line as a tool for mobilization, Xi illustrates how his belief system, as a constituent of the felt need to be related, prompts him to rely on ideas, specifically Buddhism, Confucianism, and socialism, in particular ways (Brown & Bērziņa-Čerenkova 2018). His relational lack has bred a style that neither copies Mao nor may be copied by anyone else.

The illustrative literature on how Buddhism, Confucianism, and socialism, as ideas, interact with personalities yields two impressions. On the one hand, each personality type is disposed toward a preference for certain ideas. On the other, ideas guide actions by constituting a person's belief. Therefore, under the definition of personality as a felt need for certain relations, neither ideas nor personality are stable. Personality is unstable because the felt need for certain relations necessarily evolves in line with the growth of the political actor, probably due to the experiences of success and failure in meeting the ongoing relational needs. In addition, an idea or system of ideas is unstable, even though a solid belief has already been shared by many of its subscribers and beyond the reinterpretation of the autocrat, if they are conscious of their peculiar relational need. In that case, the autocrat will appropriate the idea to meet their needs and alert their people to the selected, evolving components of the idea. This is how Xi's case is theoretically illuminating in general.

In a nutshell, the reformation of Xi's personality during the Cultural Revolution informs his use of ideas. He intended to use these ideas neither to transform his people nor to assess the world but, rather, to strategize his acceptance by the people and internalize them following his perceived success. His personality evolved into a self-perceived world benefactor only during the second half of his career. His relational need has continued to develop through his previous (successful) experiences of satisfying the relational need.

Xi Jinping's emergence from the Cultural Revolution

Methodologically, this chapter adopts an interpretative approach. However, the interpretations do not come from a prior lens selected by a personality analyst. Instead, I give Xi Jinping the benefit of the doubt by gathering clues from his own remarks to weave the development of his personality and his use of ideas. Specifically, relying on the available documents, Xi tells his own personality needs, the political ideas that attract him, and the ways he has appropriated these ideas. I will put these remarks together into a plausible personality narrative for him. Such a double-interpretive method certainly cannot claim absolute truth. Even so, this method enables me to demonstrate the influence of ideas turning inward in Xi's case.

While this book is not a focused study of Xi's personality, this chapter attends to a particular component of his belief system that characterizes an integral aspect of his personality (He 2013). It is a personality factor that affects how he is determined that his people, as well as the world in general, should relate to him in a certain way, and is inclined to read and learn from different ideas accordingly to support his quest for acceptance. Specifically, this chapter argues that Xi's experiences during the Cultural Revolution gave rise to two firm lessons that guided his learning and thinking throughout his future career. Reading Confucianism, Buddhism, and socialism/Maoism enabled him to perform and transform his experiential lessons into cultural and philosophical ones. His successful post-Cultural Revolution career enhanced his confidence to implement his cultural lessons in an increasingly creative manner.

Specifically, the two initial lessons are, first, he as an individual is vulnerable, and, second, he who coalesces into the masses can survive and triumph. The first is a claim based on many sources that have already been listed in a *New York Times* article (Buckley & Tatlow 2015). The second is widely noticeable in the public record (Xi 2003; Lee 2018; Torigian 2018). By coalescing, Xi meant investigating and satisfying the needs of the masses. Given his perceived success, he could in reverse expect the masses to desire what he would desire for them, though, given his confidence, he is ready to coalesce into his would-be and discursive masses elsewhere in the world (He 2013; Lee 2018; Shirk 2018).

The mass line idea

As a youth, Xi experienced vulnerability. With his father's fall, Xi's faced many life challenges from the age of 13. His father, Xi Zhongxun, had been a top-ranking Communist general and leader before Mao imprisoned him for 16 years. Zhongxun was rehabilitated after the Cultural Revolution but then alienated Deng Xiaoping due to his differing position on General Secretary Hu Yaobang's purge and the suppression of the pro-democracy students in 1989 (Singh 2022: 156–7). Xi lived in a cave during the Cultural Revolution, between the ages of 16 and 23. His father's tumultuous career impressed him. He suffered beatings and humiliation at school, and struggled to adjust to peasant life initially (Buckley & Tatlow 2015), but gradually regrouped to become not only a devoted peasant labourer but also a village leader (Editorial Office 2012).

Xi later recalled his lessons about "reality, pragmatism, and the masses", "gained self-confidence" seven years later, and benefited from this learning throughout "his entire career" (Xi 2003). Having felt uncomfortable initially, he ran away from his poor village on one occasion. Upon his return, he attempted to adopt a different style. After Xi proved physically capable of sustaining hard labour, an increasing number of villagers came to listen to him, including the Party secretary, whom he described as "consulting him about every village affair" (Xi 2003). Thus, he virtually turned his cave residence into the centre of the village. He recalled his father's advice that social unity is the essence of all success. According to Xi (2003), the unity sensibility inspired his coalescence into the peasant masses.

Indeed, the peasants' admiration contrasted sharply with Xi's beatings by the Red Guards. The villagers' support later persuaded the Party to recruit him after he had made ten unsuccessful applications. After two years, he was the only city youth who remained and persevered in the village. He overcame solitude by assuming the leadership to improve the villagers' living conditions. Returning to the city was probably less attractive or likely to lead to achievements than remaining where he was, with his increasing popularity. Given his family record's flaws, there would have been no opportunity for the masses to embrace him in the city or bureaucracy without nepotism. He is thus appreciative of those who once helped him with practising the mass line, like a family. The Party that he can trust is the one where he has successfully endowed these supporting comrades with leadership capacities.

Xi's felt intimacy with the discursive masses continues even today. After embarking on a political career, with his rehabilitated father's help, he had an opportunity to work for the Minister of Defence, who was simultaneously a Politburo member. However, he lacked the confidence to enter high politics or the administrative environment, and soon decided to return to the basic level (Xi 2003). Based on his earlier life, Xi had developed the confidence to win the hearts of those with whom he had direct contact. He believed that the masses could prove his trustworthy calibre to the Party better than nepotism could. He thus "loves the masses as if loving my parents" (Institute of Innovation Theory 2017: 11). Only when he coalesced into the masses could he feel like he was "standing on solid ground, with strength". The bitter lives of the poor pushed him to "think pragmatically", "face challenges courageously", and "keep calm under difficult circumstances". His "emotional attachment to the masses", thus developed, contrasted strongly with the impermanent, merciless encounters that were characteristic of the Party and bureaucratic apparatus (Xi 2003). The mass line, a political slogan and principle of the Chinese Communist Party, has been Xi's approach and also what he would recommend to all who wish to overcome individual vulnerability. Similarly, the Party, in the face of the people and the nation coping with the world, is too vulnerable to neglect the mass line.

Xi's very first policy during his term as Zhejiang Provincial Governor, a post that hinted at his candidacy for future national leadership, was to turn the bottom-up channel of petition into one of top-down gathering (Xi 2007: 24 May 2004), ensuring that his officials were in constant touch with the masses in order to "win, warm, and calm the hearts of the people" (Xi 2007: 3 March 2004). Xi refers his practice of the mass line to the historical records of Fan Zhongyan (989–1052) and Zheng Banqiao (1693–1766), both of whom were devoted Confucian officials (Xi 2007: 5 January 2004). He advised that, whenever faced with difficulties, the cadres should always rely on "the wisdom and the strength of the masses to find the answer" and develop an emotional attachment to the masses (Xi 2007: 21 June 2004). At this point in his career, the mass line has already defined his personality and policy style. From the success of the mass line adopted by both historical and contemporary leaders, as well as in his village life, Xi derives his knowledge, confidence, and mission:

> 'The practices by the masses are the richest and most dynamic practices. The ulterior wisdom and strength of the masses are immense. We insist on learning from the masses and coalescing into the masses. Always have faith in the masses, rely on the masses, and work for the masses. Resolving any conflict or problem requires in-depth investigation through coalescence into the subaltern and the masses to learn from the masses. [They are] the teacher.' (Xi 2007: 21 June 2004)

Buddhist thought

If the mass line has been a typical slogan of the Party, Xi's internalization has been distinctive, as it does not simply concern ideologically transforming, mobilizing, and romanticizing the masses into the strategic tools of an autocrat, external to the masses (Ong 2022). For Xi, his pursuit of transcendence over self-centrism denotes the spirit of his mass line. For Mao, learning from the masses ultimately enabled him to revolutionize the masses. Instead, for Xi, it is the determination to become one of them without the latter being ready to rise. Given that individuals are intrinsically vulnerable, such a transcendent consciousness appears to benefit from Xi's encounter with Buddhist teachings that stress emptiness, infinity, asceticism, and otherworldliness (Salter 2000; Shimizu 2021). While Xi is not a Buddhist himself, he has been exposed to Buddhism since childhood, as his mother was a devout Buddhist and his father an intimate friend of the tenth Panchen Lama. Besides, his wife Peng Liyuan is likewise a follower of Buddhism. The process whereby Xi selectively assimilated Buddhist wisdom is unclear. Nevertheless, he has been a rare PRC leader in that he freely sprinkles his various speeches with Buddhist axioms.

As an educational ideology, Buddhism constitutes Xi's epistemological scheme. This same scheme guided the Republican Neo-Confucians and Kyoto School philosophers during the early 1900s on how to cope with Western civilization (Shih 2019; 2012: Ch 1). In brief, a Buddhist approach to modernity protects Western learning from being reduced to individualism or materialism, because the active learners have transcended their existential interests. For Xi, however, transcendence learning is undertaken primarily for self-reflection rather than to seek any emancipative solution to his people's predicaments, given that Buddhism is politically incorrect within a Marxist state. In the longer term, however, a romanticized self-image of being transcendent (for example, through Zen meditation) can lead to a disregard for suffering on a smaller scale in the name of compassion for the entire nation, humanity, or even the universe (Hesig and Maraldo 1995; Hubbard and Swanson 1997; Stone 1999b). The sacrifice of a minority is justifiable if the leaders are devoted to a far greater, even unlimited, entity. There exists such a thread of Zen in Xi's Buddhist constituent.

Xi's quotations of Zen thought reveal a desire for some kind of transcendence – a state in which mundane concerns for self-interest are set aside. In the context of individuals, transcendence refers to setting aside one's personal welfare and security; in the context of the CCP, dissolving hierarchical consciousness; and in the context of the PRC, attenuating national interests. The incurrence of Zen thought reproduces a wider relational context, in which caring for a greater entity takes priority. Due to the opacity and political incorrectness of Zen sayings, these sporadic appearances in Xi's speeches do not appear to be aimed at enlightening their audience or satisfying any needs. Rather, they must reflect Xi's spiritual reflections on how, in various capacities, he feels such little concern for his positionality that he can comfortably coalesce into the masses in context, for example, peasants vis-à-vis the county director, billions of citizens vis-à-vis the CCP Chair, or the multiple Belt & Road sites vis-à-vis the PRC President. A county director, the CCP Chair, or the PRC President would face vulnerability unless they transcended their positionalities or melted into the masses.

Xi's explanation of Buddhism's value consistently refers to its wisdom regarding openness, learning, merging, and humility, leading to civilizational exchanges and fusion across vast territories and bodies of water (Xi 2014a). These characteristics do not translate into mass-line activism, however. They nevertheless convey Xi's ideal self. Xi mentions Zen personality traits such as "intuition" (bujue) to reflect transcendence (Xi 2014b: 4 May 2014), referring to the non-consciousness of immersion in the context, "mediation" (mian bi cheng fo) (by facing a wall) to renounce selfness (Li 2018: 8 March 2013), referring to the loss of self-awareness, "the empty-self" (wu wo) to make any personal goal meaningless (Du 2018: 22 March 2019), referring to feeling the other as the other feels herself, and the Buddha's wish (xinyuan) to relieve pain (Xi 2014a: 16 September 2014), referring to a more ambitious wish engendering a more powerful result. In short, Buddhism underlies Xi's belief system, which allows him to select from the Buddhist texts in order to justify his mass-line policy. Still, he turns to Confucianism to inculcate his cadres into a sincere mass line.

Confucian thought

The first dimension of a Confucian personality tackles the breeding of virtuous individuals, including both her cadres and herself. Since Xi became the CCP Chair, he has continued to believe that adhering to the mass line will enable the party to survive any challenge. Still, he remains unsure about the party cadres, whom he knows to be corruptible (Editors 2014). He repeatedly appeals to familiar Confucian axioms in his many addresses to Party members and learned audiences. Note, for example, in the single speech celebrating the anniversary of the anti-Confucian May Fourth Movement in 2014, Xi (2014b) paradoxically cited several Confucian classics – including *The Analects*, *The Great Learning*, *The Works of Mencius* (or *Mengzi*), *The Book of Rites*, *The Book of Historical Documents*, *The Works of Guanzi*, and *The Book of Changes* – to encourage moral education. However, these sources enable him to preach about the method of individual self-disciplining. They do not inform his personality directly. Nevertheless, his familiarity with the Confucian classics indicates early, intensive value internalization and coincides with the need to overcome solitude and vulnerability by marginalizing one's personal calculation. Xi's Confucian belief alludes to how a national self consists of his personality in terms of the need for China to overcome solitude and vulnerability by sharing the fruits of its growth.

The national self pertains to the Confucian dimension of Xi's personality. In this regard, the unity sensibilities inherited from his father, alongside Xi's acknowledgment of individual vulnerability, prompt a nationalist consciousness. Confucianism coalesces the lives of individuals into a culture of over two thousand years. Such a consciousness is crucial because he could no longer visit every village as he did during his term as county director (few county directors can achieve this, even today), not to mention being, at the same time, the nation's President. Nationalism, embedded in the longevity of a people, substituted for the mass line in places he could no longer visit, especially where his corruptible colleagues failed in their duties. A distinctive trait of Xi's nationalism is that it is less an instrument of political mobilization than a remedy for his sense of individual vulnerability. To that extent, Xi rarely presents himself as a nationalist hero at the beginning of his chairmanship until his party wheedles him into posing as a saviour after the first term. Instead, his narrative decentralizes the duty of nationalism, as if all are entitled to have their own nationalist stories, which he allegedly shares and unites; hence, "the Chinese dream is ultimately the people's dream and necessarily and thoroughly dependent on the people to accomplish" (Xi 2013: 17 March 2013). Nationalism means simultaneously constituting all as a timeless people and writing everyone's story about the people. Xi's lines of nationalism emphasize:

> '[I]t is imperative to ensure the unity of the prime status of the People and the leadership of the Party, thoroughly dependent on the people to proceed with reform and openness. Each of the breakthroughs and development of the understanding and practice, the emergence and development of new things, and the innovation and accumulation of experiences in reform and openness comes from the practices and wisdom of billions of people.' (Office of Literature Research 2013: 31 December 2012)

Xi's autocratic governmentality

Indeed, no direct evidence of any connection between ideas and governmentality is retrievable. Indirectly, Xi's practices and interpretations of the mass line show traces that align with those selected ideas derived from Buddhism, Confucianism, and socialism. The following discussion evokes three levels of Xi's collective self, accordingly. Xi's need for an accepting relation to overcome the sense of vulnerability constitutes each collective self. Self-fulfilment at all levels relies on combining ideas to practise the mass line in their contexts. Overall, these three collective selves may demonstrate different uses of ideas to substantiate Xi's inclination toward a mass-line approach, as the contexts shift.

The three collective selves are the Party self, the national self, and the international self, constituting Xi's self and, in reverse, evolving from his need for (imagined) intimate relations with the discursive masses at various levels. The Party self illustrates the influence of the Buddhist quest for transcendence and emptiness through Xi's anti-corruption campaign and a supplemental Confucian self-disciplinary sensibility. The national self exemplifies the Confucian influence through pursuing the Chinese dream and national unity, and a supplemental socialist (that is, egalitarian) anti-poverty campaign. Finally, the international self manifests the socialist influence through the quest for a shared future for humankind and a supplemental Buddhist appeal to great sympathy. Corresponding to the three levels of the self, this section presents Xi's major rationale and interpretation of his anti-corruption programmes, the Chinese dream, and the shared future for humankind rather than looking at the processes of the policy programmes.

At the beginning of his term as county party secretary in the late 1980s, Xi was determined to fight corruption fearlessly. Despite his close colleagues' advice to do the contrary, he considered his offence against a few thousand cadres as trivial compared to the benefit of millions (Editors 2014). His time as Party Chair similarly began with a stress on anti-corruption, which led to nearly 500 ministerial officials and over four million Party cadres being purged by the end of 2021 (Chen, Y. 2022). Anti-corruption is unambiguously a mass-line campaign for Xi, as almost all of his speeches on anti-corruption end with a demand for coalescence into the masses. The Buddhist spirit informs his determination that the Party must remove any remaining self-centrism to transcend its limitations. Xi speaks of a need "to screw the mass line firmly" (Li 2013) and requires the Party to clean self-centrism in terms of "formalist, bureaucratic, pleasure-driven, and extravagant habits" (Xi 2013: 17 March, 2013). Once the Party has been freed from self-interest calculi, that is, it achieves a state of "self-purification", it can form a "flesh-and-blood relationship with the masses" (Xi 2017). Xi specifically evokes a Buddhist dyadic notion of "a demon" ('mo') and Buddha's way, warning that anti-corruption measures form a long battle that requires perseverance and also inspires the cultivation of a pure mind so that, when "the demon grows a foot, Buddha's way, a yard" (Xi 2021: 16 October 2014). Despite "the limitation of each individual's capability" and "time", the Party can overcome limitation as a result of the Party members "wholeheartedly serving the people" (Xi 2012a: 15 November 2012).

Nevertheless, the Party's selflessness is possible only if each Party member is adequately prepared. Confucianism's self-disciplining is the method that Xi prescribes for the Party members to learn the mass line (Chen & Shen 2014). With the Party cadres taking a leadership role, their virtue and constant self-rectification are crucial for building the people's trust. Xi requests that the leading cadres at the centre of the Party, his closest colleagues within the Politburo, should be the first to demonstrate virtue (Xi 2018: 4 December 2012). He cites Confucius' teaching that all will act righteously if the ruler does so first (Editors 2015: 14 January 2014). Through this citation, Xi clarifies his view that the Party cadres occupy a higher status in the people's eyes. For him, this higher position imposes a demand for greater selflessness, to be enforced through "self-purification, perfection, reform, and enhancement" – the "four self-becomings" that he reiterated during the following decade (Xi 2012a: 15 November 2012). Note that Xi has never employed Confucianism to allude to the state's institutional arrangement or ideological goal. These ideas of self-rectification are individual ethics that cannot be applied to a collective actor. A Confucian self with a Buddhist transcendence of the self-centrism of the Party exemplifies Xi's understanding of anti-corruption.

At the beginning of Xi's first term, the 'Chinese dream' emerged to characterize his leadership during the following decade. For him, the Chinese dream enjoys a symbiotic relationship with the Chinese nation's 'great rejuvenation', a term that has been around since 1997 but is by no means established. The first reference to it usually reflects a motivation to use an idea. Xi's initial reference to the Chinese dream, a few days after his inauguration on 29 November 2012, is telling. On this particular occasion, Xi (2012b) was unambiguous in his desire regarding "uniting all the Chinese contemporaries", literally "sons and daughters" ('er nü'), thereby engaging in a heredity discourse by insinuating a link to a continuum from the past to the future. In this Confucian-style togetherness, no one has any excuse not to prepare themselves to be part of the dream. Between these lines, the mass line is implicit but powerful in the notion of the Chinese dream, that benefits and connects all as the members of a great nation. This desire is to be fulfilled by "building well our Party". Hence, Xi, the Party, and the people, who are insignificant when acting separately, become powerful when all are selflessly faithful to the entire nation. The dream:

> '... is the shared desire of every Chinese contemporary. History teaches us that everyone's fate in the future tightly hinges on the state and nation's future fate. With the state and nation being good, everyone can be good. It will be an honourable but challenging task that requires the Chinese to work together, generation after generation.' (Xi 2012b)

If the Confucian method reifies the Buddhist spirit of transcendence of the Party self, the socialist method reifies the Confucian spirit of unity of the national self. Appealing to socialist ideas, Xi's (2012b) very first use and interpretation of the term "Chinese dream" expressly referred to China as ready to "become a well-off society", so that it was "ultimately a people's dream". He also predicted that such a day would precede the Party's centenary. At the 18th Party Congress, that nominated him Party Chair, Xi revealed his plan to eliminate poverty before July 2021. Celebrating the Chinese Communist Party's centenary on 1 July 2021, Xi pronounced the plan's realization to be "the critical first step toward" fulfilling the Chinese dream. The material base and advancement of the Chinese dream attest to the mass line, the essence of which is, for Xi, consistently that everyone is being, and must be, taken care of. Nevertheless, the mass line, informed by Confucian unity, is not the same as solidarity in a liberal tradition, since individuals are not equally responsible to each other under Confucianism but to the national self that constitutes all.

The materialist approach to the mass line is particularly relevant at the level of the international self because the Confucian unity, that assumes a heredity sensibility, or the Buddhist transcendence, that requests mediation, hardly applies. For Xi to overcome China's vulnerability as a nation-state in the world, materialism is inevitable. The international mass line points to an international anti-poverty or comprehensively well-off world. Xi's first diplomatic attempt was to transform Deng Xiaoping's 'keeping a low profile' into 'striving for achievement'. Specifically, striving means sharing China's growth with its neighbours (Yan 2014). With the Belt & Road Initiative (BRI) evolving quickly, a substitute conception that arose was the 'Common Destiny of Humankind', that later became a 'Shared Future for Humankind'. A Confucian underpinning can be detected in the gift-giving style of this BRI investment (Bunskoek & Shih 2021). However, this would be too value-laden for the hosts of BRI to make sense of the goodwill. In any case, in addition to all of the strategic and economic analysis of the BRI projects worldwide, the determination to connect the world into a relational entirety, in which China is accepted and liked, cannot be fully comprehended without falling back on an analysis of Xi's personality.

With Confucianism a distinctive culture of East Asia, the methodological discourse to make sense of China's BRI goodwill for the rest of the world turns to the Buddhist narrative, informed by a love for unlimited varieties, all prospering, as well as a move away from binaries (Ling 2020). Primarily, the narrative evokes civilizational exchanges and openness. While the socialist/egalitarian narrative emphasizes win-win situations, the Buddhist narrative incurs a romanticized history of the historical Silk Road (Winter 2020; 2021). Buddhism has been one of the most frequently cited examples of civilizational learning in the Chinese context. Xi alludes explicitly to a Buddhist spirit in his praise of the BRI's civilizational openness, reminding his audience that: "Twenty pieces of beautiful glaze excavated from the underground palace of Xian's Buddhist Famen Temple include those imported from the Eastern Roman Empire and the Islam world during the Tang Dynasty" (Li 2018). He elaborates on the spirit being a "transcendence of spatial temporality and national borders" which "revitalizes relics, legacies, and rune-like symbols and enables them to achieve immortality" (Li 2018).

Involution and caveat

Xi's need to coalesce into the discursive masses is not static. A note on involution provides clues to follow-up research. All ideas, personalities, regimes, and subsequential politics suffer involution. When an idea about the proper relations between people or the autocrat and their people emerges, this is also when it begins to involute. Given people's different needs and the ideas appropriated to meet these, relations evolve and reconstitute both ideas and personalities. Confucianism is linked to individuals' self-discipline, while Buddhism is the transcendence of self-centrism, with socialism, to cater for the material benefits of the needy. Reconstitution occurs either because: 1) a need for acceptance, once satisfied, engenders a taken-for-granted obligation of the alters to reproduce the relationship; or 2) an unsatisfied need prompts criticism of alters – as ungrateful dissidents and incompetent cadres, who are perceived to have abandoned their roles. In other words, forcing specific others to coalesce into the self-as-the-masses indicates involution. As a result, there was a Xi before December 2012, and has been another since 2013.

Involution inevitably occurred as Xi's successful career rose, compelling him to face a population that could neither be visited in person due to its size nor convinced, due to the lack of a shared idea, to imagine their common relationality. He encountered his first embarrassing moment when he reached beyond the county level and has, ever since, relied on the Party apparatus and enforced a top-down mass line. A more significant challenge is the international encounter, in which his mass line approach can hardly move beyond sheer material giving. No request for self-disciplining or unity would make sense internationally. No longer automatically appreciated by the recipient or the onlooking communities through Confucianism or Buddhism, preaching in artificial terms such as the shared future of humankind may prove estranging, or even threatening, to some. The artificial discourse could incur more material giving by China and the heightened expectation of a performed liking for China. While the BRI intends to be egalitarian, its practices may ironically appear hierarchical, unilateral, and revisionist.

In the domestic context, a successful career could give rise to a self-image of being naturally transcendent and appreciated. Transcendence sensibilities substitute for the vulnerability consciousness to shape Xi's personality within the national leadership. An emptied or self-sacrificing self, which is demanded of Xi's self by Buddhism, desensitizes alter-sacrifice, which is considered conducive to achieving the Party or nation's collective transcendence. A self-disciplining Xi who achieves Confucian unity justifies the demand on alters likewise to practise self-discipline. Material redistribution to achieve socialist egalitarianism enforces the sacrifice of the perceived affluent. As a result, embracing the unlimited possibilities of living things, loving them, and relieving their pain can involute if the autocrat conceives that the goal of total coalescence has already been achieved. Indeed, based on his past experiences, Xi might easily believe that the welcome that he receives is genuine – because he had treated the people well. In reality, however, the people he can care for directly are, at best, an insignificant sample of the entire population.

A significant caveat when looking at personality and ideas, accordingly, pertains to the relevance of the regime and political culture that prompts the entire Party and the state apparatus to report the success of the mass line thoughtlessly and mislead their ruler into hallucinating their own transcendence, and hence a vicious circle of involution (Dimitrov 2023). The autocrat and the autocracy, as regimes, can thus strategize a political idea in different ways, with Xi overcoming the various levels of the self's vulnerability but the CCP instrumentalizing ideas to enhance control. Nevertheless, the lack of a checking mechanism in terms of such a self-romanticizing tendency reinforces those ideas that silence disapproving opinions, that the Party regards as the self-centrism of all who fail to exhibit support or praise. If the autocrat feels anxious about coalescence into the masses but their subordinates worry about romanticizing only successful coalescence to demonstrate their loyalty, neither personality, idea, nor their constantly reconstituted hybridity can sufficiently explain Xi's ever-expanding scope of the mass line, based on Buddhist and Confucian ideas.

Conclusion

Although it is a cliché to claim that both the personality and the idea cause a consequence, this chapter uses Xi Jinping's case to complicate the analysis of personality as a process of the idea leading to outcomes. Specifically, this case study shows how ideas can strategize and adapt the self besides shaping one's attitude toward the world. Given the need to be related, it is inevitable that previously learned ideas will be selectively appropriated. Ultimately, the idea still reconstitutes the personality in ways that no structural determinant can predict. The appropriation and practice of the idea provide a clue to the autocrat and reconfigure their relational need. In terms of Xi Jinping's evolving personality, an initial need overcomes individual vulnerability through coalescence into the masses. Xi's personality has grown into a quest for his transcendence, informed by: 1) Buddhism while practising the Party self; 2) a reminder of the Confucian unity to prepare the self-disciplining Party cadres while practising the national self; and 3) a socialist sensibility regarding the material needs of the disadvantaged while practising the international self. The illustrative programmes include anti-corruption, the Chinese dream of anti-poverty, and the shared future of humankind. As these programmes enter maturity, what merits further discussion is the involution that Xi's mass-line personality has increasingly suffered. The anchor of autocracy – the people – starts shaking when the autocrat becomes self-involved.

6

Relational Democracy of Confucianism

Relations and governability

This chapter provides empirical evidence of the relational governmentality of democracy composed of a Confucian component. Relational democracy informs a pluriversal agenda of governability to substitute for the binary of democracy versus autocracy. The regime of regimes, which includes both, is composed of relationality that breeds a sense of resemblance between leaders and their people and their consciousness of mutual belonging. According to the inclusive definition outlined in Chapter 1, which incorporates both liberal and Confucian beliefs, in broad terms, democracy refers to policy making that is exempt from a monopoly. This definition provides the space to allow various threads of relational culture to be a component of broad democracy that may constitute a system of constraint on the (governmental) monopoly of power, while at the same time having the capacity to prevent endless involution of constitutional or electoral designs (Ackery 2005; Xu 2006).

Relational democracy is the kind of democracy in which the authorities and the people refrain from severe options to reflect unity and solidarity sensibilities. These sensibilities arise because the members of the system believe that they resemble one another in some significant way. Unity is informed by a sense of obligation to yield, and solidarity by a passion to support (see Chapter 3). They accept each other's mutual belonging and practise self-restraint when making decisions. According to this definition, the lens of relational democracy can be applied to all regimes, even stereotypical autocracy (Collier 2017; Brinkmann 2019; Kirkpatrick 2022), dependent on the people's cooperation (Haugaard 2021; Chuliá 2023). These sensibilities inform the systemic identity to restrain confrontational appeals from turning policy making into extremity or monopoly. This definition facilitates a more comprehensive understanding of how il/liberal democracy survives cleavages through relational sensibilities rather than checks and balances (C&B).

The remainder of the chapter proposes a theory of 'relations and balances' (R&B) that can exist alongside the familiar 'C&B' theory or the related idea of the separation of powers within liberal traditions, particularly the US system. R&B means that *the authorities and the people within the same system readily relate both to each other and among themselves in order to caution all against engaging in extreme behaviours.* The democratic processes can remain stable only if the members face no threat of exclusion. Without relational consciousness, liberal democracy cannot recover from an involution caused by stratification, cleavages, regression, and discrimination (see Chapter 2). The sense of security and belonging in particular requires self-restraint on the part of the incumbent and the advantaged, which is a known virtue not only in liberal and Confucian democracies (Allison 1995; Berkowitz, 1999: xi; Baxley 2010: 57–9) but also in illiberal and autocratic regimes (Wright 2008; Goes Aragão Santana 2020). Every system contains a component of relational democracy, the ways to reproduce it, and experiences with periodical involutions, long or short, frequent or rare. Self-restraint is a relational inevitability that keeps a system governable.

Systemic governability through 'relations and balances'

Wherever ethnic, religious, class, ideological, or merely power cleavages deprive the consensual entitlements of the members who belong to the same il/liberal society, the virtue of self-restraint must exist in order to transcend the imagined binaries and restore a sense of inclusive belonging. One such practice is to embed the self in a systemic relationship, symbolized by a common leader, idea, mission, history, or identity, that can exemplify the existence of a greater systemic (that is, selfless) consciousness, to calm the rival groups into reciprocally concealing their extreme self-concerns (see Introduction). This is how and why, eventually, the people will refrain from engaging in threatening views and activities.

The spirit of unity to preserve the sense in all of belonging to the system is intrinsic to illiberal or autocratic governmentality, where some members possess the power to disenable the entitlements of others (Collier 2014). Both a culture of solidarity (Adler 2008; Goh 2011) and unity (Bell 2006; Kim 2019) can restore the governability of a system that suffers from a distinctive kind of involution. A system is governable when self-regarded members of the system feel their belonging and basic needs are secure. Compared with governability, governmentality can alternatively refer to 'the readiness of individual members to coordinate in ensuring governability'. Confucian and liberal societies can enlighten each other on the relational potential of those losing governability (Peys 2021). Ultimately, abusive autocrats sometimes prompt unpredictable solidarity between subalterns to struggle for the restoration of reciprocal benevolence. Likewise, cleavages and exclusion within a liberal system facilitate intense politics of identity, sometimes with the compromising consequence of substituting sacrifices for the entitlement of the victim groups to reclaim their belonging and basic needs.

Based upon the previous chapters, in terms of the difference between solidarity and unity in denoting relational consciousness, the following discussion will argue, philosophically as well as empirically, that Confucianism encourages a spirit of unity through making concessions to inform and deconstruct the binary of democracy versus autocracy. R&B is the behavioural consequence of Confucianism. That said, solidarity-based self-restraint within liberalism and unity-based self-restraint in Confucianism operate on different levels. R&B constitutes systemic-level governmentality, while C&B and solidarity represent intra-systemic governmentality, which primarily focuses on desiring and enforcing due process and the system's norm that defines the political relations among its components. In comparison, the functions of R&B and concomitant Confucian self-restraint ensure the system's inclusiveness regarding who is entitled to belonging and benevolence. Both are important for democratic governmentality. Without sound R&B, even a well-designed C&B structure will prove incapable of precluding exclusion. In contrast, sound R&B cautions against excluding a related member as tantamount to self-exclusion.

Although the R&B theory draws on Confucianism, it addresses the previously mentioned governmentality shared by all communities – self-restraint qua relation. The theorization of self-restraint under liberalism is an established agenda (Kautz 1995; Spragens 1999; Thompson 2019). In comparison, R&B reveals that Confucianism by no means encourages the unrestrained power of the allegedly moral autocracy. Rather, the evidence reveals a style of stability that welcomes rather than suppresses pluralism (Chu et al 2010; Shin 2011). Confucianism achieves stability via fostering reciprocal relations between the autocracy and the people. Despite desiring moral leadership, the Confucian constituency is lukewarm about granting the autocrat an ideological or political monopoly in order for the system to remain inclusive and stable in the long run. Confucianism's pursuit of systemic stability indicates that the various contending versions of democracy probably all share the same need to maintain an inclusive systemic identity to ensure the governability of the polity. By no means is inclusiveness restrictively liberal or Confucian in nature, neither of which is consistently inclusive as both can suffer involution of various kinds.

Aborted civic nationalism

Western political thought treats constitutional limitations on power so seriously that preventing the authorities from doing evil is its paramount aim. On the one hand, power is not trustworthy, given that having desires is the original sin in the Christian tradition. On the other hand, pursuing desires is the common people's right by nature. Therefore, all resemble one another in terms of having desires. The shared prior understanding that rights need protection and power needs limitations constitutes the governmentality that enables them to engage in trade, competition, and coordination. Since they see each other as belonging to the same kind and therefore capable of being reasoned with, the US presidential and legislative power relies heavily on informal persuasion and networking rather than written rules (Redman 1973; Neustadt 1980).

With the sense of original sin becoming increasingly obscure, philosophers of constitutional democracy have yet to provide an alternative discourse on how the citizens and the authorities who allegedly belong to their systems are of the same self-restraining kind (Sheets et al 2011). One candidate that comes close is civic nationalism, which claims to protect everyone's civil liberties wherever they come from. Unfortunately, the tides of migrants and refugees everywhere suggest that civic nationalism proves to be weak in protecting their rights and increasingly weakening in the 21st century. Facing the national identity crisis, for example, US President Obama appealed, in his 2012 election night speech, to an abstract sense of 'togetherness' (Obama 2012). In short, a comprehensive theory of democracy, and autocracy for that matter, must simultaneously address how its members relate to one another as qualified members of the same system. Such an issue of belonging is intrinsically about governmentality.

The practice of constitutional democracy has faced two acknowledged challenges since the end of the Cold War. One challenge is illiberal democracy (Zakaria 1997). Electoral politics, that evolved from the colonial legacies everywhere, fails to quell the confrontation between either ethnic or religious groups that belong to different cohorts of migration or transnational yet cohesive groups that belong to different political systems. The other related challenge is the rising social regression, which leads to a sense of aversion toward newer immigrant populations and their children. The US presidential elections of the 21st century, to continue the above mentioned US example, have witnessed a campaigning style that increasingly echoes the fundamentalist securitization of, and resulting aversion to, difference. Formal rules cannot cope with contradictive claims to rights, power, and desires. The once-triumphant wish for the advent of the end of history, in which the troika of individualism, capitalism, and democracy will prevail over nationalism, socialism, and authoritarianism, has failed to materialize anywhere.

Solidarity, romanticized by civic nationalism, is thus volatile. The problems associated with the illiberal turn appear to be twofold in nature: the people have no choice regarding their sub-national label, which was initially colonial (that is, externally and historically imposed), so electoral defeat incurs a fear of suppression or discrimination by the victorious group. As a result, power is a virtue rather than a sin. Electoral politics expediently excavates, reproduces, or contrives social cleavages to force voters to take sides (Lipset & Rokkan 1967; Przeworski & Sprague 1986; Brooks & Manza 1997; Kitschelt 2000). Liberal democracy used to have a solution, as it is presumably built up of civic politics, where individualized citizenship connotes no immediate relevance of their group identity to civic rights. The defeat of their candidate at an election does not allude to the group's fate. In this way, citizens of different ethnicities are similarly entitled to a national due process, that entails individualizing all groups and indiscriminately protecting all citizens (Greenfeld 1992; Tamir 1993).

Civic nationalism cannot cope with the age of globalization, however, where the victims of former slavery, colonialism, militarism, imperialism, and forced labour mix in host communities that reluctantly concede such victims rights but suspect their intelligence, loyalty, religion, hygiene, networking, and even diet. The virtue of solidarity fades in the face of a perceived outgroup during real or imagined political and economic tension. In short, self-assertion, rather than self-restraint, emerges powerfully. Intra-systemic solidarity between all collapses. The alert to perceived disintegration testifies to the aborted governmentality of civic nationalism (Schlesinger 1998; Huntington 2005). Ultimately, some form of sacrifice is necessary to ensure unity at the systemic level before claims to the entitlements of the victim groups can be convincingly restored.

As Chapter 3 painstakingly demonstrates, while self-restraint is a norm that is similarly stressed under Christianity and Confucianism, important contrasts exist in terms of their philosophy, institution, and practice. Liberal self-restraint acknowledges the entitlement of all to the protection of their rights. It works most powerfully among non-acquaintances belonging to the same communities of practice (Adler 2008), where procedures organize all into synchronized participants who are restrained from encroaching on others' rights. Comprising self-respect, liberal self-restraint thus confirms the self-worth of all. Relational security, indicated by the citizens' self-conscious observance of procedure, can then achieve solidarity among non-acquaintances. Self-restraint simultaneously attests to the shared identity with the political system that institutionalizes due process. Solidarity becomes, accordingly, a product of rationality (Adler 2008) and civilization (Linklater 2021). Even anarchical conditions within international politics can evolve into regimes through the self-restraint of rational states, both liberal and illiberal (Ikenberry 2001; Steele 2019).

On the contrary, Confucian self-restraint demands the unity of a greater self, whose security and well-being represent a guarantee of the security and welfare of its members collectively. This greater self usually adopts the metaphor of the family. A subscription to unity incurs self-sacrifice, and so does not concern a reciprocal exchange for the rights of all between equals but, rather, it is an absolute duty to ensure the survival of the greater self, hence disregarding immediate self-worth. Unity around a selfless leader, as opposed to solidarity informed by prior binding universal values and procedures, reconfirms mutual acceptance between seeming strangers. For Confucius himself, people of different ethnicities, customs, classes, religions, and so on, are kin by default (Tan 2009: 151), except that they are unsure which kinship, without gift-exchange, symbolizes a mutually acceptable relation. This relation ultimately relies on a common leader to honour because they represent the selfless heavenly order. The coexistence of dissimilarities is preserved by shunning the synchronization of any universal rules and rights, camouflaging differences through ritual qua decency, and reciprocating benevolence, periodically (Roach 2019).

The reference to Confucianism in the following discussion is primarily linked to cosmological beliefs (Hofstede & Bond 1988; Hwang 2012; Han 2013), rather than sagehood, institution, or ritual. Such an attitudinal orientation contrasts significantly with the liberal premise that individuals are autonomous actors that are only bound together by the due process of rights protection (Park & Shin 2006; Bell 2007; Richey 2013). Due processes in multilateral settings among self-restraining non-acquaintances would probably deprive the Confucian actors of the relational security provided by belonging to the greater self. Abiding by allegedly due processes might damage the integrity of the greater self by privileging individuals over the group or imagining their sameness at the expense of differences. Under Confucianism, self-restraints mean belonging, as indicated by proper rituals to worship the common leader, ancestor, or Heaven (Yang & Rosenblatt 2008; Lew 2011). Sacrifices, rather than rights, confirm the desire for belonging; belonging guarantees benevolence rather than solidarity. That is why the constituents of self-restraint under Confucianism are negotiable according to the context, thus attending to the flexibility and inclusiveness of the system and involving a kind of 'actionism' (Peys & Steele 2021: 3).

In order for democracy embedded in the individualist epistemology of rights to remain socially cohesive, some degree of social and cultural governmentality to comfort both parties of the encounter between ontological strangers (that is, the former colonizing and colonized populations) is required. They used to be socially and economically familiar to each other but, once they enter the postcolonial period, the adoption of individualizing liberalism in the postcolonies provides no discursive room to blame anyone but themselves for continuously being the primitive and mineral and cash crop plantations, hence reinforcing, rather than emancipating, their racial inferiority. However, this status of quasi-slavery appears to be a rational choice for individuals in aggregate. In the eyes of the parasite colonial societies, immigrants are reduced to absolute otherness to be guarded.

Consequently, the promise of inclusion speaks mainly and in depth, albeit indirectly, to the racially, sexually, religiously, and economically advantaged strata, domestically as well as internationally (Monroe 2020; Schramm 2020; Sabelo 2022). Ironically, accordingly, exclusion and discrimination are the components of liberal governmentality in practice. Fear of an anticipated political defeat due to the shifting balance of numbers leads to democratic failure (West & Jeffrey 2006: 19; 22). In short, the cleavages at the systemic level, caused by the legacies of the past and practically continuous colonialism, automatically destroy the intra-systemic solidarity. If they pre-empt becoming less advantaged, the due processes will suffer due to hypocrisy, and the system will become illiberal.

The subsequent discussion on a survey draws on Confucian wisdom in both China and Taiwan to illustrate how a thinking route to inclusiveness at the systemic level enables the people to stay related and balance extreme tendencies in thought. This does not mean that China and Taiwan are the same kind of Confucian state. Nevertheless, the different institutional arrangements of China's one-party and Taiwan's electoral rule neither fully relate nor guarantee the alert to the monopoly of each polity. Rather, the Confucian self-restraint at the systemic level reduces the significance of the differences between the institutional arrangements of the two societies.

Epistemicide in constitutional democracy

The postcolonial century, which began in the 1960s, has mainly suffered a systemic identity crisis. To the extent that it ignores the absence of a stable systemic identity everywhere (Hu 1998), modern political theory (including the long-lived system theory (Almond & Verba 1963; Easton 1965) which deals with intra-system behaviour) is generally racist in nature, as applied to postcolonial societies in particular (Sabelo 2018; 2022). In a nutshell, it is tantamount to a civilizing project to liberate people from their colonized racial identities so that they may act as independent individuals and so transcend their unfortunate past. To that extent, relying on the individual members' trust in due process is an intrinsically flawed programme. Internally, individualization misconceives the colonized population as aggregate free labourers, an identity that silences their collective past and continuously subjects each one of them to the same productive role that was assigned by the former colonial powers, disguising colonization as their rational choice. Externally, the massive exploitation of raw materials likewise continues under the guise of a free exchange between nations, based allegedly upon national interest calculi.

Consequently, the racial distinction at the systemic level is justifiable. The spirit of solidarity cannot prevent the discriminative or violent treatment of the perceived inferior out-group. However, contemporary constitutional liberalism attends primarily to the relation between the various branches of the authorities as well as that between the individual citizens and the authorities, to the negligence of the need for an integrative mechanism, be it national or post-national (Abizadeh 2002; 2004). Lingering slavery, colonization, or even genocide escape individualizing constitutionalism and ring no bells in liberal governmentality.

Constitutional democracy relies on the conviction that, to protect individual citizens from the abuse of power, the government's power should be divided or limited, multiple parties may compete for public office at elections, and elections should be regular (and hence 'due') processes. None of these institutional or practical checks on the administrative power guarantees constitutionalism unless the actors, in their relevant capacities, decide to apply measures to check the abuse of power. In fact, a democratic constitution can succumb to the people's volition to enhance rather than limit their leaders' discretion (Fromm 1942; Pye 1985), usually renouncing self-restraint toward a perceived out-group and resulting in illiberal politics. Illiberal politics, which has plagued constitutionalism, usually involves constructed racism. As such, the history of the US is linked with slavery, while Europe witnessed the Holocaust. Both legacies linger on. The use of constitutionalism to institutionalize the self-restraint of elected leaders and their constituencies is, therefore, indefinite.

A culture of self-restraint is only intermittently reliable, too. Even in the US, where liberalism enjoys both constitutional and cultural support, national security advisors could not resist taking advantage of the 911 terrorist attacks, for example, to launch a war against the virtually fabricated ground of Iraq's possession of weapons of mass destruction. The people could believe in them not only because they all subscribed to the liberal governmentality but also because misinformation about a Muslim Arab is either conveniently believable or harmless to liberal governmentality. The same leaders even approved the torture of Iraqi prisoners-of-war (Cerf & Navasky 2008; McMurtry 2013).

The condition for constitutionalism is certainly less sanguine, where no such tradition of liberalism at all exists, as in the US. In modern Chinese history, for example, appealing to the extra-systemic call for unity has been effective in convincing the presumably separate branches to renounce their duty regarding C&B. This included Yuan Shikai's (1859–1916) infamous short-lived attempt to regain the emperorship in 1916 through convening an extra-constitutional body – the Representative Assembly. Another example, in then newly democratized Taiwan, is Li Denghui's (1923–2020) acclaimed amendment from a parliamentary constitution toward presidential leadership via the convening of a similar ad hoc body of the Representative Assembly.

Nevertheless, civic nationalism remains an attractive programme for transcending illiberal politics. Civic nationalism offers an alternative to deliberate democracy (see Chapter 2) as a remedy to the involution of liberal democracy, which is now reduced to a synonym for cleavages, corruption, and war. Consider that illiberal politics draws on an attitude of aversion to an ethnic target group. In that case, liberalism strives to individualize one's ethnic identity to create the illusion that this is a matter of choice (Glass 1995). Nevertheless, civic nationalism, as a theory, faces serious challenges in the age of globalization, because globalization sensitizes ethnic representations and undergirds them with a politically irresistible ideology of sub- or cross-national tribalism. At the end of the Cold War, in the 1990s, 'ethnic cleansing' occurred in the Balkans, and fundamentalist discourses have spread within US politics in the 21st century (Campbell 1998; Smidt et al 2010). Illiberal democracy is, accordingly, not simply the patent of the Global South.

It appears that neither individual citizens nor ethnic groups that institutionally belong to the same political system can automatically relate through a solidarity consciousness. They are increasingly estranged from one another. In times of difficulty, liberal democracy consistently fails the test of exercising self-restraint at the systemic level. Individual rights as the boundary of the system become blurred, due to the struggle of who should be in and who out. After all, self-restraint, motivated by rights consciousness, is not aimed at group unity, nor does constitutionalism, in itself, help to determine the criteria for membership of the system. On the other hand, however, religious, ethnic, or regional identities, enacted to protect specific sub-national groups, are not, in themselves, subject to democratic procedures. Therefore, for a democracy to sustain the challenge posed by politics of difference, other mechanisms must lead divergent components of the system toward mutual acceptance (Haugaard 2021), and hence relational democracy. Such a systemic mechanism of mutual relating is not discursively evident in liberalism. A clue exists in Confucian self-restraint, which deliberately breeds an overarching systemic identity that neutralizes religious, regional, or ethnic divides.

Self-restraint as relational democracy

In his peculiar reinterpretation of illiberal democracy, Daniel Bell defends Confucian societies' illiberal politics (Bell 1996). His illiberal politics is not infected with ethnic confrontation but, rather, refers to the benevolent ruling of the entire system by gentlemen. Implicitly, Confucianism pertains to national politics, which transcends ethnic division. Confucianism stresses the greater self (Hwang 2012: 280– 81; 340– 1). All should be cared for, regardless of their contribution to the welfare and security of society. Ethnic politics has no legitimacy under Confucianism. If not necessarily welcome, ethnic difference is rarely a source of alarm in Confucian society. Instead, mixed kinship has been regarded, conventionally, as a positive measure, designed to transcend the ethnic boundary (He 2004). Caring for the vulnerable is one of the most important rituals for Confucianism, because decent leaders rule under the pretension that all are related as brothers (Roach 2019). Ethnic and religious cleavages are governable through rituals of the greater self that are designed to calm the people, despite the discrimination that continues in practice.

For Bell, whose perspective comes from within Confucianism, the puzzle concerns, not ethnic conflict, but, rather, how to alleviate the disintegrating consequence of the self-centric values of liberal democracy, which are partly embedded in the C&B device (Bell 2007). Bell and his colleagues find that Confucianism is far more advanced in terms of conceiving good governance, presumably because selfless leaders are responsible for the welfare of the entire system rather than primarily their own constituency. Another interrelated Confucian ideology, that is opposed to the assumptions of constitutional democracy, is the nature of politics. Empirical findings show that constitutional democracy's treatment of the government as a necessary evil contradicts Confucianism's regard for it as a symbol of the highest moral order.

That said, a set of survey data, acquired from the East Asia Barometer (2005– 8) and discussed in the following paragraphs, registers an ostensible contradiction, indicating a desire for moderation; namely, the respondents from China and Taiwan favour neither a dominant government nor potentially chaotic participation qua C&B. (To access the data, researchers should apply via: http://www.asianbarometer.org/newenglish/surveys/Data Release.htm.) This makes sense to the cultures of unity and self-restraint, however, as unity promotes inclusiveness while combatting extremity. Inclusiveness averts the monopolizing authorities that abort consultation, while extremity, that causes chaos, is a perceived danger. The people's wish to restrain extremity carries the key message of the culture of unity.

Symbolic unity is a major mechanism of relationality. Indeed, 86% and 69% of the Chinese and Taiwanese respondents to the East Asia Barometer survey responded positively to the statement, 'Government leaders are like the head of a family, we should all follow their decisions'. Informing the same relational governmentality, 79% and 75% of the Chinese and Taiwanese respondents, respectively, responded positively to the statement, 'The relationship between the government and the people should be like that between parents and children'. The government and the people alike are obliged to practise self-restraint and consider each other's needs.

Because of this moral pretension, Confucianism could approach liberalism with caution and qualification, lest individual rights' consciousness should stimulate self-concerns and, consequently, dissolve their unity consciousness. The East Asia Barometer shows that 57% of the Chinese and Taiwanese respondents responded positively to the statement that the 'harmony of the community will be disrupted if people organize many groups' (although almost 38% of the latter did not). The same tendency appears regarding the statement that, 'If people have too many different ways of thinking, society will be chaotic', to which 56% and 65% of the Taiwanese and Chinese respondents responded positively, and 26% and 31% negatively, respectively. Two related propositions that arise are: 1) if the authorities are conceived of as a necessary evil, a relational democracy must install C&B; and 2) if the authorities are a necessary moral, a relational democracy must ensure that all can relate to them, however incongruently.

On the one hand, C&B cannot guarantee the rights of different races, beliefs, or classes; on the other, Confucianism alone is insufficient to restrain autocrats' abuse of power. C&B may backfire under Confucianism because multiple candidates compel all to present one another either as sharing partial interests or as traitors. In comparison, candidates fail to represent their particular constituency under Confucianism. Public campaigning in the latter context is zero-sum, with no option for pursuing a middle way (Pye 1981: 1). The competition to win the entire population necessarily generates anxiety. Power contenders tend to earmark their opponents as either outsiders or traitors (Shih 1999; 2007). Otherwise, it would be impossible to explain why someone else would oppose one's presumably selfless stance. In this regard, the national politics that suffers cleavages could, even under an ostensibly liberal system, risk sparking a witch hunt, with the worrisome irony of destroying unity (Schmitt 1996).

Being disquieted by their clash, the people can only remain calm and supportive when politicians display self-restraint. Hence, 59% and 80% of the Chinese and Taiwanese participants, respectively, responded positively to the statement that, 'Open quarrels (criticisms) among politicians are harmful to society'. With Taiwan witnessing intense political rivalry, open quarrels enhance the possibility that extremism will arise. Therefore, the Taiwanese are more anxious than the Chinese about open quarrels. Similarly, 50% and 52% of the Chinese and Taiwanese interviewees, respectively, responded negatively to the statement that, 'Conflict among political groups is not a bad thing for our country'. Note, though, that, having suffered an intense cleavage in their national identity, the Taiwanese respondents who agree with the statement display a relatively low but impressive rate of 40%. With the authorities lacking dominant power, some people certainly hope that there exist politicians who will protect their identities.

Self-restraint proves to be a widespread norm, that is expected of politicians, the authorities, and the people. Indeed, 72% and 71% of the Chinese and the Taiwanese respondents, respectively, responded positively to the statement that, 'If a government policy serves the interests of the majority of people, I should support it, even if it jeopardizes my private interests'. Furthermore, 76% and 51% of the Chinese and Taiwanese respondents, respectively, responded positively to the statement that, 'For the sake of the national community/society, the individual should be prepared to sacrifice his/her personal interest'. The national identity cleavage does not prevent the Taiwanese respondents from alleging loyalty to their own national identity with the same unwavering attitude as their Chinese counterparts, with 84% and 82% of the Chinese and Taiwanese participants responding positively to the statement that, 'A citizen should always remain loyal only to his country, no matter how imperfect it is or what wrong it has done'.

Regarding the leader, restraint is likewise a proper norm. Fewer respondents support the idea of a government wielding an ideological monopoly to disqualify politically incorrect articulation. Therefore, the East Asia Barometer records that 49% and 22% of the Chinese and Taiwanese respondents, respectively, responded positively to the statement that, 'The government should decide whether certain ideas should be allowed to be discussed in society', while 24% and 71%, respectively, responded negatively to it. Granted a more submissive Chinese performance, the support for a platform to insist on ideological consistency is by no means absolute. To that extent, an autocrat enjoys no sure legitimacy to create policy arbitrarily, given that 35% and 33% of the Chinese and Taiwanese respondents responded positively, but 44% and 63% responded negatively, respectively, to the statement that, 'If we have political leaders who are morally upright, we can let them decide everything'.

Indirect evidence shows that the relational balance that the constituency seeks is linked to how the members of the society can act without having to side with extreme positions. Multiple links between candidates and their constituencies are typical. This is not unlike the repeated cases throughout Chinese dynastic and modern history, in which the local gentry negotiated for peace with each ruling force that arrived in turn, regardless of the latter's family tree, ethnicity or loyalty (Skinner 1964–5: 3–43, 195–228, 363–99; Naito 1983; Shue 1988). The threat of disunity is dissolved through this multiple networking, when the multiple bilateral relationships with each political force remain stable, regardless of the electoral results. Therefore, the respondents who are in need of care are better at private than public participation, for the literature suggests that lobbying in the process of street-level administration makes far better sense to Confucian society (King 1975; Shi 1997) compared with C&B, which stresses lobbying for a general change in the legislation.

This by no means suggests that relational democracy is sheer opportunism, negligent of justice, or pseudo-liberal in nature. Confucianism seeks long-term stability and unity, to balance the passion for justice at the present moment, based on the assumption that no state or version of justice can outlive the greatest good of peaceful coexistence. Patience, rather than pushing, entails the appropriate practice of self-restraint. Immediate resolutions are accordingly counterproductive. Of the Chinese and Taiwanese participants, 39% and 17% responded positively to the statement that, 'When dealing with others, securing one's immediate interests should be more important than developing a long-term relationship', while 46% and 78% responded negatively, respectively. A noteworthy difference between the Chinese and Taiwanese respondents is that 44% and 20% responded positively to the statement that, 'The best way to deal with complicated political issues should be to leave them to the future', while 26% and 66% responded negatively, respectively: so far more Chinese respondents than Taiwanese respondents agreed with this statement. The Taiwanese respondents' strong alienation from the future may be attributed to the uncertainty of the national identity in Taiwan.

Even currently, the respondents at both sites seem to consider the monopolizing authorities unhelpful, as 62% and 76% of the Chinese and Taiwanese participants, respectively, responded negatively to the statement, 'We should get rid of parliament and elections and have a strong leader decide things'. Regarding the opposition party, 83% of the Taiwanese participants responded negatively to the statement concerning a system in which 'only one political party is allowed to stand for election and hold office'. While chaos is undesirable, restraining unity is acceptable, provided that a minimum level of governability is maintained (Shih et al 2019: Ch 6), hence leading to inclusiveness and stability. Governability incurs no C&B. It exemplifies a selfless quality through the coexistence of the incompatible. The aesthetic characteristics of governability tend to privilege pragmatism over rationalism (Hall & Ames 2003).

These empirical results reflect Confucian governmentality in China and Taiwan. It denotes the coexistence of a deference to authority and group unity, on the one hand, and the acceptance of the differing opinions of individuals and politicians, on the other. In East Asia, Doh Chull Shin finds that Confucian communities embrace traditional values that are incompatible with liberalism (Shin 2011; Kim 2019). This finding is in line with the R&B argument that the concern with C&B does not motivate tolerance, in the way that relational security does. The latter quest camouflages the ethnic, religious, and ideological binaries through certain unity rituals and bypasses the issue of sincerity. The essence of R&B is governability, undergirded by stable relationality and, to that end, the cognitive capacity to restrain from interrogating differences.

Governability as restraining extremism

Relational democracy prefers governability to C&B. An inductive factor analysis of the East Asia Barometer yields three essentially R&B factors that are informed by the mutual acceptance sensibilities to assess the quality of governability. I label these: 1) the strength of other orientation, 2) the disposition for unity, and 3) the readiness for restraint. These three relational factors, which are drawn from a list of 14 Chinese and 11 Taiwanese factors in total, based on all of the responses to the 40 statements regarding attitudes toward democracy, include one Chinese R&B factor and two Taiwanese R&B factors. Combined, these three factors operate independently of a belief in liberalism. Within the scope of R&B analysis, the in/tolerance of differences reflects the people's relational concerns rather than their internalization of liberalism. As a result, the people may appear to perform inconsistently when measured on a scale of liberalism. However, relational governmentality may be aligned with their answers. The governmentality of R&B is that both the authorities and their constituencies must constantly judge the conditions in order to decide which of the unrestrained actions and thoughts they should balance and how – by endorsing or disapproving them.

Specifically, the 'R&B' factor in the Chinese poll – the other orientation – indicates that the people consistently expect the same degree of moderation in the actions of both the government and the people (see Table 6.1). Regarding the people's other orientation, the four positively associated statements are 'placing personal interests second to those of the family', 'supporting government policy that is personally disapproved', 'accepting the parent-child metaphor for the government-people relation', and 'difficulty in discussing politics with those who disagree'. These four variables are also negatively associated with the statement that 'morally right leaders should decide everything', which advises that moral leaders still must listen to others. The other orientation factor explains the level and direction of governability,

Table 6.1: The Chinese R&B factor: other-orientation

+.471	For the sake of the family, the individual should put his personal interests second.
+.407	People should always support the decisions of their government even if they disagree with them.
+.367	The relationship between the government and the people should be like that between parents and children.
-.344	If we have political leaders who are morally upright, we can let them decide everything.
+.329	Would you have a hard time conversing with your friends or co-workers about politics if you had differing opinions?

Notes: Factor analysis is based upon the survey data acquired from East Asia Barometer (2005–8). To access the data, follow the procedures provided at https://www.asianbarometer.org/survey.jsp?page=s10. The five variables in the table can be respectively labelled as familism, authoritarianism, patriarchy, collective leadership, and harmony.

because it denotes how prepared the people are to adapt according to the perceived needs of others. The constitution of the self through a concern for others (or a lack thereof) affects the imagined unity of the community more deeply than does the monopoly of policy making (or lack thereof) by a moral leader.

The first factor in the Taiwanese poll – the unity factor – combines the variable that suggests that 'one should not insist on one's disputed opinion', with the two other variables showing negative attitudes toward the views that 'harmony will be disrupted if people organize lots of groups' and 'society will be chaotic if people have too many different ways of thinking' (see Table 6.2). These three variables represent attitudes toward disputation, multi-party or interest groups, and plural thinking. While the two variables of multi-party and pluralism can be conceived of as either liberal or relational attitudes, the first does not concern liberalism, but a recognizably relational disposition. Therefore, with the association of all three being statistically significant, this factor plausibly reveals a relation rather than a belief in liberalism.

The second factor in Taiwan – the restraint factor – includes a consistent lens with which to guide the attitudes toward the government and the people (see Table 6.3). Thus, at the social level, the restraints (or lack thereof) on 'immediate interest concerns' in one's life planning and social capital calculation in one's 'altruist action' are associated with, at the political level, the expectation (or lack thereof) that politicians will refrain from engaging in 'open quarrels' and that the government will refrain from 'attaining unreserved support'. This factor empirically testifies to an attitudinal force that is essential in influencing governability performance.

Governability denotes, in terms of the three R&B factors, refraining from extreme actions. Of the Chinese and Taiwanese participants, 34% and 56% responded positively to the statement that, 'If the government is constantly checked [that is, monitored and supervised] by the legislature, it cannot possibly accomplish great things', while fewer of them, respectively 21% and 34%, responded negatively. Two lessons can be learned here. First,

Table 6.2: The first Taiwanese R&B factor: unity

-.349	Harmony of the community will be disrupted if people organize lots of groups.
-.316	If people have too many different ways of thinking, society will be chaotic.
+.300	A person should not insist on his own opinion if his co-workers disagree with him.

Notes: Factor analysis is based upon the survey data acquired from East Asia Barometer (2005–8). To access the data, follow the procedures provided at https://www.asianbarometer.org/survey.jsp?page=s10. The three variables in the table can be respectively labelled as multi-party, pluralism, and articulation.

Table 6.3: The second Taiwanese R&B factor: restraint

+.305	When dealing with others, securing one's immediate interests should be more important than developing a long-term relationship.
−.310	Open quarrels (criticisms) among politicians are harmful to society.
+.334	People should always support the decisions of their government even if they disagree with them.
+.449	Do you agree or disagree with the following statement: By helping people in trouble today, someone else will help me when I am in trouble someday.

Notes: Factor analysis is based upon the survey data acquired from East Asia Barometer (2005–8). To access the data, follow the procedures provided at https://www.asianbarometer.org/survey.jsp?page=s10. The four variables in the table can be respectively labelled as: short-term benefits vs long-term benefits; unrestrained politicians vs restrained politicians; authoritarianism vs qualified authoritarianism; and social capital vs altruism.

relatively more respondents feel uncomfortable about the legislative checks on the administration in both China and Taiwan. Second, the more active legislature in Taiwan yields weaker support for legislative checks than that existing in China. The implication is that legislative activism matters more than the level of liberalism in determining the attitude toward C&B, and that such activism is conceived of as a *negative* attribute. Governability rests upon the moderation of all sides. Indeed, 86% and 69% of the Chinese and Taiwanese participants, respectively, responded positively to the statement that, 'Political reform should be introduced little-by-little instead of all-at-once'.

Note that the quest for governability also embraces more room for individuals than the authorities. Consider the results of two survey questions conducted by the East Asia Barometer. Of the Chinese and Taiwanese participants, 63% and 48% responded positively and 30% and 48% negatively, respectively, to the statement that, 'Sometimes one has to follow one's own beliefs regardless of what other people think' (with an equal split between the Taiwanese respondents). Moreover, 25% and 11% of the respondents responded positively to the statement that, 'The most important thing for political leaders is to accomplish their goals even if they have to ignore the established procedure', while 35% and 82% responded negatively, respectively. It is notable that both the Chinese and Taiwanese respondents displayed greater support for the idea of themselves acting assertively, rather than the authorities (at 63:25% and 48:11%, respectively). Meanwhile, a significant 55% and 68% of the Chinese and Taiwanese participants, respectively, responded negatively to the statement that, 'When the country is facing a difficult situation, it is OK for the government to disregard the law in order to deal with the situation'.

Ultimately, the notion of 'legitimacy' has no exact Chinese equivalent (Jiang & Bell 2012). What is justifiable requires a shift in perspective (Lerner

2002: 28–9). When legitimacy is denied to a regime or political figure ruling in the Chinese context, they may recover from the image of corruption or suppression to win a selfless reputation at a later stage. A regime claims legitimacy by transcending the interests of the regime itself (Bell 2011: 143). Pardoned due to the people's need to restore governability, 'barbarians', 'imperialists', 'bandits', and any brutal forces of intrusion can stage an inclusive ritual to restore legitimacy, even if they have committed mass killings. The massive suppression of a pro-democracy rally on 4 June 1989 exemplifies this irony. The crackdown on students and workers on that day discredited the same autocrat, Deng Xiaoping, who established a worldwide reputation decades later for restoring governability to facilitate reform.

As with the 4 June anomaly, the people feel uncomfortable about extreme measures. The authorities are expected to adopt a relaxed approach. Let us take as an example the question of whether Taiwan's political future will be that of an independent nation or a piece of lost territory that will be reunited with China (Huang 2006). A governability problem exists between the pro-independence constituency and the lukewarm others within the same system. Increasingly, mutual estrangement threatens R&B. An R&B pursuit of inclusiveness and liberalism share the preference for tolerance. However, the liberal constituency will probably resort to illiberal exclusion to perceived 'absolute' alterity or otherness, such as the migrants of former colonies, once they grow weary of the due processes (Nordin & Smith 2019). In comparison, a Confucian autocrat is likely to adopt, instead, enduring preferential treatment, albeit interrupted at intervals by periods of punitive measures.

Given this, reinterpreting Taiwan's liberalism from the perspective of relational democracy can shed light on the democratic perspective of Chinese politics. In short, a positive Taiwanese attitude toward liberal institutions may reflect an R&B attempt to restore inclusiveness rather than a preference for liberalism. The former is a systemic issue, while the latter an institutional or intra-systemic one. Despite a willingness to express dissatisfaction that appears to confirm liberalism, the higher dissatisfaction displayed by the Taiwanese constituency regarding the performance of the authorities may well reflect a problem of systemic identity rather than failed liberalism. In fact, 72% of the Taiwanese participants responded negatively but 54% of Chinese participants responded positively to the statement that, 'Everyone is treated equally by the government'. The Taiwanese are thus open about and, arguably, comfortable with failed liberalism.

When the systemic identity is relatively stable, the constituency ought to be more willing to remain patient when facing challenges to the reciprocal relationship. This parallels the notion of 'holding', discussed in Chapter 3. The holding force in East Asia, however, is a collective concept, as opposed to the aggregate of individuals within liberalism. The call for a harmonious society in China reaffirms the classic wisdom that the members of the polity should be related to one another in imagined reciprocal ways rather than distinguished from one another as the holders of differentiated rights or distinctive identities. Consider the discursive people discussed in Chapter 1. The imagined reciprocity can extend the idea of discursive people to the governmentality of members of society. Therefore, concession, rather than dominance, is the sensible way to cope with a minor challenge when governability is not an issue. On the contrary, to keep an already disturbed systemic identity inclusive requires not only the authorities to be tolerant but also its members to withdraw, at times, from self-restraint in order to signal a lack of the greater self and trigger the autocrat's counter-governmentality sensibilities. The authorities and the people are culturally prepared to invoke a systemic perspective to imagine a horizon that is broader than their own living conditions. The R&B theory indicates how restoration via self-restraint is always possible.

Democratic governability reaches its zenith when a system performs two kinds of concession: first, the members of the system are ready to concede their interests for the sake of systemic stability in the long run; and, second, the authorities are prepared to make concessions to the system's disadvantaged or estranged sections in order to maintain reciprocal bilateral relations. They respectively make a case for governmentality and counter-governmentality. Empirical evidence from the East Asia Barometer suggests that both the people and the government qua the greater self fully understand the importance of conceding.

Balance of relationships in relational democracy

The following principles of conduct, based upon the previous discussion, should apply to all relational democracies, which rely on R&B to secure systemic stability in the long run. Paying attention to relations, restoration, and repair at the expense of immediate resolution to ensure a harmonious future always pays. Such future rationality is more a governmentality than a calculation. Of the Chinese and Taiwanese participants in the East Asia Barometer statement, 77% of both agreed with the statement that, 'By helping people in trouble today, someone else will help me when I am in trouble someday'. The implication is that, in the long run, governability privileges relations with one another over designing and enforcing rules. Even when preparing for the long-term is not a typical value under certain conditions, given the need to restore governability in a constantly changing world, all will predictably revise any allegedly universal rules at a different site and time.

With governability as a substitute for the binary of democracy and autocracy, a research agenda on how a community is culturally prepared to combine unity and solidarity-embedded restraint in various ways can incorporate a pluriversal foundation of a methodologically-inclusive approach. To keep the system governable and stable, the governability principles necessitate that all must choose between restraining the self, the other, or a little of both:

- adapt sooner or later, with no rule lasting forever;
- practise inclusiveness occasionally by bypassing the rules; and
- incentivize self-restraint when encountering a perceived extreme action on the part of the other.

The governability principles may fail at a specific site and moment. Members of the system interact according to their judgment of the nature of the breakdown facing them, and choose between:

- negotiating to bypass the synchronic rules and norms on this one occasion;
- abiding by or qualifying the rules, but receiving or giving compensation, in cycles; or
- resisting the rules when the existing ways of life face the threat of destruction.

Governability obliges counter-governmentality of the authorities to:

- make exceptions to the norms/rules in order to restore stability if the challenge is minor;
- mix suppression and compromise when the challenge is judged to be indirect; and
- suppress in the name of the norms/rules when the challenge is judged to be direct.

Governability obliges the governmentality of the people to:

- seek remedy within the system if the suppression or corruption are judged to be temporary or minor;
- mix protest, lobby, and disengagement when the suppression or corruption are judged to be non-systemic but perpetual; and
- dishonour the authorities by sabotage, alienation, or resistance if the suppression and corruption are judged to be severe.

All contemporary synchronic values or institutions are, at best, transient in the long run. What remains constant is that, for the system to be governable, both the authorities and the governed must agree on their systemic membership and act in coordination in order to keep the system inclusive. Moreover, the quickest way to reach a consensus on the scope of the system is through compromise and suppression. This is by no means exclusively Confucian in nature. Non-Chinese conditions, likewise, consciously tolerate, if not encourage, value compromises in specific contexts to ensure systemic stability. All authorities and their governed members must make subjective judgments to determine if their mutual relations have deteriorated and how this perceived change should be remedied according to the procedures and norms. The judgment reflects the comfort or discomfort of the people with their systemic membership. The exact composition of the governable procedures varies according to the ideology and institution of the time. C&B represents merely one of the varieties, that cannot be sustained without R&B support. R&B lays the deep groundwork that enables the members of the system to stick with an institutional arrangement that is already failing to fulfil its promise.

The problems associated with autocracy and challenges to liberal democracy similarly concern the lack of an R&B theory, which all systems begin with but gradually lose, due to a preoccupation with choosing and reproducing a particular synchronic ideology and institution. Civic nationalism cannot cope, as its advocates once assumed, with the increasingly diverging political identities, that are rooted in as well as constructed on the postcolonial cultural politics. They will adapt by relaxing on the ideological, class, and racial fronts to enact systemic inclusiveness, upon which C&B is based. They will also make concessions to immigrant groups periodically, to ensure their sense of belonging and so, subsequently, systemic stability. If one considers Taiwan an illiberal society due to its national identity cleavage, its illiberal democracy does not, after all, arise from a typical ethnic conflict. Rather, Confucianism provides a clue about how to resolve the governability issue via the evolution of an inclusive style of R&B.

The problem with Confucian societies that practise electoral democracy is the lack of C&B, resulting from the lack of an institutional setting that is embedded in the historically specific context of European modernity. The Confucian constituency expects a lofty leader, who is above politics, on the one hand, to symbolize the systemic identity, and yet is sufficiently flexible, on the other, to avoid the leader's intervention in differing ways of life. In practice, the people dislike challenges being made to the authorities for the sake of systemic stability. Still, in theory, they disapprove of the use of dictatorship or top-down control to maintain reciprocity with the authorities. Finding a position between the two is the essence of R&B. Typically, this would entail deciding the extent of the support for the ideological stance of the authorities in exchange for exemption from the duty derived from the same ideological stance (Pye 1968; 1988). Both the people's ambivalence toward authority and the authorities' undecidable self-positioning between kings and politicians unintendedly echo the governmentality and counter-governmentality of R&B.

7

A Pluriversal Dialogue with Ubuntu

(Co-authored with Raoul Bunskoek)

Introduction

The notions of the regime of regimes, law-like inevitability, unity, short-lived nationalism, mass-line personality, and relational democracy, as discussed in the previous chapters, have led the hearts of the people to proceed through the hardnosed and multiple cycles of benevolence and involution up until the 2020s. The Confucian state of nature, which is constituted by heaven, earth, and ten thousand living things, including humankind, may nevertheless appear archaic to the Lockean or Hobbesian states of nature. The cosmological configuration of the latter stresses the desires and the rights of individuals instead and represents the arrival of the Enlightenment and demise of the medieval 'Dark Ages'. From such a modernist (and patriarchal) tradition of human versus human and human versus nature, the cosmologically indistinguishable boundaries of men/women or humankind/nature under Confucianism easily cause discomfort, for Confucianism discourages individual identities, self-interests, and the rule of law, that protects them from any rule unless by consent. In the modernist light, Confucianism cannot help but suppress and silence the people. In the 21st century, though, this Europe-centric view has an opportunity to unlearn its state of nature into a pluriversal relationality.

Chapter 7 makes a rare attempt to conduct a direct dialogue between two non-Western cosmological relations; namely, Southern African Ubuntu and Chinese Tianxia. Their dialogue characteristically differs from those between any one of them and the European cosmological tradition of the state of nature because there is no attempt in either Tianxia or Ubuntu to convert the other. The purpose of this chapter's intellectual exercise is not merely to encourage learning about others. Learning assumes that the self is the main subject to determine what others mean. The purpose is, rather, for all to unlearn their own self so that all can appreciate how they may be accommodated by different cosmological relations. Therefore, the dialogue between Tianxia and Ubuntu is not designed to express a 'correct' view of each other, but intended to challenge one to unlearn one's self-understanding. Through unlearning, it becomes incomplete, insufficient, and inconsistent, and therefore not a universal reference to appraise the world.

Moreover, the gap in the existing scholarship on Ubuntu and Tianxia provides a further reason for their dialogue. The rich literature on Tianxia needs reader-friendly access in order for its strangers to find their points of engagement. The spirit of spontaneity within the philosophy of Ubuntu challenges the Tianxia actors to create an exit from the layers of their discourses. Pluriversalism, that occurs in practical life, does not rely on literature, so the understanding of pluriversalism must transcend the literature. Ubuntu is, therefore, both a therapy that allows Tianxia's increasingly self-involving stance to overtake the currently dominant neoliberal order and also a lesson on how pluriversalism characterizes the inevitable dynamics of Tianxia to unlearn its limitations. In turn, practitioners of Ubuntu can unlearn its 'naturalness' by regarding how ignorance about it supports the civilizational self-image of believers in other cosmologies.

Joining Ubuntu as unlearning

The continuously increasing frequency of the so-called 'South-South cooperation' (SSC) between China and Southern African countries over the last few decades highlights the need for an understanding of the epistemologies of the actors involved. To achieve such an understanding requires 'serious and emphatic engagement with "other" traditions' (Behr and Shani, 2021), instead of being trapped in the familiar suspicion of an anti-Western 'alliance of autocracies' (Myers 2021) In order to bypass the modernist epistemological fixation, this chapter juxtaposes two post- and pre-Western cosmologies and epistemologies from the Global South: namely, the Bantu/Southern African concept of Hunhu/Ubuntu and the Chinese concept of Tianxia. Rather than reiterating the cliché that they are different from the neoliberal order, the final chapter of the book will elaborate on the tendency of cosmological thinking to universalize and theorize the inevitability of their mutual adaptation, especially in terms of people as nature. In brief, (re)worlding Ubuntu and Tianxia, as well as the Western rights of nature, enables us to answer why and how the Western, African, and Chinese relationalities, each according to their own formulations, *must have already* enlightened all of the actors due to the colonial and postcolonial experiences, unknowingly, and regardless of the seeming uniqueness of each.

In Southern African communities, particularly the Zimbabwean and South African neighbourhoods, the cosmological and epistemological concept of Hunhu/Ubuntu has been (re)attracting attention since the 1990s, 'for the simple reason that both Zimbabwe and South Africa needed home-grown philosophies to move forward following political disturbances that the liberation war and apartheid had caused, respectively' (Mangena 2020: 1). In particular, there was a strong need for an epistemology (a way to understand the world) that would allow former enemies, victims, and perpetrators, to 'coexist' peacefully rather than continue the vicious circle of revenge (Mamdani 2015; Ndlovu-Gatsheni 2018). In Mamdani's (2015: 82) words, '[t]he point of it all was not to avenge the dead, but to give the living a second chance'. This way of dealing with transitional justice differed considerably from the idea behind how the Nuremberg Trials were set up, which assumed 'that there would be no need for winners and losers to live together after victory' (Mamdani, 2015: 66). Instead, '[p]erpetrators would remain in Germany and victims would depart for another homeland' (Mamdani, 2015: 66) – that is, Israel. (Naturally, in practice, this did not entirely work, since not all of the victims left Germany and not all of the perpetrators stayed.) Mamdani finds it highly problematic to apply the latter type of justice, which he coins 'victim's justice', to postcolonial contexts in African countries, because it perpetuates the distinction between fixed 'perpetrators' and 'victims', whereas, in reality, the relations between these entities are often cyclical – that is, the perpetrators of today become the victims of tomorrow, and vice versa. Therefore, he argues in favour of the concept of 'survivor's justice', which encompasses both victims and perpetrators, since '[r]econciliation cannot be between perpetrators and victims; it can only be between survivors' (Mamdani, 2015: 77). This is in line with Hunhu/Ubuntu thinking, which stresses the importance of the community or group rather than focusing on the individual. This makes Ubuntu an inherently relational concept, which is underscored by the Nguni/Ndebele phrase '*umuntu ngumuntu ngabantu*' (a person is a person through other persons) (Mangena 2020: 1). In other words, perpetrators and victims are also themselves through each other.

In short, Hunhu/Ubuntu was, on the one hand, a response to the remnants of Western colonialism, while on the other constituting a reappraisal of the traditional Bantu/Southern African thought with the goal of (re)inventing tradition to constitute a distinct, '(Pan-)African' identity. This particular form of Pan-Africanism (Walden 1974; DuBois 2015 [1903]) erases the artificial boundaries/borders that were forced upon the African continent by Western imperialism/colonialism, and has culminated in, for instance, the African Union passport, that was introduced in 2016. Kenyan UN ambassador Martin Kimani highlighted this during a speech at the UN Security Council on Russia's invasion of Ukraine. He said, "we commented that we would settle for the borders that we inherited, but we would still pursue continental economic, political, and legal integration, rather than form nations that looked ever backwards into history with a dangerous nostalgia" (Kimani 2022).

In the Chinese context, the concept of Tianxia ('all-under-heaven') has similarly (re)emerged as a response to Western worldviews that emerged from neoliberal social sciences. The two theories constitute two sides of the 'bifocal lens', that shows either the 'China threat' or the 'China opportunity' paradigms (Pan 2012). The concept of Tianxia also alludes to an aspiration to return to the traditional Chinese worldview, in which China resumes the role of a 'moral/virtuous/symbolic' centre in a relational universe (Shih 2011; Zhao 2019). Yet, as Babones (2020: 131) points out, "[j]ust as the Greek word *hegemonia* became the English hegemony and the Latin word *imperium* became the English empire, the Chinese word *tianxia* is entering English-language political discourse as something related to, but distinct from, its original Chinese meaning(s)'. According to Babones (2020: 131), Tianxia may describe a more spiritual form of international society not dominated by a single, central state.

Both Hunhu/Ubuntu and Tianxia constitute concepts that are readily used to 'reimagine' how people belong to their group. However, there is a danger that they essentialize 'China' – or 'Africa' for that matter – as inherently and perpetually 'different' from the so-called 'West'. Any cosmology must have 'universal implications' (Acharya 2014), though, because a cosmology that leaves behind strangers who belong to another cosmology is neither natural nor supernatural, and is hence failing. All cosmologies adapt and save room for outsiders and subscribers alike, to detect and develop their associability.

Still, this book must confront two kinds of ambivalence. One concerns the question of whether or not we should operationalize Ubuntu and Tianxia to provide an empirically universal foundation for comparison. The other concerns whether or not we should stretch a cosmological discourse to embrace policy discussions in order to achieve a corrective effect on the currently biased monopoly of the neoliberal order. Chapter 7 chooses to take the middle way regarding both agendas. Therefore, for the first question, the remainder of the chapter does not engage in operationalization lest this inadvertently turns a discursively evasive expression into a technically fixed value. However, it still tries an abstract definition that is sufficiently linguistically distinctive to provide an exit to subscribers from their beliefs. On the second question, the discussions refrain from practical policies to avoid engaging in over-interpretation or unintended mundane interferences but, on the other hand, suggest policy proclivities to enable unlearning.

The following discussions in this chapter thus posit that:

- relational cosmology is always inclusive and, therefore, open, that is, no one is a complete or ultimate stranger; and
- it is always both normative and analytical.

In a nutshell, regarding their abstraction definitions, Ubuntu indicates 'the necessity of all to nurture all', while Tianxia indicates 'the state of all belonging to kin'. We will review the potential of both Ubuntu and Tianxia to form a symbiosis with a broadly conceived Western relationality, embedded in the imagined state of nature, that indicates 'the entitlement of all to the rights of nature'. Accordingly, Ubuntu and Tianxia are relational cosmologies that explain, in addition to prescribing, the governmentality of all actors, as does Western relationality. Specifically, the two non-Western traditions encourage the adoption of a non-solution to cope with disputes rather than participation in a checks-and-balance or rule-based system.

A pluriversal approach to relational worlds

The recent literature on Ubuntu focuses mainly on the pedagogical school curriculum, prescriptive policy orientation, or normative business theory (see, for example, Hailey, 2008; Lutz, 2009; Murove 2012). All three styles create the impression that Ubuntu is neither commonsensical nor practical in daily life, when, in fact, it is. The literature nevertheless reflects the urge discursively to restore it to a conscious level in the social as well as the policy world. However, such an approach neglects the analytical aspect of the study of Ubuntu, as if it were currently irrelevant to policy thinking. A similar neglect of the cosmological constitution of behavioural rationality applies likewise to the study of Chinese Tianxia, with the effect of reducing Tianxia to a worldview with the potential to shed light on the reform (or revision) of international relations.

To that extent, a parallel relational turn in Western political sciences, rooted in the modern European thought of the anarchical state of nature, the rights of nature, and the autonomous system of self-help, remains the only cosmology that can simultaneously achieve allegedly objective explanation and subjective morality. Being objective refers to independence from individual discretion but a constraint on individual choice. Without detecting the objective forces of Ubuntu relationality, Ubuntu would be no more than a revisionist attempt at disruption.

From the perspective of intellectual history, the evolving cosmological order bred a collective identity. It gave rise to the evolving values and institutions, which became stable, apparent, and legitimate over time, finally leaving the constituting cosmology as subconscious and in oblivion. What used to be normative and prescriptive for all members of the group, combined, to survive their challenging conditions of nature became something structural and rational (see Chapter 2). Mbembe thus interrogates how a Eurocentric canon attributes truth only to the Western way of knowledge production while disregarding other knowledge traditions (Mbembe 2015: 9). Alternative cosmological orders, that espoused differing values and institutions, were erased, eclipsed, ignored, and, hence, unnoticeable during encountering and conquest in a process that de Sousa Santos (2014) refers to as 'epistemicide'. Discursively, to the extent that the mimicry of Western political science dominated the postcolonial relations after WWII, these orders are irretrievable. The system of liberal democracy, more than anything else, is cast as the only vehicle by which the suppression and exploitation caused by colonialism may be overcome.

The re-emergence of Ubuntu, as well as Tianxia, inspires an unlearning of the rights of nature only after democratization has involuted into each practising a different combination of: 1) failing states, for example, Southern Sudan, Myanmar, and those suffering ethnic cleavages that colonially drawn borders impose upon them; 2) rogue states, for example, Iran, North Korea, and those resisting assimilation into the natural rights or global governing institutions; 3) revisionist states, for example, China, Russia, and those taking advantage of global regimes effectively without simultaneously engaging in democratization; and 4) pupil states, for example, the newly industrialized countries of South Korea, Taiwan, and those affirming colonial legacies through their alleged success with regard to democratization. Many more states (for example, Brazil, India, Vietnam, and Turkey) are arguably combinations, contingent on the context or historical timing. For African 'Ubuntu states', it is, however, the most urgent but also the most difficult to unlearn their premodern identities due to the lack of legible alternatives to their artificially crafted sovereign identities, that inflict 'internal' and 'regional' cleavages.

Disappointed by the repeated genocides and other mass atrocities associated with African politics, critics may quickly lose confidence in Ubuntu and lose sight of its continuing legacies. An agenda of Ubuntu aims to attain a level of abstraction that can provide analytical perspectives not only to reveal the policy orientations of the African leadership(s), but also the salience for others to seriously engage with it. Similar efforts are appropriate as well in order to understand Tianxia. The attempts at abstraction to achieve universalization are not unlike the situation in which a practitioner, who undertakes policy analysis of autonomous individuals based upon the binary of state and society, must appreciate its underpinning cosmological belief in the state of nature. Alongside abstract Ubuntu and Tianxia, liberalism constitutes merely *a* lens that can be juxtaposed with others, as opposed to *the* lens. While much has been written about Ubuntu, particularly about conflict resolution, peacebuilding, and human rights, it remains at the fringes of scholarly analysis (Smith 2017: 8). In comparison, even Tianxia, the literature on which is accumulating impressively in the international relations domain, remains marginal because dominant observers (for example, Callahan 2008; Pillsbury 2016; Wang 2017) perceive and portray it as little more than a Chinese intellectual manoeuvre, designed to legitimate the dominance and expansion of the Chinese autocracy.

Specifically, in the case of Ubuntu, the term appeared in the title of South Africa's 2011 foreign policy White Paper, 'Building a better world: the diplomacy of Ubuntu' (Smith 2017: 8). Even so, Tieku argues that the individualist ontology has undermined our understanding of 'collectivist social entities such as those in Africa' (Tieku in Smith 2017: 7). He describes three features arising from a more collectivist approach: consensual decision-making, group-think, and the Pan-African solidarity norm (based on the work of Mazrui [1963, 1967] and Clapham [1996], cited in Smith 2017: 8). In addition to its potential explanatory value, the notion of *Ubuntu* can also help to refocus the attention on important principles, such as shared humanity, given that it emphasizes cooperation, mutual understanding, and a greater sense of responsibility toward the collective well-being (Smith 2017: 9).

Let us contrast this with the clash of civilizations and consider a repertoire of cosmological relations, including the rights of nature, Tianxia, and Ubuntu, all of which are learnable to anyone through practice and intellectual sense-making. There would be no reason why an actor, who is motivated by the fear of losing their entitlement to the rights of nature while living in a different context, could not pre-empt events by practising Tianxia and Ubuntu. The practice of Tianxia would rely on the crafting of benevolent roles that affirm mutual acceptance by conceding reciprocal prerogatives. The practice of Ubuntu would engender, within the rising power, a sense of being nurtured and secured, and trigger the need to reciprocate nurturing. In this hypothetical example, all three cosmological relationalities are conceived of as naturally given. All generate values and institutions that will become the structures and rationalities of subsequent generations, each probably to a different degree of strength, and all are retrievable, with the proper triggers. This example reifies what Ling and Agathangelou (2009) called 'one world of many worlds'. It embraces the quest for pluriversalism by Trownsell et al (2022). That said, initially deriving a level of abstraction from the traditions of these cosmological relationalities to enable a mutual association that poses no threat of cultural assimilation due to its *acultural* nature is key to accessing such pluriversal worlds, that do not simply conquer, divide, or estrange, as in the scenario of the clash of civilizations. Pluriversalism is the dynamic *coexistence* of all cosmologies, each in their own adaptable terms. It is the relation of relations and the world of worlds, but its governmentality is yet to inspire the people of the world.

Confucianism and the rights of nature compared

The cosmological origin of the state of nature, the laws of nature (Beate 2000; Carlson & Fox 2013), and modern civil society profoundly affect the theory and the practice of democratization everywhere. While the state of nature has been a foundational concept of Western political thought, despite its various versions, parallels have been present in the history of political thought elsewhere, noticeably in ancient Chinese political thought (Hu, T. 1927; Hu, S. 2013), albeit these are retrievable only through inference. One significant Western feature that appears to be widely accepted, even among historians of natural science, is that, within the Judeo-Christian tradition, the rational creator, the author of nature, is external to what He creates. The consensus is that this transcendental power does not exist in the Chinese history of thought. The Heavenly reason, Dao ('way') or Qi ('vapour'), informs the phenomenon of oneness that proliferates and constitutes everything, despite its constantly changing and different forms (Needham 1956; Bodde 1957). This cosmology led to two dramatically different paths of development in subsequent generations concerning the nature of the state of nature (Ames 2008), which arguably resulted in different understandings of the contemporary state and society (Qin 2018; Shih et al 2019; Zhao 2019).

Although sporadically noticed elsewhere (for example, Lutz 2009), what has escaped the literature is a relational sensibility, shared by the modern European and ancient Chinese history of thought, respectively, concerning the way in which the people in the state of nature relate to each other. Modern European thinkers, such as Hobbes, Locke, Rousseau, and Kant, embraced incongruent imaginations about the security conditions for humankind or the realistic/idealistic state of governance, that provides order for them. Even so, for them, all individual persons own the entitled rights of nature that God allows them. God is the consensual lord in their formulations, albeit these are not always uttered by them, and His laws of nature render all as related to each other. Therefore, the people – who are strangers to one another – and states – which are involuntary rivals, due to the lack of a common authority in the mundane world – cannot be absolute strangers to each other. They share the sameness and the original sin provided by God, and know each other as joint subscribers of the laws of nature, even though they are unacquainted with each other (Buber 1965, 1970). The anxiety would be huge if even a non-acquaintance should suffer the violation of their rights of nature because the offence would allude to the breakdown of the laws of nature that constitute the identities of all men and women. Accordingly, a rational person gives consent to a social contract that protects them from the threat of the breakdown of their rights.

Even so, as Mills points out in *The Racial Contract* (2022), these 'rights of nature' were originally limited to White people, who were the only ones seen as human (Grosfoguel 2015). Likewise, 'Kant's use of reason is not for the pursuit of universal rights, but rather, universal rights for whites, and racist, colonial occupation for others' (Shilliam 2021: 38). Nevertheless, to allow the majority of the believers in universal rights the benefit of the doubt, this discussion is based on a definition of the universality of the rights of nature as was truly intended by its subscribers.

In comparison, without an external authority to govern the relations between people in ancient Chinese political thought, people are nonetheless considered related in their genesis as, cosmologically, Heaven and the earth are believed to give life to all phenomena. In other words, a certain quality of sameness – an indebtedness to life-sustaining belonging, that is ultimately rooted in Heavenly worship – likewise constitutes the living and the non-living in ancient Chinese thought. Their varieties and differences are natural; hence the necessity to improvise mutual belonging contingent upon the needs of the other in context. No objective, almighty force provides the laws of nature, that could oblige the people to respect each other's rights of nature. Consequently, sameness within ancient Chinese thought denotes natural belonging rather than natural law. Different to the 'natural rights' point of view is the ontological insignificance between being and non-being, with the effect that life is not an entitlement of an individual person, but an indistinctive ontological state. Instead, the life that continues in a variety of forms and through cycles belongs to oneness, yet belonging, while inevitable in guaranteeing life, does not accentuate 'the right' to life. Instead, belonging prioritizes sacrifice over rights for the sake of survival and the interest of the greater self qua (metaphorically Heavenly) kin. To that extent, causing death or suffering, which indicates the demise of the greater self, is ontologically destructive and governmentally suicidal.

In practice, this belonging sensibility produces a variety of platforms that value lives in the long run; for example, Confucianism adopts the metaphor of kinship to oblige benevolence in substitution for killing. Daoism neutralizes the meanings of and desires for killing because all of the justifications for killing disrupt natural relationality. Moism preaches military deterrence in the name of universal love, to relinquish killing eventually, while legalism resorts to the threat of killing to establish unity and discipline.

In short, in this ancient Chinese thought, the people are bound to be related and to belong by nature. Still, in practice, they must depend on the guidance of the princes and their advisors, who create differential roles for the princes to adopt and practice belonging accordingly. Deeply rooted in these discourses lies the same anxiety of the Western thinkers regarding anarchy and the threat to life. Briefly, a fear of the loss of relational order, to which the people can subscribe both intellectually and in practical terms, is distinctive of neither the Chinese nor European history of thought. That said, none of these ancient Chinese schools are preoccupied with an ontological narrative that has been distinctively crafted for humankind. No Christian kind of transcendence makes sense. Instead, these thoughts are primarily norms, each undergirding a particular art of governance. The art consistently concerns how the rulers and the people relate to each other through benevolent, pedagogical, or disciplinary role-making and -playing, rather than observing durable rules. As a result, mutual anxiety easily emerges between European ontological sensibilities that abhor the lack of the rights of nature in multiple streams of Chinese thought and the Confucian preoccupation with the reproduction of belonging that is not essential to the European state of nature, which alludes to individuals' autonomy.

Let us now consider an anecdote. Noteworthy and critical reflections in the Chinese literature on belonging, that resonate with the concerns for the state of nature, likewise emerge in the 21st century. Specifically, the literature raises the notion of villagers' exclusive 'descendant entitlement' (or 'zu fu ren quan', literally 'human rights of assets left by ancestors') to land in a 'natural village', as opposed to an 'administrative village'. The same heredity presumably sanctions the entitlement of all descendants of the same ancestors. Descendants are spontaneously obliged to accept redistribution according to the deceased's leaving and the newborn's joining. Therefore, ancestry is a relational binary designed to exclude outsiders (that is, relational strangers) whose identities do not depend on which sides of a border they reside. In a nutshell, descendant entitlement is noticeably a combination of Confucianism and natural rights.

On the other hand, exclusive land rights are likewise a relational binary that is designed to reproduce the relevance of the imagined sameness of ancestry to contemporary identities. That said, it is, in practice, necessary and virtual to relate beyond gene relations. That is why Confucian role relations, embedded in metaphoric kinship, strive for ever-expansive relations until all are ready to connect. Improvising kin metaphors is the ultimate resort of Confucianism in order to imagine mutual belonging, cut across binaries, prevent estrangement, and reconcile strangeness. That is why friendship (among a social circle), partnership (in a project), neighbourship (in a region), and Chineseness (through a shared culture), are added to kinship and metaphorical kinship in modern times in China's internationalism.

For the sake of convenience, a relation is used here as an antonym to strangeness and referred to as 'imagined resemblance', which denotes a condition of mutual constitution whereby the actors are discursively acquainted or psychologically comfortable with each other. The key to Confucian relations is (metaphoric) kinship, which presumably guarantees natural and reciprocal benevolence. Confucians use metaphorical kin relations to naturalize benevolent relations between the people of the world. Metaphors invoke role-making and role-taking. Performing metaphorical (or extended) kin roles is the Confucian technique for making a stranger related. European thought is not qualitatively different, to the extent that the state of nature is likewise a metaphor (Rolf 2014), and the law of nature that substantiates the social contract is, by all means, a role scheme, calling for role-making and role-taking. That said, the laws of nature in European thought oblige each member of society to craft their roles vis-à-vis the state. At the same time, Confucian relationality requires the intensive interrogation of role relations in context before they can adequately and properly reciprocate benevolence.

In any case, strangeness is the common indicator of political incorrectness in both the Christian and Confucian traditions. However, the ways in which they overcome strangeness differ. For Europeans, the social contract, embedded in the laws of nature, reconciles strangeness except for those deficient in Christianity. Christianity, consent to rule, equality, and the rights of nature, combined, ensure solidarity between women and men of sameness. Such sameness makes possible the system analysis of comparative and even international politics, according to Kenneth Waltz (1979). Even though there is no central authority to coordinate states or allocate values among them, they all think that they know whom they are dealing with in terms of the same original sin and aspirational and behavioural patterns. They differ only in terms of their capability, skill, opinion, and priority of preference, none of which is ontological.

In contrast, Samuel Huntington's (1996) theory of the clash of civilizations connotes an essentially different threat, which is intellectual and ontological. The laws of nature are not consensual across Huntington's civilizational divides nor a relevant reference to allow the anticipation of solidarity. It is precisely in this kind of context of civilizational discourse that critical reflections on the state of nature have become pertinent and timely again in the 21st century.

In a pluriversal world, however, neither the Huntingtonian clash of civilizations nor the Waltzian systemic sameness of all actors, that necessitates surveillance over and rivalry with ontological strangers, is apparent. After all, merely the philosophical technicality of managing strangeness differentiates them from Confucianism. Other imagined states of nature and humanity than Christianity and Confucianism are by all means present. In this regard, Ubuntu, the main topic of this chapter, provides a comparable lens relative to Christianity and Confucianism. According to this cosmology, humans share a nature, which is not external to humanity as the Christian God is. Therefore, humans can only be who they are if they sustain one another, each in their own identity/subjectivity/individuality, embedded in the commonly constituting humanity. The readiness and capability to meet the necessity of mutual sustaining inspire self-consciousness and self-becoming. Thus, Ubuntu contrasts with the drive for self-disciplining to submerge individuality into restrictive kin relations under Confucianism. Comparatively, the notion of individual subjectivity creates a common point of reference for all three cosmologies and yet incongruent approaches to reconcile strangeness, with: 1) individuals related through God – attaining the absolute rights of nature for each obliged to accept and protect the same absolute subjectivity of each other; 2) individuals related through their mutual nurturing – sustaining indiscriminately the relative subjectivity of each other that alludes to their own; and 3) individuals related through ancestry and the metaphorical oneness of all – being entitled to belonging, outside of which, spatially as well as temporally, the individual subjectivity is free from interrogation.

Ubuntu as the cosmological necessity to nurture

To bring Ubuntu into a conscious strategy inevitably reflects a contrast to a perceived Western civilization. The difference sensibilities thus prevail in the discourse on Ubuntu. In a study of African diplomacy, Tieku (2008) argued that the African and Western understanding of personhood differ. The African notion of personhood is embedded, and contrasted against the individuated Western idea. This alienation from individualism results in the easy cultivation of communitarian thinking, since a person is said to achieve their full being only in others (Thakur 2015: 221). An Ubuntu approach will, in the first instance, attempt to cultivate a sense of togetherness, foster cooperative relations, and improve others' quality of life, with the latter based on sympathy. Hospitality is then a matter of aiming to forge a relationship of (active) belonging and (compassionate) benefiting, neither of which a Kantian gives any intrinsic or inherent moral weight (Bell and Metz 2011: 90).

Note the 'isiXhosa saying *Ubuntu ungamntu ngabanye abantu*, meaning "people are people through other people"' (Jackson 2014: 904). The individualistic ontology adopted by the mainstream Western social sciences is problematic for dealing with certain issues in African contexts: transitional justice (Ndlovu-Gatsheni 2018), individual human rights, imposing embargoes on Zimbabwe under Mugabe and Sudan under Bashir. Following the spirit of Ubuntu, in contrast, a consensus is essential when dealing with issues for, as Julius Nyerere puts it: "We talk until we agree" (Smith 2017: 8).

For Naude (2019: 26), there is the lingering risk of Western-centrism in pursuing an exclusively African Ubuntu. One of his condensed pages painstakingly excavates such a colonial thread in the discourses on Ubuntu, for Naude first cites Mbiti (1969: 108–9, cited in Naude 2019: 26):

> Whatever happens to the individual happens to the whole group, and whatever happens to the whole group happens to the individual. The individual can only say: '"I am, because we are; and since we are, therefore I am.' This group orientation is a cardinal point for understanding the African view of man.

Naude (2019: 26) pays particular attention to Mbiti's discussion of kinship, that can be extended to the living dead (ancestors) and even includes animals and non-living objects through the totemic system, leading to a 'deep sense of kinship, with all it implies, [which] has been one of the strongest forces in traditional African life'. Naude (2019: 26) continues to discuss Metz's (2007b) contention that there is indeed an indigenous African ethics, that expresses the communitarian approach of African ethics in distinction to the individualism of Europe. He quotes Metz (2007b: 338; see Metz 2012): '[a]n action is right just insofar it promotes a shared identity among the people grounded on goodwill; an act is wrong to the extent that it fails to do so and tends to encourage the opposites of division and ill-will' (Naude 2019: 26).

The caveat is that Ubuntu would fail as a project of decolonization if it were merely used to 'essentialize' Africans; namely, as an elite abstraction, the provincialization of Ubuntu mirrors the colonial power structures that exactly inhibit the move to release Africans from their oppression under coloniality (Naude 2019: 28). Naude (2019: 35) then offers a criticism:

> But on the stronger claim of actual epistemic decolonisation, it is apparent that the *ubuntu* project – like all forms of theoretical-scientific knowledge – is invariably steeped in Western knowledge forms and rules of validation. From this perspective, and judged by the more fundamental epistemic demands of decolonisation, *ubuntu* is in fact a perpetuation and further reinforcement of a colonial mindset.

Nevertheless, difference or distinction sensibilities are the rationale for mutual learning and unlearning, that enable the realization and knowledgeable practice of pluriversalism, for Metz's moral theory aligns with Ali Mazrui's (1994: 40–1) observation, 'What is distinctive about Africans is their short memory of hate'. To that extent, Bell and Metz (2011: 84) find that, '[t]he prizing of forgiveness likely emerged from small and relatively stable communities, where it made social sense to find ways of letting go of resentment in the interest of restoring harmonious relations'. Just as with transitional justice, the people still had to live together (coexist), so forgiveness became more important than punishment. This approach to conflict resolution, arguably, applies also to large-scale postcolonial societies, where conflict has not ended yet and, in fact, has provided the main moral motivation for South Africa's Truth and Reconciliation Commission (TRC) (Bell and Metz 2011: 84) and, more importantly according to Mamdani (2015), the Convention for a Democratic South Africa (CODESA).

In recent years, Piet Naude (2019) has conducted important advanced analytical work in this field. He points out that, in the saying 'I am, because we are', the 'we' that shapes the 'I' has a particular ethnic and kinship character, rather than a universal ('I am through all others') connotation (27). Translated into the current contexts, *ubuntu* could mean that I use my power in society to benefit those who are 'of my own' (27). Even so, he maintains that 'so far as [he] can tell, *it is a fact* that there are several judgments and practices that are spatio-temporally extensive in Africa, but not in the West" (Metz 2007a: 333, our emphasis) (28). What was then lost was the epistemic legitimacy of Africa. Put simply, epistemicide fundamentally means the denial of one's knowledge and imposition of that belonging to someone else (de Sousa Santos 2014).

Still, it is useful to note Pieterse and Parekh's (1995) caution that decolonizing knowledge is not simply about inversion or reversal. The risk is either that a purely Southern episteme will replace a supposedly Western one or that centuries of knowledge production will effectively be erased in a serious attempt to reach back to an older, more 'authentic' folk knowledge. According to Ndlovu-Gathseni, 'In the process [of racism], epistemic racism deprived humanity of the chance to benefit from rich knowledge cascading down from diverse geo-political sites of thought' (Ndlovu-Gathseni 2018: 137). Conversely, Africa, or indeed the non-European world, is never given but constituted through the ideological and epistemic gazes of colonial modernity and its politics of alterity (Wai 2020: 65). As such, the majority of the knowledge about Africa, or China for that matter, is also always already immersed in the contexts and configurations of a Western epistemological order and its conceptual categories (Wai 2020: 68).

Rather, pluriversality needs to focus on social processes as already and always constituted from connectedness. Bhambra and Santos (2017: 6) focus on historical connections that were 'generated by processes of colonialism, enslavement, dispossession and appropriation' (also see Mawdsley et al 2019: 17). Wai (2020: 74) summarizes Mudimbe's (1991) suggestion that we deal with this problem (as he does masterfully in *Parables and Fables*) by: 1) the dissolution of the antimonic tensions in disciplinary 'discussions about what is false or true' in local cultures and texts, to do away with 'the myth of historical roots so widespread in African studies'; and 2) the dualistic thinking at the heart of essentialist conceptions of African identities and cultures, fashioned by the colonial library and its temporal formations/categories.

The discussions bring to the (re)worlding of Ubuntu, inductively, an acultural abstraction of heavily cultural practice, or translation, that makes sense to those actors who subscribe to different cosmologies, requires no exotic lens to appreciate, and triggers similar sensibilities in their policy making. By lining up the terms mentioned earlier – including group, kinship, community, people, extensiveness, relationality, togetherness, hospitality, belonging, forgiving, benevolence, consensus, sympathy, we are, and I am – the chapter is ready to propose the following cultural translation of Ubuntu for all to detect it within their own (sub)consciousness. In a nutshell, then, Ubuntu is 'the necessity of all to nurture all'. Failing Ubuntu, that is, aborting the need to nurture or the need to be nurtured, I can no

Table 7.1: Mini-pluriversalism

	Ontology	Community	Relation	Individuality
Christianity	God	Social contract	Rules of law	Rights
Ubuntu	All-being	Spontaneity	Interdependence	Nurturing
Confucianism	Oneness	Kinship	Ritual and role	Cultivation

longer be who I am. To develop this line further, those who nurture are neither superior nor inferior. Ubuntu is, accordingly, inevitable as well as practical; individualized as well as collective; rational as well as cosmological, dynamic, moral, and universal. The people do not practise Ubuntu all the time, and neither do South Africans. Even so, the people are always capable of Ubuntu. Then, it becomes a social science project to study culturally, socially, politically, economically, and psychologically when, why, and with whom we practise, shelve, or preach Ubuntu.

Note the caveat that the chapter provides a definition for Ubuntu, a notion that is not supposed to be defined as what it is or is not. Defined nevertheless, Ubuntu attains its aforementioned definition specifically for the purpose of unlearning Tianxia and the state of nature. In other words, other definitions that target the unlearning of other cosmologies are certainly plausible. The current definition compels the Tianxia thinkers to reflect critically on how the silencing of self-fulfilling individuality contributes to the cycles of involution of Chinese autocratic governmentality. Likewise, liberal practitioners of the state of nature must face the need for rights owners to relate through reciprocal nurturing in addition to protection from interference. Such a version of Ubuntu furthers pluriversalism in the world of worlds (see Table 7.1).

A common disposition for non-interventionism

Chapter 7 has so far discussed three different cosmologies and the epistemologies derived from them. Certain kinds of relational sensibilities constitute all three, as the necessity to nurture, the rights of nature, and destined kinship are considered spontaneous and imperative for the survival of all. Nevertheless, there are challenges and opportunities related to their mutual appreciation. Ubuntu and the rights of nature attend to the self-fulfilment of individuals. Still, an Ubuntu person achieves her goal by contributing to her group and accepting the contributions of others rather than protecting the rights to each to pursue their own desires. The rights of nature and Tianxia share an alert to the presence of seeming strangers. Still, a Tianxia person improvises metaphorical kin roles for them rather than converting them into rules of conduct regarding the entitlement to rights. Tianxia and Ubuntu embrace group consciousness, but benevolence incurs a reciprocal obligation and the control of self-interests for a Tianxia person rather than the dynamics of self-becoming for all.

Without romanticizing Ubuntu into a policy principle or guideline, this section considers Ubuntu as a governmental disposition. Specifically, it concerns the attitude toward interventionism that enforces neoliberal as well as globalization rules upon autocratic governments. In practice, the three cosmologies display different interventionary tendencies, with the rights of nature the only one prone to interventionism for the sake of universalizing rules regarding the rights of nature. Referring predominantly to Africa and China, interventionary policies, designed to convert failing states, defeat rogue states, and contain revisionist states, prompt a sense of intimacy between the targets of the intervention or containment.

The overall favourable opinions about China among Africa's elite are not merely the result of China being more able to provide funds/money and thus (indirectly) because of corruption. Another argument is that the 'no strings attached' (or 'no conditionalities') adopted by Chinese actors in providing loans and aid is attractive because it highlights an approach by China that is essentially 'judgment free' or 'non-paternalistic': that is, according to the practice of Tianxia that exempts individual subjectivity from interrogation, Chinese actors do not tell African actors what to do or how, unless the latter ask their advice (as, for example, Ethiopia, see Fourie 2015). For China, a reciprocal exchange of goodwill, without worrying about or checking each other's differences, is only available outside the Western circle and is most warm-hearted toward a China that is constantly under the moral scrutiny of the West. Given the spirit of mutual nurturing, the South-South relations between China and African nations can be more favourable because of the compatibility of the 'African' inherent epistemology of Ubuntu and the 'Chinese' Tianxia.

First, failing Ubuntu's mutuality and self-becoming to fulfil the necessity to nurture, interventionary policies are used to wear a superior, and at times racist, lens toward African 'others', in defiance of the spirit of equality presumed for the prospective subscribers to the rights of nature. In contrast, Tianxia's benevolence requires no homogenization of values. Instead, Chinese actors are quite upfront about their reason for being in Africa; namely to develop together in order to achieve 'win-win' situations in a material sense. The fact that Chinese actors have self-interests causes many Western observers to see a Western self in Tianxia, that carries the original sin to be checked and balanced. It likewise induces African receivers of investment to suspect exploitation rather than togetherness. The Western discourse on Africa-China relations echoes broader concerns about the essentially extractive nature of this relation (Pieterse and Parekh

1995; Comaroff and Comaroff 2012; Bhambra and Santos 2017). That said, Tianxia, as a cosmology, still places enormous pressure on the Chinese state to amend the role-improvised/improvising relations with suspicious partners by balancing the alleged exploitation with a nurturing policy sporadically, to promote the partners' welfare. Therefore, periodical debt cancellations have become common and are expected by both Chinese lenders and their over-burdened debtors.

Arguably, the 'Collectivist Worldview' (Tieku 2012) of Ubuntu of the African leaders, which leads them to prefer working with Chinese actors rather than Western ones, is partly a response to Western colonization. The Western colonizers saw their colonial populations as inferior to themselves and therefore in need of 'civilizing'. Epistemicide is particularly acute wherever the twins of individuals' market value and discursive style overtake other standards of judgment on an aggregate of people of colour, confirming and reproducing the stereotype of the civilizational superiority of the White race. The historical 'white man's burden' consisted of raising inferior populations to the level of Western civilization, a process internalized by many colonized populations. Yet, as Frantz Fanon points out, in his seminal work *Black Skin, White Masks* (1967), even if colonized populations managed to reach this level, they were still not accepted, because they were unable to escape from their skin colour. In other words, adopting the civilizational knowledge of the colonizers became a condition for the colonized to be treated as 'human' by the colonizers. Yet, even then, they were not accepted. This is why the 'no conditionalities' approach, adopted by China, is seen so favourably by Africans all over the continent.

Festus Mogae, who was president of Botswana at that time, for instance, said in 2006 that he found that: "the Chinese treat us as equals. The West treats us as former subjects … I prefer the attitude of the Chinese to the West's" (Hilsum 2006). Wade (in 2008), the former president of Senegal, echoed Mogae's sentiments when he declared that "China's approach to our needs is simply better adapted than the slow and sometimes patronizing post-colonial approach of European investors, donor organizations and non-governmental organizations" (quoted in Hodzi 2018: 196). In contrast, Chinese actors are perceived to be mutually nurturing. This explains why the more locally embedded Chinese actors in Africa are usually more successful – that is, if they adapt their Confucianism-inspired relational practices to suit Ubuntu-inspired ones. The social bonds thus created are here "a source of indebtedness and obligations" (Jackson 2012: 196).

What distinguishes Ubuntu-Tianxia relationality from the rights of nature is the (externally bestowed) prior nature of the latter; namely, the prior consensus on the rights of nature and the associated institutions and rules define the relations. This prior relation also determines how the West can make an encountered stranger a legitimate member of the relations. In comparison, for the nurturing Ubuntu actors or the reciprocal kin role-takers, the conditions of the encountered strangers, as well as the acquaintances, are essential for the improvisation of relations. The points of resemblance that constitute the relations with the other parties are contingent, other-oriented, and context-sensitive, rather than being ontologically fixed before encountering. In addition, improvised relations are accustomed to changes in the long run, as no one remains exactly the same over time. Such an emphasis on improvised resemblance, as opposed to prior resemblance, has significant policy implications.

As already discussed, prior resemblance invokes interventionism. A relation informed by prior resemblance may induce a conflict with strangers, to be examined, taught, or converted according to the consensual rules agreed upon by other extant members of the same relation. In contrast, relations that require mutual consultation proceed on the governmentality that actors are consciously alerted to self-centrism. Sensitivity to the conditions of the other side, embedded in differently felt needs, may lead to two policy tendencies. The first is strategic patience when specific benevolence proper for each other is still unavailable. Second, strategic patience enables one to tolerate, and sometimes even promote, non-solutions as a temporary solution in order to establish a minimum level of coexistence with others who are either strangers or rivals. Relations for relations, whose contents are flexible and revisable, are preferred to rule-oriented relations in Ubuntu and Tianxia. After all, solutions and points of resemblance evolve with the self-identity, the parties involved, and the issue. In the end, staying somehow related is more pragmatic and sustainable than enforcing any specific relationship or rule.

For the Ubuntu actor, who is ready to exercise hospitality, politeness, and concerns at the end of rivalry, obsession with the memory of rivalry is transient. For the Tianxia actor, provided that there exist ways to reproduce nominal kinship roles, as is always the case, conflicts of a certain sort need not define the overall, nor the future, relations. Even for the rights of nature actors, patience is not atypical at all in a situation where violations cannot be punished or stopped immediately because other more significant mundane interests or practical incapacity prescribe the preservation of a minimum relationship. As time passes, reluctant patience develops into strategic patience and non-solution becomes the acceptable status quo. However, non-solution would appear troublesome from the rights-of-nature point of view. Ubuntu poses an invincible challenge to the subscribers of the rights of nature. The latter prioritizes self-centred desires over the need for mutual nurturing, to the racist result of forgetting the colonized population as its lasting nurturer despite its estrangement from liberal governmentality. Both Ubuntu and Tianxia are ready to theorize the reluctant status quo into a regular relational decision. After all, maintaining the status quo is nurturing, relative to rivalling, and role-improvising, unlike rule-binding.

Conclusion

The abstraction tried here may commit philosophical violence to each of the three cosmologies due to the neutralizing effect on their historical and cultural contexts. However, the purpose of this discussion is not to celebrate a proud tradition that no hegemonic dominance can successfully silence, block, or erase. Rather, given that all are bound to be related, it is worth interrogating how these cosmologies can contribute to a more comprehensive acknowledgment of the people in the pluriversal relations of governmentality. As Mawdsley et al (2019: xv) put it, 'perhaps the way to newness lies in seeing all knowledge systems as providing but partial insights into the truth'. For Mbembe (2015: 10), '[t]he problem – because there is a problem indeed – with this tradition is that has become hegemonic'. The abstraction that brings forth cosmological encounters that did not exist in the past enables mutual intellectual accessibility and empowers practitioners by becoming conscious of their previously unnoticed relational capacity for patience, mutuality, and goodwill. When the people are ready to make room for each other by recognizing their rights to desire and opinion, camouflaging incongruence through benevolence and rituals, or forgiving and nurturing others, nothing concrete has to be achieved in order for all to adapt and coexist continuously. Non-solutions that enable minimum mutual nurturing are widespread and logical in daily life. The people endure, sustain, inspire and/or compel the eventual/cyclical restoration of corrupt, suppressive regimes, democratic as well as autocratic, periodically, with a governmentality of belonging (and dominance) from which no one can escape.

To reiterate, the necessity of all to nurture all, and the state of all taking metaphoric kin roles are also present in the Western state of nature. Similarly, exercising one's right to enhance one's self-interests is likewise familiar in Africa and China. A pluriversal governmentality will allow all three to coexist in parallel in the same universe and recognize the potential of all communities to become practised and responsible in fulfilling their relationalities. To cite Mawdsley et al (2019) again, 'to be free of all inherited legacies … This is truly Svaraj [freedom] in ideas.' Ubuntu is of particular value because it underscores a certain decentred pluriverse, to which African actors are implicitly assumed to adhere. At the same time, Tianxia is hierarchical, presumably with China at the top, and the cosmology of the rights of nature is exceptionalist in an American way. While Tianxia sometimes relies on shaming to induce others into adopting kinship roles, Ubuntu contrarily advises against shaming others in public. Both suggest solving issues in private through a consensus achieved through talk.

Currently, Tianxia and the rights of nature rival each other as the representatives of different universes. The recognition of Ubuntu as an alternative cosmology compels them to engage in critical (self-)reflection. Ubuntu reminds a rights-of-nature actor of their other relationality – being nurtured by nature, society, and the population (especially postcolonial and populations of colour) elsewhere and nurturing others through engaging in voluntary, philanthropic actions. It reminds a Tianxia actor of the dynamic and joy of self-becoming through mutual nurturing, whereas they are exclusively accustomed to self-sacrifice and inexpressible self-interests. Ubuntu and Tianxia are especially illuminating in their joint readiness to embrace strategic patience and the adoption of a non-solution to protect the relations within the dynamics of the status quo. In a nutshell, communities and their citizens engage in all of these relationalities in the pluriversal world. Epistemological renovation through the allusion to Ubuntu brings pluriversalism to the consciousness of all and empowers them to embrace a more comprehensive self-unlearning and mutual reconciliation.

Conclusion: Balancing Dominance and Belonging

A regime cannot operate unless its members readily coordinate in ways that ensure that their common belonging to the regime and the perceived entitlements of each are mutually accepted. This quality of regime survival calls for governmentality and counter-governmentality that prepares the people and their political leaders, respectively, to remain vigilant regarding their belonging need to keep the regime relationally intelligible and agreeable. To that extent, we are unlikely to empathize with how the Chinese socialist autocracy evolves without analyzing the governmental impacts of Confucianism. Submerged in their liberal governmental breeding, contemporary social sciences acquire the function of justifying, consolidating, and spreading liberal democracy but fail badly in terms of making sense of socialist autocracy. That said, liberalism can still speak of the blind spot of Confucianism, which is the inattention to the idea of rights as a normative option in the case of abusive autocracy. Conversely, liberalism can similarly unlearn its own obsession with the preferences of individuals, as well as their aggregate, to the neglect of caring as a regime inevitability.

Democracy and autocracy are on the same governmental tracts, with two discursive identities. Democracy and, for that matter, autocracy are not about measuring rights or equality, but about balancing dominance and belonging. This book suggests that neither democracy nor autocracy can operate without a level of relational imagination to prepare the members of its political system to mind the needs of each other, especially between those acting in the name of the authorities and their people. Given that 'the people' are an essential constituent of all political systems, the liberal agenda that separates democracy from autocracy by merely reviewing how readily the former embraces the institution and culture of participation can prove awkward and misleading. Instead, relational democracy attends to the systemic capacity for limiting any system from committing extreme exploitation and suppression. Democracy and autocracy, as stereotypical categories, can each suffer such involution but tentatively adopt each other's relational style when attempting to restore the relational default. These cycles of relational order and chaos are not uniquely liberal or Confucian. In a nutshell, autocracy and democracy are neither linear in time nor binary in space, since the same population is always capable of shifting between relationalities that yield the two categories. Rather, the same processes of belonging and dominance constitute them.

Appraising democracy and autocracy to determine which protects human rights and provides good governance yields a problematic comparison. Moreover, the comparison between the two systems at particular points in time overlooks each system's pace of cycles. Such comparison reproduces the myths that democracy encourages the people's participation to protect and enhance their rights and that autocracy side-lines it in order to guarantee effective, quality governance. Both myths position the people against the regime although, indeed, they conversely privilege one of the two capacities over the other. This book interrogates governmentality, that necessarily encompasses the people and the regime simultaneously. The puzzle is how governmentality is preached, practised, compromised, and restored regarding the relation sensibilities that bind the regime to the people. This shared puzzle thus approves no general measurement for all. Both rights and good governance can be conceived of as entitlements, taking turns, if not existing simultaneously. Rather, the puzzle is a qualitative interrogation, relying on critical/cultural translation.

This book critically translates solidarity and unity as two forms of relational foundation that are essential to support different communitarian identities. Solidarity is essential to contemporary neo/liberalism. In the liberalist tradition, in the premodern state of nature, all people have a need to protect their special interests and pursue their desires. Based on their understanding of and sympathy for each other's special needs, philanthropy and, thereafter, solidarity emerges among them. These needs evolve into entitlements, norms, and rules, that move gradually toward modern capitalism, which is presumably applicable to all individuals equally. Once rules have evolved, they transform solidarity into duties, so even the losers are still guaranteed their basic needs. The contemporary agenda of comparative politics, accordingly, studies how those who do not abide by rules, supposedly due to their entrapment in premodern or postcolonial relationalities, can be converted to join former colonizer societies of aspiring individuals. In their intellectual history and the sociology of philosophy, modern thinkers contrived their formulation of the state of nature in response to premodern configurations of the (Christian) churches and the (feudal) kingdoms, that involuted from time to time and ignored the right of individuals to pursue interests and desires.

On the other hand, the existence of the state and church implied people's stronger and more spontaneous need in the state of nature for belonging, that would require the limiting of people's pursuit of interests and desires through their acknowledgment of fear and guilt. Both belonging and limiting echo Confucian necessities.

According to Confucianism, coordinating people into residential communities calls for trustworthy leaders to ensure that the sacrifices that are made by the individual members contribute exclusively to their groups. Leaders rely on common cosmological beliefs, rituals, and performance to establish their credit for acting selflessly. With commonly accepted selfless leadership, its followers can emulate its self-sacrifice, support its dominance and prerogatives, transcend differences between their identification traits, overcome mutual estrangement, and form unity around the leader qua collective interests. Together, reciprocal benevolence creates the regime of regimes, enabling all to adopt the same lens of political assessment: bad autocrats ultimately fall. Without the regime of regimes, individuals do not care about the welfare of others, and their leaders feel no obligation to ensure the unity of the autocrat and their people. Who would wish to follow the autocrat, then? If they refuse to let go, who would lack the legitimacy to slay them?

It is possible that those regimes that failed to care lacked the evolutionary skill to survive natural selection, and so no longer exist. Unity reflects a strong need among the people to survive in the state of nature. It is a brutal inevitability. The regime of regimes emerged in the premodern period, to be undergirded by cosmological beliefs of various sorts. It gradually evolved into institutions, values, discourses, practices, interests, and so on (for example, the sovereign state, equal rights, constitutionalism, market capitalism, social welfare, and environmentalism) to become unnoticeable for either practitioners or contemporary theoreticians. The capacity to fall back to the regime of regimes, when a specific regime decays, points to restoring the care for the living conditions of people. Confucianism, socialism, and liberalism all caution against the monopoly of resources, be it by autocrats, the bourgeoisie, the state, or the hegemonic power. Liberal democracy appears particularly vulnerable in this regard, as no cosmological foundation (such as 'original sin') exists to urge the elite circle to worry about the maldistribution, cleavage, corruption, or anything other than their re-election. Solidarity used to be a norm that celebrates a claim to civilizational progression, but the rampant cleavages in today's liberal democracy merely weaponize it.

Relational skills matter to the people, who must improvise ways of belonging to the community or system in order to pre-empt systemic involution. Whenever the regime fails to guarantee a sense of belonging, meaning that the leaders or a portion of the population are disqualified from belonging, the people seek other alternatives. For a Confucian example, the emergence of solidarity amid the population indicates the abortion of the selfless role by the leadership. This book mentions a peculiar kind of solidarity at the time of abuse by a Confucian autocrat – unpredictability. Unpredictability occurs when a bizarre deed spreads instantly – that is, faster than a virus – among docile people. It exposes the isolation of the leadership and the loss of the collective lens. In other words, solidarity is a derived need to limit the involution of unity when bad autocrats emerge under Confucianism. For a liberal example, in response to a rise in cleavage and illiberalism, the identified incorrect groups can improvise sacrifices as their appeals to unity and retrieve belonging.

While all communities are equipped with both relational capacities, they have tendencies according to their cultural preparation, with liberal democracy being inclined toward solidarity and Confucian autocracy toward unity. Unity targets the welfare of the entire population at the expense of self-concerns. Solidarity cares about the individual's entitlement to equal rights. Translating between them facilitates a reassessment in four senses. First, the other is not an anomaly to the extent that the people are the shared concern, despite a contrast between the aggregate of individuals and the collective without individuals. Second, the translation enables a rediscovery of the other relational capacity in the self. Third, the dominant relational capacity places an internal limit on the capacity to pre-empt abuse. Fourth, alienation from the regime is the cross-board signal to inspire mutual sympathy and support with an alternative mode of relationality, that is, alternation between solidarity and unity. In short, the people of both systems are equipped with alternative relational skills, although usually only one of the two defines the default of the regime.

Ultimately, the difference lies in the relational skill that supports or restores governmentality rather than a specific relation at work. The relational analysis points to the impossibility of a power monopoly, for the leaders themselves subscribe to the same relational configurations as the people. The regime nonetheless estranges the people periodically and causes a monopoly issue. Democracy and autocracy differ with regard to how people respond under a perceived over-monopoly circumstance. They do not differ systematically in terms of the required length of time, the depth of the revision, and the cost incurred for them to restore. Thus, the people's participation cannot dissuade a liberal regime from illiberal mobilization. In our discussion, modern capitalism has produced a liberal democracy that is unable to recover from involution. People must find a way, through unity, to transcend their political cleavages. This sometimes points to war. Similarly, people's selflessness can be insufficient to rescue a Confucian autocracy from defying self-restraint. They must support each other in order to isolate the regime. In short, democracy and autocracy are not crucial points of comparison to understand the people or the capacity to restore governmentality during involution.

The regime's estrangement from prior relationality may arise for many reasons. One widely shared reason in modern Chinese history is the incurrence of statist nationalism or political sub-nationalism, which likewise ruins the opportunity for the liberal spirit of solidarity among autonomous individuals to grow. Nationalism, likewise, redirects the Confucian unity spirit embedded in the regime's selfless benevolence toward an assertive, extractive urge. Conveniently agitated by binary thinking, nationalism, under Confucian autocracy, can nonetheless be exempt from a clear target, such as Wuhan-based nationalism during the COVID-19 pandemic. Even so, all kinds of binaries existed alongside the outbreak of the pandemic. Against the widespread impression, however, the CCP's manipulation of nationalism has a built-in limit. Before over-stretching and over-exciting the population, with the effect of harming their minimal living conditions, the autocracy is prepared to engage in counter-governmentality by retreating from nationalism. The people can also adapt relationality to remind the autocracy of the regime of regimes, however harmful, slow, and indirect that process may be. Regardless of the type of system, top-down political/statist nationalism cannot help but be short-lived in order to prevent the regime, liberal as well as Confucian, from perpetuating a monopoly induced by its own echo and committing isolation.

Autocracy fails to persevere in selflessness because, sooner or later, it begins to take the people's relational governmentality for granted and abuse it. The regime will then suffer a split in its unity, as its leaders eye each other's relative power instead of focusing on the welfare of the entire population. The people comply with their mobilization to divide the community along the binary of correctness and incorrectness. In modern times, the seeming power of statist nationalism to unite but inevitably trap the regime into further committing a monopoly – including internal scapegoating, external demonizing, and self-romanticizing – will backfire eventually, due to the relations-and-balances (R&B) governmentality. Such autocratic cycles are essentially relational cycles, that are unfamiliar to social sciences, which is preoccupied with detecting the seeds of liberalism in these cycles. Each seed informs a point of civilizational conversion. This way, social sciences commit a policy fallacy that is deeply submerged in the ontology of individual rights. Emancipating the targeted population from feudalism, the church, or any other collectivist cosmology reveals the teleology and praxis of the thinktank scholarship in the contemporary liberal world. However, the relational governmentality in liberal democracy that inspires social science research is likewise, unnoticeably and unknowingly, cyclical in terms of internal cleavages, external intervention, and corruption.

Thus, the widespread cross-boundary population, such as migrant communities, bilingual persons, multi-religious families, transnational businesses, and so on, that reveal the pluriversality of relational worlds, are worthy topics of research. Pluriversalism is so prevalent that silencing it by social science discourses can no longer sustain the incapacity of the science and policy circles to remedy the ontological rigidity of liberalism and other forms of binary correctness. As the regime mobilizes its people to unite around a liberal spirit, their mutual nurturing across boundaries, that qualifies correctness, is often left in oblivion. Pluriversalism, in practice, is both a source of anxiety from the political correctness point of view and a therapy that prevents exacerbation. Tracing the pluriversal relations, informed by the intersections of liberalism, Confucianism, Ubuntu, and so on, together with the cycles of relational governmentality at every allegedly liberal as well as Global South site, and substituting them for the binary agenda, still has a long way to go.

Finally, for liberal democracy to move beyond its incessant rounds of involution and loss of a caring capacity, this book mentions three remedies. The first is deliberative democracy – an institutional remedy. It cannot work because the people lack a compelling reason to try to reconsider, from a solidarity perspective, by standing in the shoes of each other, at a precarious time that threatens their own well-being. The second is civic nationalism – an ideological remedy. This is unavailing for the same reason that the people cannot but resort to aggression and regression in order to cope with the breakdown of mutual belonging. The third is the original sin consciousness – a cosmological remedy. The idea of original sin comes close to the Confucian counter-governmentality, rooted in the belief in the inevitability that all bad autocrats fall. The modern version of origin sin can be colonialism. With a sin no one can do without, the sense of guilt might motivate the leaders and the elite, in an involuted liberal democracy, to rehabilitate the impulse to care again.

Appendix: The Diagrammatic Logic of Counter-governmentality

This appendix provides seven diagrams to illustrate in a simplified and logical way the dynamics of counter-governmentality. The diagrams each contain two dimensions. One dimension is composed of the mass line/dominance, denoting the collective choices of the people and the autocrats. The other is composed of belonging/unpredictability to indicate the state of relations between the autocrat and the people. These diagrams include, in order, the presentation of the demand and supply of counter-governmentality (Figure A.1), the governmental involution of liberalism (Figure A.2), the gap between universal and benevolent love in Hong Kong (Figure A.3), the difference in the effects of top-down and bottom-up nationalism (Figure A.4), Xi Jinping's counter-governmentality needs before and after 2012 (Figure A.5), the self-restraint in the dynamics of relational democracy (Figure A.6), and the mini-pluriversalism of Ubuntu, Tianxia, and liberalism (Figure A.7).

Four macro definitions underpin the diagrams:

- the mass line: leaders learning from the people about reality and the ways to improve it (Chapter 2); the policy makers and the administrative organs investigating and satisfying the needs of the masses (Chapter 5);
- governmentality: all practising mutually conducive governing normalcy (Chapter 2); the readiness of individual members to coordinate in ensuring governability (Chapter 6);
- counter-governmentality: (an autocrat) believing in their duty and desiring to adapt the self to suit the people's conditions (Chapter 1); and
- unpredictability: uncertainty in the force and direction of arousal of the people, what triggers it, and when triggered (Chapter 1).

An enhanced implementation of the mass line can enable more precise benevolence delivery, increase the sense of mutual belonging between the leadership and the people, and heighten the degree of acceptance of the governing dominance. The decrease in such a sense will discourage the leadership from the mass line, reduce the information flow, and

APPENDIX

Figure A.1: Demand for and supply of counter-governmentality

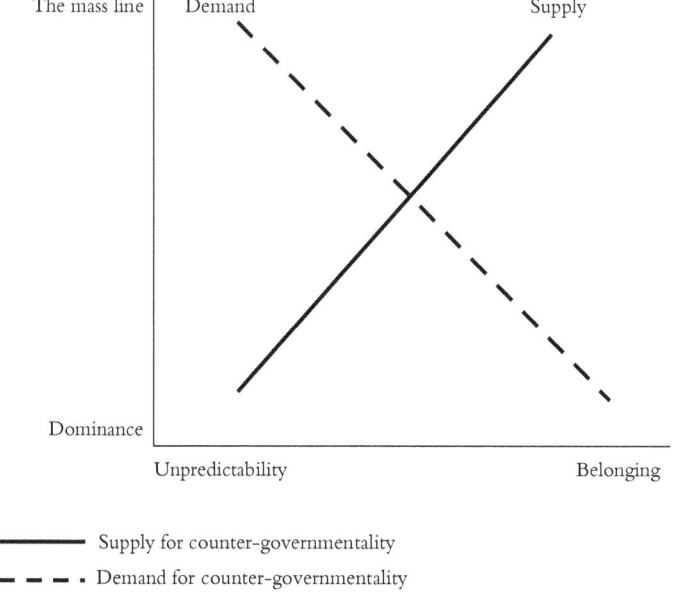

add the unpredictability of the people's response to the government's policy. Unpredictability demands strengthening of the mass line to improve counter-governmentality but ironically induces the authorities' disposition for dominance. Depending on the prior preparation of counter-governmentality, which can be indicated by the slope, dominance that improves the perception of belonging and then revives the mass line investigation can either deliver the desired policy or overstretch the capacity of the leadership (see Figure A.1).

An overall shift of the equilibrium to a lower level of belonging and the mass line indicates involution. The people's heightened demand for counter-governmentality in liberal democracy causes no more unpredictability and reaches the floor at the point of election as the people each consider themselves individually responsible for their choice of leadership after the election. The people's solidarity and support for the leadership easily reach a ceiling at the point of the election, beyond which point the leadership has no felt duty to investigate the people's needs (see Figure A.2).

With the perception of a high level of belonging, the Beijing authorities offered exemption from socialist planning and extraction as well as hybrid elections for the legislature and the executive at the point of the return of Hong Kong to China. International and Hong Kong liberal forces perceived instead an illiberal regime taking over, demanding accordingly

Figure A.2: Supply and demand of counter-governmentality during involution under liberal democracy

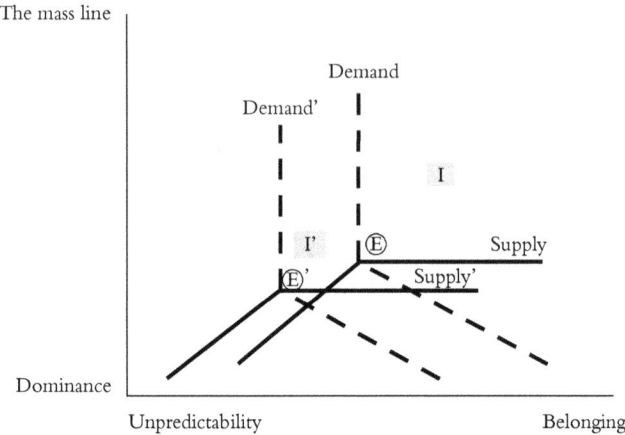

Notes: I = beginning involution, the gap between maximal supply and minimal demand; I' = deteriorating involution; Demand' = demand during involution; Supply' = supply during involution; Ⓔ = election that begins involution; Ⓔ' = election during continuous involution.

Figure A.3: Hong Kong, 2014 and 2019

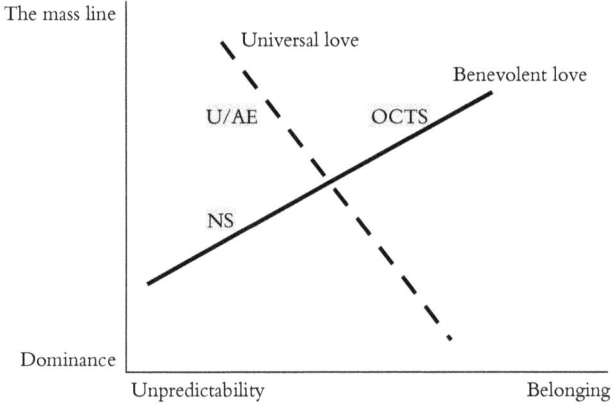

Note: Universal love = the affective aspect of the culture of solidarity that breeds the felt obligation to enable each other's consensual entitlement (see Chapter 3); Benevolent love = the affective aspect of the culture of unity that breeds the felt obligation to align with each other to conceal incongruent self-concerns (see Chapter 3); OCTS = One Country, Two Systems including capitalism and limited election; U/AE = 2014 Umbrella Revolution/2019 Anti-Expedition Movement; NS = National Security Laws.

direct elections to honour their entitlement to execute regular consents to be governed. Frustrated, the two unpredictable uprisings in 2014 and 2019 reversely prompted Beijing to move toward dominance and adopt national security laws (see Figure A.3).

Figure A.4: Nationalist supply for counter-governmentality

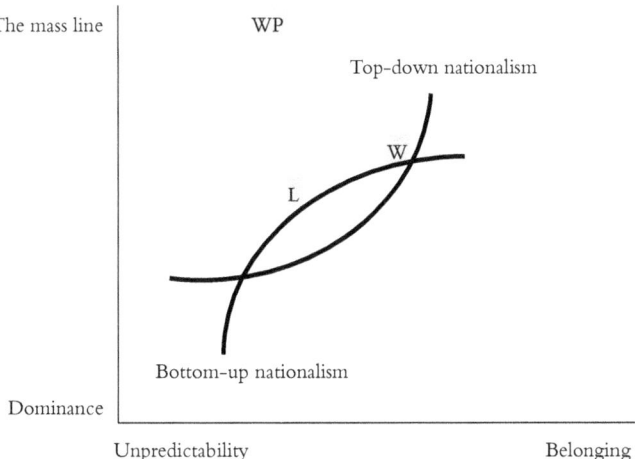

Notes: Nationalism: the practice of caring for the national group to which one claims to belong (see Chapter 4); L = Dr Li Wenliang's death and the arousal of the people's unpredictable solidarity; W = Wuhan nationalism transformed to become a top-down Chinese nationalism; WP = White Paper Protest reflected aroused unpredictability.

Nationalism inspires the people to engage in self-restraint in support of the leadership's pursuit of national unity to cope with an Other that challenges either the existence of the self-other boundary or the credits of the leadership to maintain the boundary. It distracts people from otherwise reduced welfare at the present time. Nationalism embraces the characteristics of counter-governmentality to the extent that the people internalize the boundary and desire its protection by the leadership. However, top-down nationalism has a limit in terms of engendering a mutual sense of belonging between the leadership and the people. This is because it relies on the leadership to deliberately reproduce the boundary and sooner or later strains and squeezes the people's welfare. Bottom-up nationalism is so spontaneous that the leadership has to adapt and support it in order to survive it. However, it can eventually backfire from a counter-governmentality point of view because it produces solidarity between the people to the consequence of neutralizing the leadership. Therefore, the leadership will not go along with it continuously but will try to transform it into top-down nationalism (see Figure A.4).

Xi was highly sensitive to the people's needs and engaged in investigating the people's living conditions regularly and responsively before his inauguration in December 2012. After the inauguration, the leadership has increasingly taken the people's support for granted and invested less in investigating, compared with top-down preaching (see Figure A.5).

Figure A.5: Xi Jinping's counter-governmentality before and after 2012

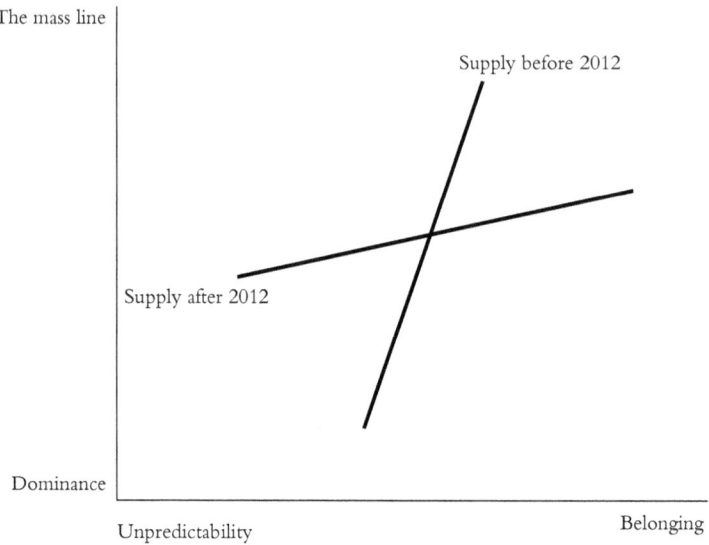

Figure A.6: Self-restraint as governmentality in relational democracy

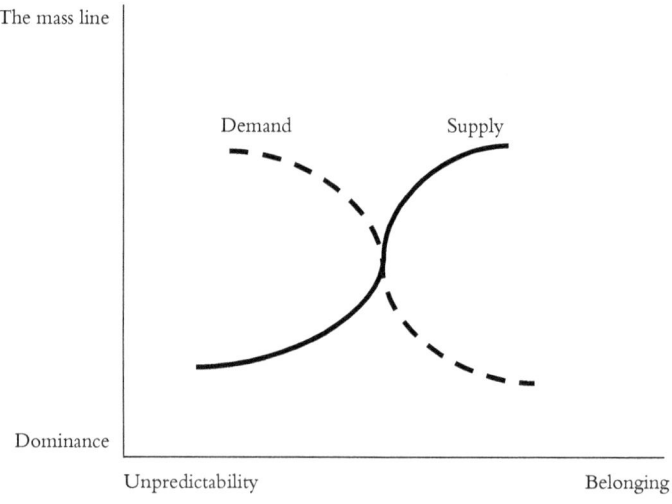

Neither demand nor supply of counter-governmentality will go beyond a certain limit to ensure a mutually acceptable relation between members of the system as well as between members and the leaders at the systemic level (see Figure A.6).

Figure A.7 reproduces Table 7.1 in a different form.

APPENDIX

Figure A.7: Pluriversal relations between governmentalities

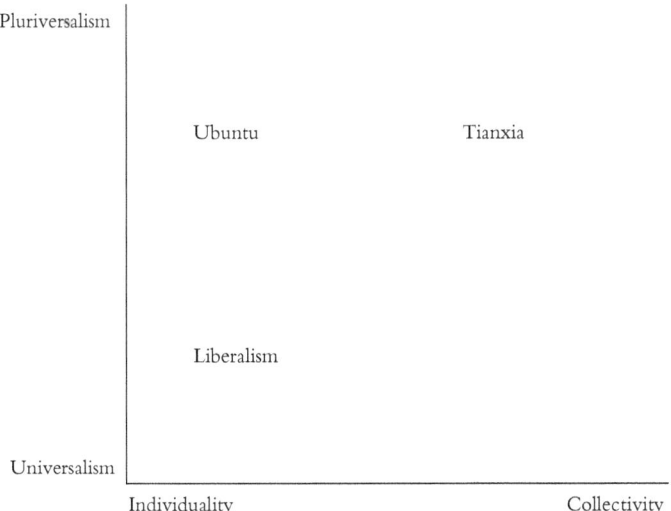

Notes: Pluriversalism: the dynamic coexistence of all cosmologies each in their own adaptable terms (see Chapter 7), the world of worlds and the relation of relations (see Chapter 7); Ubuntu = the necessity of all to nurture all (see Chapter 7); Tianxia = the destiny of all belonging to kin (see Chapter 7); Liberalism = the entitlement of all to the rights of nature (see Chapters 1 and 7).

References

The 13th Central Committee of the Chinese Communist Party (1990) 'The CCP Center's Decision on Strengthening the Connection of the Party with the Masses' (中共中央关于加强党同人民群众联系的决定) 12 March, Available from: http://cpc.people.com.cn/GB/64162/64168/64566/65389/4441853.html [Accessed 7 March 2024].

Abizadeh, A. (2002) 'Does Liberal Democracy Presuppose a Cultural Nation? Four Arguments', *American Political Science Review*, 96(3): 495–509.

Abizadeh, A. (2004) 'Liberal Nationalism Versus Postnational Social Integration: On the Nation's Ethno-Cultural Particularity and "Concreteness"', *Nations and Nationalism*, 10(3): 231–50.

Abizadeh, A. (2021) 'Counter-Majoritarian Democracy: Persistent Minorities, Federalism, and the Power of Numbers', *American Political Science Review*, 115(3): 742–56.

Abraham, K.J. (2022) 'Midcentury Modern: The Emergence of Stakeholders in Democratic Practice', *American Political Science Review*, 116(2): 631–44.

Acharya, A. (2014) 'Global International Relations (IR) and Regional Worlds: A New Agenda for International Studies', *International Studies Quarterly*, 58(4): 647–59.

Achiume, E.T. (2021) 'Transnational Racial (In)Justice in Liberal Democratic Empire', *Harvard Law Review Forum*, 134(7): 378–97.

Ackery, B.A. (2005) 'Is Liberalism the Only Way Toward Democracy? Confucianism and Democracy', *Political Theory*, 33(4): 547–76.

Adamidis, V. (2021) 'Democracy, Populism, and the Rule of Law: A Reconsideration of Their Interconnectedness', *Politics*, https://doi.org/10.1177/02633957211041444

Adebanwi, W. (ed) (2022) *Everyday State and Democracy in Africa: Ethnographic Encounters*, Athens: Ohio University Press.

Adler, E. (2008) 'The Spread of Security Communities: Communities of Practice, Self-Restraint, and NATO's Post-Cold War Transformation', *European Journal of International Relations*, 14(2): 195–230.

Adorno, T., Frenkel-Brunswik, E., Levinson, D. et al (1950) *The Authoritarian Personality*, New York: Harper & Row.

REFERENCES

Agamben, G. (2020) 'The Enemy is not Outside, it is Within Us', *The Book Haven*, [online] 14 March, Available from: https://bookhaven.stanford.edu/2020/03/giorgio-agamben-on-coronavirus-the-enemy-is-not-outside-it-is-within-us/ [Accessed 31 August 2023].

Ahrens, P. and Kantola, J. (2022) 'Political Group Formation in the European Parliament: Negotiating Democracy and Gender', *Party Politics*, https://doi.org/10.1177/13540688221106295

Ai, L. and Wang, Z. (2020) 'Unequal and Universal: The Opposition and Unity of the Confucianism and Mohism in the View of Distributive Justice', *Philosophy Study*, 10(10): 663–66.

Albert, E. (2020) 'How a Pandemic Drew China and Serbia Closer', *The Diplomat*, [online] 27 March, Available from: https://thediplomat.com/2020/03/how-a-pandemic-drew-china-and-serbia-closer/ [Accessed 31 August 2023].

Albertoni, N. and Wise, C. (2021) 'International Trade Norms in the Age of Covid-19 Nationalism on the Rise?', *Fudan Journal of the Humanities and Social Sciences*, 14(1): 41–66.

Al Jazeera (2020) 'Chinese premier visits Wuhan, epicentre of coronavirus outbreak', *Al Jazeera*, [online] 28 January, Available from: https://www.aljazeera.com/news/2020/01/chinese-premier-visits-wuhan-epicentre-coronavirus-outbreak-200127153309730.html [Accessed 31 August 2023].

Allan, J. (1998) 'Liberalism, Democracy, and Hong Kong', *Hong Kong Law Journal*, 28: 156–67.

Allen, K. (2020) 'Coronavirus: Cement mixers become celebrities in China lockdown', *BBC News*, [online] 31 January, Available from: https://www.bbc.com/news/world-asia-china-51315238 [Accessed 31 August 2023].

Allison, H.E. (1995) *Kant's Theory of Freedom*, Cambridge: Cambridge University Press.

Almond, G.A. and Verba, S. (1963) *The Civic Culture: Political Attitudes and Democracy in Five Nations*, London: Sage Publications, Inc.

Almond, G.A., Powell, G.B. and Mundt, R.J. (1996) *Comparative Politics: A Theoretical Framework*, New York: Harper Collins College Publishers.

Ames, R.T. (2008) 'Using English to Speak Confucianism: Antonio S. Cua on the Confucian "Self"', *Journal of Chinese Philosophy*, 35(1): 33–41.

Ames, R.T. (2020) *Confucian Role Ethics: A Vocabulary*, Albany: State University of New York Press.

Ames, R.T. (2021) 'A Cosmological Aestheticism: The Interpretive Contexts for Confucian Role Ethics', in M. Ghilardi and H.G. Moeller (eds) *Handbook of Chinese Aesthetics and Philosophy of Art*, London: Bloomsbury Academic, pp 63–78.

Andrej, K. and Anders, S. (2020) 'Leader Succession and Civil War', *Comparative Political Studies*, 53(3-4): 434–68.

Ang, Y.Y. (2016a) *How China Escaped the Poverty Trap*, Ithaca: Cornell University.

Ang, Y.Y. (2016b) 'Co-optation & Clientelism: Nested Distributive Politics in China's Single-Party Dictatorship', *Studies in Comparative & International Development*, 51(3): 235–56.

Ang, Y.Y. (2018) 'Autocracy With Chinese Characteristics: Beijing's Behind-the-Scenes Reforms', *Foreign Affairs*, 97(3): 39–46.

Angle, S.C. (2015) 'Western, Chinese, and Universal Values', *Telos*, 171: 112–17.

Appleby, R.S. (2000) *The Ambivalence of Sacred: Religion, Violence, and Reconciliation*, Lanham: Rowman & Littlefield.

Arendt, H. (1977) *On Revolution*, New York: Penguin Books.

Arneil, B. (2021) 'Jeremy Bentham: Pauperism, Colonialism, and Imperialism', *American Political Science Review*, 115(4): 1147–58.

Babones, S. (2020) 'From *Tianxia* to Tianxia: The Generalization of a Concept', *Chinese Political Science Review*, 5: 131–47.

Backer, L.C. (2022) 'Linking People to Governing Institutions Through Leninist Political Parties: 全过程民主 (Whole Process Democracy), Socialist Consultative Democracy, and 中国新型政党制度 (China's New Political Party System)', *SSRN*, 11 June, http://dx.doi.org/10.2139/ssrn.4134483

Ball, T. and Dagger R. (2008) 'Democratic Centralism: Communist Policy', *Encyclopedia Britannica*, [online] 5 June, Available from: https://www.britannica.com/topic/democratic-centralism [Accessed 31 August 2023].

Baloyra, E.A. (ed) (2019) *Comparing New Democracies: Transition and Consolidation in Mediterranean Europe and the Southern Cone*, New York: Routledge.

Bandurski, D. (2020a) 'Reclaiming Doctor Li', *China Media Project*, [online] 19 March, Available from: http://chinamediaproject.org/2020/03/19/reclaiming-doctor-li/ [Accessed 31 August 2023].

Bandurski, D. (2020b) 'Turning on the Kitsch', *China Media Project*, [online] 26 February, Available from: https://chinamediaproject.org/2020/02/26/turning-on-the-kitsch/ [Accessed 31 August 2023].

Bandurski, D. (2020c) 'Coronavirus: The New and Ingenious Ways Chinese Citizens are Evading Censorship to Learn About the Outbreak', *Hong Kong Free Press*, [online] 13 March, Available from: https://hongkongfp.com/2020/03/13/coronavirus-new-ingenious-ways-chinese-citizens-evading-censorship-learn-outbreak/ [Accessed 31 August 2023].

Banki, B.F. and Mchombu, K. (2008) *Pan-Africanism/African Nationalism: Strengthening the Unity of Africa and Its Diaspora*, Trenton: The Red Sea Press.

Barbara, G., Joseph, W. and Erica, F. (2014) 'Autocratic Breakdown and Regime Transitions: A New Data Set', *Perspectives on Politics*, 12(2): 313–31.

Barry, A., Osborne, T. and Rose N. (eds) (1996) *Foucault and Political Reason: Liberalism, Neo-Liberalism and Rationalities of Government*, Chicago: University of Chicago Press.

Baum, R. (1964) '"Red and Expert": The Politico-Ideological Foundations of China's Great Leap Forward', *Asian Survey*, 4(9): 1048–57.

Baumann, C., Winzar, H. and Viengkham, D. (2020) *Confucianism, Discipline, and Competitiveness*, New York: Routledge.

Baxley, A.M. (2010) *Kant's Theory of Virtue: The Value of Autocracy*, Cambridge: Cambridge University Press.

BBC News (2020) 'Coronavirus: Pregnant nurse "propaganda" sparks backlash', *BBC News*, [online] 21 February, https://www.bbc.com/news/world-asia-china-51583186 [Accessed 31 August 2023].

Beate, J. (2000) *The Cultural Construction of International Relations: The Invention of the State of Nature*, New York: Palgrave.

Beattie, P., Chen, R. and Bettache, K. (2022) 'When Left Is Right, and Right Is Left: The Psychological Correlates of Political Ideology in China', *Political Psychology*, 43(3): 457–88.

Behr, H. and Shani, G. (2021) 'Rethinking Emancipation in a Critical IR: Normativity, Cosmology, and Pluriversal Dialogue', *Millennium*, 49(2): 368–91.

Bell, D. (1995) 'A Communitarian Critique of Authoritarianism', *Society*, 32(5): 38–43.

Bell, D. (ed) (1996) *Toward Illiberal Democracy in Pacific Asia*, New York: Macmillan.

Bell, D. (2006) *Beyond Liberal Democracy: Political Thinking for an East Asian Context*, Princeton: Princeton University.

Bell, D. (ed) (2007) *Confucian Political Ethics*, Princeton: Princeton University Press.

Bell, D. (2011) 'Jiang Qing's Political Confucianism', in R. Fan (ed) *The Renaissance of Confucianism in Contemporary China*, New York: Springer, pp 139–52.

Bell, D. (2016) *The China Model: Political Meritocracy and the Limits of Democracy*, Princeton: Princeton University Press.

Bell, D.A. and Metz, T. (2011) 'Confucianism and Ubuntu: Reflections on a Dialogue between Chinese and African Traditions', *Journal of Chinese Philosophy*, 38(5): 78–95.

Ben-Eliezer, U. (1993) 'The Meaning of Political Participation in a Nonliberal Democracy: The Israeli Experience', *Comparative Politics*, 25(4): 397–412.

Bennett, M., Brouwer, H. and Claassen, R. (eds) (2022) *Wealth and Power: Philosophical Perspectives*, London: Routledge.

Berger, P. (1983) 'Secularity: West and East', in Editors n. a. (eds) *Cultural Identity and Modernization in Asian Countries: Proceedings of Kokugakuin University Centennial Symposium*, Tokyo: Kokugakuin University, Available from: https://www2.kokugakuin.ac.jp/ijcc/wp/cimac/index.html [Accessed 21 January 2024]

Berkowitz, P. (1999) *Virtue and the Making of Modern Liberalism*, Princeton: Princeton University Press.

Bhambra, G. and Santos, B. (2017) 'Introduction: Global Challenges for Sociology', *Sociology*, 51(1): 3–10.

Bieber, F. (2020) 'Global Nationalism in Times of the COVID-19 Pandemic', *Nationalities Papers*, https://doi.org/10.1017/nps.2020.35

Bieber F. (2022) 'Global Nationalism in Times of the COVID-19 Pandemic', *Nationalities Papers*, 50(1): 13–25.

Bilba, C. (2011) 'The Parent-Child Relation in Hobbes: Beyond Private Life and Public Reason', *Revista De Cercetare Si Interventie Socia,* 32: 172–93.

Blecher, M. (1983) 'The Mass Line and Leader-Mass Relations and Communication in Basic-Level Rural Communities', in G.C. Chu and Francis L.K. Hsu (eds) *China's New Social Fabric*, London: Routledge, pp 63–86.

Bo, L., Bohm, S. and Reynolds, N.-S. (2019) 'Organizing the Environmental Governance of the Rare-Earth Industry: China's Passive Revolution', *Organization Studies*, 40(7): 1045–71.

Bodde, D. (1957) 'Evidence for "Laws of Nature" in Chinese Thought', *Harvard Journal of Asiatic Studies*, 20(3/4): 709–27.

Boer, R. (2023) *Socialism in Power*, Singapore: Springer.

Boese, V.A., Lindberg, S.I. and Lührmann, A. (2021) 'Waves of Autocratization and Democratization: A Rejoinder', *Democratization*, 28(6): 1202–10.

Bohman, J. and Rehg, W. (eds) (1997) *Deliberative Democracy: Essays on Reason and Politics*, Cambridge: The MIT Press.

Bollyky, T.J. and Brown, C.P. (2020) 'The Tragedy of Vaccine Nationalism: Only Cooperation Can End the Pandemic', *Foreign Affairs*, 99(5): 96–108.

Borgström, B.-E. (1980) 'The Best of Two Worlds: Rhetoric of Autocracy and Democracy in Nepal', *Contributions to Indian Sociology*, 14(1): 35–50.

Bowers, F. (2020) 'Covid-19 in Ireland: A Tale of Two Countries', *Raidió Teilifís Éireann*, [online] 18 April, Available from: https://www.rte.ie/news/analysis-and-comment/2020/0417/1132230-tale-two-countries/ [Accessed 31 August 2023].

Boylan, B.M., McBeath, J. and Wang, B. (2021) 'US–China Relations: Nationalism, the Trade War, and COVID-19', *Fudan Journal of the Humanities and Social Sciences*, 1–18, https://doi.org/10.1007/s40647-020-00302-6

Brennan, D. (2019) 'Taiwan calls for democracy in Hong Kong as anti-China forces on both islands face down Beijing', *Newsweek*, [online] 23 July, Available from: https://www.newsweek.com/taiwan-calls-democracy-hong-kong-anti-china-activists-both-islands-face-down-beijing-1450661 [Accessed 31 August 2023].

Breslin, S. (2010) 'Great Expectations: Competing Domestic Drivers of Chinese Policy Deliberations', *VoxEU*, [online] 16 April, Available from: https://voxeu.org/article/great-expectations-competing-domestic-drivers-chinese-policy-deliberations [Accessed 31 August 2023].

Brewster, K.R. (2020) 'Reflections of Self and Other: Discursive Possibilities for Solidarity in Conceptions of Sameness and Difference', *Qualitative Psychology*, 7(3): 267–84.

Brinkmann, S. (2019) *The Art of Self-restraint in an Age of Excess*, Medford, MA: Polity.

Brissett, N.O.M. (2013) 'Reading Conformity, Resistance, and Hybridity in Jamaica's Educational Policy Reform Approaches', *Journal of Postcolonial Cultures and Societies*, 4(4): 82–116.

Bromme, L., Rothmund, T. and Azevedo, F. (2022) 'Mapping Political Trust and Involvement in the Personality Space – A Meta-analysis and New Evidence', *Journal of Personality*, 90(6): 846–72.

Brooks, C. and Manza, J. (1997) 'Social Cleavages and Political Alignments: U.S. Presidential Elections, 1960 to 1992', *American Sociological Review*, 62(6) (December): 937–46.

Brown, K. and Bērziņa-Čerenkova, U.A. (2018) 'Ideology in the Era of Xi Jinping', *Journal of Chinese Political Science*, 23(3): 323–39.

Brown, W. (1995) *States of Injury: Power and Freedom in Late Modernity*, Princeton: Princeton University Press.

Brumberg, D. (2002) 'Democratization in the Arab World? The Trap of Liberalized Autocracy', *Journal of Democracy*, 13(4): 56–68.

Buber, M. (1965) *Between Man and Man*, New York: Macmillan.

Buber, M. (1970) *I and Thou*, New York: Charles Scribner's Sons.

Buckley, C. and Tatlow, D.K. (2015) 'Cultural Revolution shaped Xi Jinping, from schoolboy to survivor', *New York Times*, [online] 24 September, Available from: https://www.nytimes.com/2015/09/25/world/asia/xi-jinping-china-cultural-revolution.html [Accessed 31 August 2023].

Bunskoek, R. and Shih, C-y. (2021) 'Community of Common Destiny as Post-Western Regionalism: Rethinking China's Belt and Road Initiative from a Confucian Perspective', *Uluslararası İlişkiler*, 18(70): 85–101.

Bureau of East Asian and Pacific Affairs (2019) 'Hong Kong Policy Act Report', *US Department of State*, [online] 21 March, Available from: https://www.state.gov/2019-hong-kong-policy-act-report/ [Accessed 31 August 2023].

Bush, R.C. (2016) *Hong Kong in the Shadow of China: Living with the Leviathan*, New York: Brookings.

Buu-Sao, D. (2021) 'Extractive Governmentality at Work: Native Appropriations of Oil Labor in Amazon', *International Political Sociology*, 15(1): 63–82.

Cachero, P. (2020) 'The next Tiananmen Square? Chinese citizens are demanding increased free speech after the death of a coronavirus whistleblower doctor. China is censoring their calls', *Business Insider Australia*, [online] 8 February, Available from: https://www.businessinsider.com.au/calls-free-speech-online-doctor-li-wenliang-death-censored-china-2020-2?r=US&IR=T [Accessed 31 August 2023].

Callahan, W. (2008) 'Chinese Visions of World Order: Post-hegemonic or a New Hegemony,' *International Studies Review*, 10(4): 749–61.

Calu, M.-I. (2018) 'Unintended Consequences of State-building and the Management of Diversity in Post-conflict Kosovo', *Nationalities Papers*, 46(1): 86–104.

Campbell, D. (1998) *National Deconstruction: Violence, Identity, and Justice in Bosnia*, Minneapolis: University of Minnesota Press.

Capan, Z.G., dos Reis, F. and Grasten, M. (2021) *The Politics of Translation in International Relations*, Cham, Switzerland: Palgrave Macmillan.

Carlson, J.D. and Fox, R.A. (2013) *The State of Nature in Comparative Political Thought: Western and Non-Western Perspectives*, Lanham: Lexington Books.

The Carter Center (2018) *Scripturally Annotated Universal Declaration of Human Rights*, Atlanta: The Carter Center.

Cerf, C. and Navasky, V.S. (2008) *Mission Accomplished: Or How We Won the War in Iraq*, New York: Simon & Schuster Paperbacks.

Cervinkova, H. (2020) 'Citizenship after COVID-19: Thoughts from Poland', *Social Anthropology*, 28(2): 238–9.

Chakawata, W. (2022) 'Africa's Response to COVID-19: A Governmentality in Disguise Masterclass', *International Review of Sociology*, 32(1): 141–73.

Chakrabarti, S. (2014) 'Empty Symbol: The Little Red Book in India', in A.C. Cook (ed) *Mao's Little Red Book: A Global History*, Cambridge: Cambridge University Press, pp 117–29.

Chambers, C. (2013) '"The Family as a Basic Institution": A Feminist Analysis of the Basic Structure as Subject', in R. Abbey (ed) *Feminist Interpretation of Rawls*, Pittsburgh: Penn State Press, pp 75–95.

Chan, A. (1985) *Children of Mao: Personality Development and Political Activism in the Red Guard Generation*, London: Macmillan.

Chan, A. (2022) *Xi Jinping*, Oxford: Oxford University Press.

Chan, C. and Strabucchi, M.M. (2020) 'Many-faced Orientalism: Racism and Xenophobia in a Time of the Novel Coronavirus in Chile', *Asian Ethnicity*, 22(2): 374–94.

Chan, F.G. (1980) 'Introduction: China at the Crossroads, 1927–1949', in F.G. Chan (ed) *China at the Crossroads: Nationalists and Communists, 1927–1949*, Boulder: Westview, pp 1–17.

Chan, J. (2014) *Confucian Perfectionism: A Political Philosophy for Modern Times*, Princeton: Princeton University Press.

Chan, J.C.W. (2011) 'Confucianism and Human Rights', in J. Witte and M.C. Green (eds) *Religion and Human Rights: An Introduction*, Oxford: Oxford Academic, pp 87–102.

Chan, J.M.M., Fu, H.L. and Ghai, Y. (2000) *Hong Kong's Constitutional Debate: Conflict over Interpretation*, Hong Kong: Hong Kong University Press.

Chan, K.K.L. (2019) 'Hong Kong in the World: Continuities and Changes', *Asian Education and Development Studies*, 8(2): 197–207.

Chang, A., Chu, Y-h. and Welsh, B. (2013) 'Southeast Asia: Sources of Regime Support', *Journal of Democracy*, 24(2): 150–64.

Chang, D. (2007) 'The Imperative of One Country, Two Systems: One Country Before Two Systems?', *Hong Kong Law Journal*, 37(2): 351–62.

Chang, K.-s. (1978) *Mao Tse-tung and His China*, Dusseldorf: Heinemann.

Chapman, R.A. (1956) *Rousseau: Totalitarian or Liberal?* New York: Columbia University Press.

Chapman, R.A. (1975) 'Leviathan Writ Small: Thomas Hobbes on the Family', *American Political Science Review*, 69(1): 76–90.

Cheek, T. (1997) *Propaganda and Culture in Mao's China: Deng Tuo and the Intelligentsia*, Oxford: Clarendon Press.

Cheek, T. (1998) 'From Market to Democracy in China: Gaps in the Civil Society Model,' in J.D. Lindau and T. Cheek (eds) *Market Economics and Political Change: Comparing China and Mexico*, Lanham: Rowman & Littlefield, pp 219–52.

Cheek, T. (2021) 'Xi Jinping's Counter-Reformation: The Reassertion of Ideological Governance in Historical Perspective', *Journal of Contemporary China*, 30(132): 875–87.

Chemouni, B. and Mugiraneza, A. (2020) 'Ideology and Interests in the Rwandan Patriotic Front: Singing the Struggle in Pre-genocide Rwanda', *African Affairs*, 119(474): 115–40.

Chen, D. and Kinzelbach, K. (2016) 'Democracy Promotion and China: Blocker or Bystander?', in N. Babayan and T. Risse (eds) *Democracy Promotion and the Challenges of Illiberal Regional Powers*, London: Routledge, pp 20–29.

Chen, J., Pan, J. and Xu, Y. (2016) 'Sources of Authoritarian Responsiveness: A Field Experiment in China', *American Journal of Political Science*, 60(2): 383–400.

Chen, N. and Xiao, B. (2020) 'Ideological Formation, National Development, and the "Mass Line": The Historical-political Complexity of Cultural Policy and Chinese Socialism', *The Journal of Law, Social Justice and Global Development*, 25: 146–62.

Chen, Q. (2022) 'Confucianism and the Shaping of Modern Social Order in China', in G. Sun (ed) [D. Sun (trans)] *Chinese Culture and Its Impact on China's Development*, Singapore: World Scientific, pp 157–88.

Chen, Y. (2022) 'Xi Jinping's "Zero-Tolerance" Crackdown on Corruption Achieves Dual Goals', *Voice of America*, [online] 25 January, Available from: https://www.voacantonese.com/a/Xi-Jinping-s-zero-tolerance-crackdown-on-corruption-achieves-dual-goals-20220125/6411453.html [Accessed 31 August 2023].

Chen, Z. and Shen, M. (2014) 'Anti-Four Tendencies Molds Four No-Exceptions: The Anniversary of the Practical Programs for the Mass Line Education', *The Chinese Communist Party News Net*, [online] 2 July, Available from: http://cpc.people.com.cn/n/2014/0702/c83083-25228489.html [Accessed 31 August 2023].

Chen, Z. and Wang, C.Y. (2020) 'The Discipline of Happiness: The Foucauldian Use of the "Positive Energy" Discourse in China's Ideological Works', *Journal of Current Chinese Affairs*, 48(2): 201–25.

Cheng, J.Y.S. (1988) 'The Constitutional Relationship Between the Central Government and the Future Hong Kong Special Administrative Region Government', *Case Western Reserve Journal of International Law*, 20(1): 65–97.

Cheng, Y. (2006) 'Ideology and Cosmology: Maoist Discussion on Physics and the Cultural Revolution', *Modern Asian Studies*, 40(1): 109–49.

Cherney, A. and Murphy, K. (2019) 'Support for Terrorism: The Role of Beliefs in Jihad and Institutional Responses to Terrorism', *Terrorism and Political Violence*, 31(5): 1049–69.

Cheung, S.K. (2017) 'From Transnational to Chinese National? A New In-betweenness of Hong Kong Cinema in the Postcolonial Politics of Disappearance', *Social Transformations in Chinese Societies*, 13(2): 106–17.

Chien, C.-L. (2016) 'Beyond Authoritarian Personality: The Culture-Inclusive Theory of Chinese Authoritarian Orientation', *Frontiers in Psychology*, 7 (Article 924), https://doi.org/10.3389/fpsyg.2016.00924

Chu, Y.-h. (2013) 'Sources of Regimes' Legitimacy and the Debate over the Chinese Model', *China Review*, 13(1): 1–42.

Chu, Y.-h., Diamond, L., Nathan, A.J. and Shin, D.C. (2010) *How East Asians View Democracy*, New York: Columbia University Press.

Chuliá, E. (2023) 'Mothers of Mid-century Spanish Families: Agents of Social Change in the Context of Dictatorship and Patriarchy', *Contemporary European History*, 32(2): 186–202.

Chung, S.N.-S. (1982) 'Will China Go 'Capitalist'? An Economic Analysis of Property Rights and Institutional Change', *Hobart Paper* 94, *The Institute of Economic Affairs*, Norfolk: Thetford Press Ltd.

Ciorciari, J.D. (2014) 'China and the Pol Pot Regime', *Cold War History*, 14(5): 215–35.

Collier, P. (2014) 'The Ethics of Natural Assets', *Journal of Global Ethics*, 10(1): 45–52.

Collier, P. (2017) 'The Institutional and Psychological Foundations of Natural Resource Policies', *Journal of Development Studies*, 53(2): 217–28.

Comaroff, J. and Comaroff, J. (2012) 'Theory from the South: A Rejoinder', *Fieldsights: Theorizing the Contemporary, Cultural Anthropology Online*, February 24, Available from: http://nrs.harvard.edu/urn-3:HUL.InstRepos:11204673 [Accessed 30 Januray 2024].

Congleton, R.D. (2020) 'Governance by True Believers: Supreme Duties with and without Totalitarianism', *Constitutional Political Economy*, 31(1): 111–41.

Connors, M.K. and Pathmanand, U. (eds) (2021) *Thai Politics in Translation: Monarchy, Democracy and the Supra-constitution*, Copenhagen: NIAS Press.

Cooper, K. and Dyer, J.B. (2017) 'Thomas Jefferson, Nature's God, and the Theological Foundations of Natural-Rights Republicanism', *Politics and Religion*, 10(3): 662–88.

Cooper-Cunningham, D. (2020) 'Drawing Fear of Difference: Race, Gender, and National Identity in Ms. Marvel Comics', *Millennium*, 48(2): 165–97.

Costello, T.H., Bowes, S.M., Stevens, S.T. et al (2022) 'Clarifying the Structure and Nature of Left-wing Authoritarianism', *Journal of Personality and Social Psychology*, 122(1):135–70.

Crouch, C. (2004) *Post-Democracy*, Cambridge: Polity.

Crouch, C. (2020) *Post-Democracy After the Crisis*, Cambridge: Polity.

Curato, N., Sass, J., Ercan, S.A. et al (2022) 'Deliberative Democracy in the Age of Serial Crisis', *International Political Science Review*, 43(1): 55–66.

Dahl, A. (2018) *Empire of the People: Settler Colonialism and the Foundations of Modern Democratic Thought*, Lawrence: University Press of Kansas.

Das, R.N. (1993) 'Hong Kong: An Experiment in "One Country, Two Systems"', *China Report*, 29(2): 153–64.

Davies, M. (2016) 'Everyday Life as Critique: Revisiting the Everyday in IPE with Henri Lefebvre and Postcolonialism', *International Political Sociology*, 10(1): 22–38.

Dawson, R.S. [trans] (2008) *The Analects*, Oxford: Oxford University Press.

De Leeuw, S.E., Rekker, R., Azrout, R. et al (2020) 'Are Would-be Authoritarians Rights? Democratic Support and Citizens' Left-Right Self-placement in Former Left- and Right-Authoritarian Countries', *Democratization*, 28(2): 414–33.

de Sousa Santos, B. (2014) *Epistemologies of the South: Justice Against Epistemicide*, Oxfordshire: Taylor & Francis.

Dean, M.M. (1999) *Governmentality: Power and Rule in Modern Society*, London: Sage Publications.

Dean, M.M. (2019) 'Rogue Neoliberalism, Liturgical Power, and the Search for a Left Governmentality', *South Atlantic Quarterly*, 118(2): 325–42.

Deng, J. and Smith, C. (2018) 'The Rise of New Confucianism and the Return of Spirituality to Politics in Mainland China', *China Information*, 32(2): 294–314.

Deng, X. (1984) 'One Country, Two Systems', minutes of Deng's meeting with a group of Hong Kong visitors (22 and 23 June), http://www.71.cn/2008/0402/500845.shtml [Accessed 18 November 2023]

Derous, M. and De Roeck, F. (2019) 'On Foucault and Foreign Policy: The Merits of Governmentality for the Study of EU External Relations', *European Politics and Society*, 20(3): 245–59.

Diamond, L. and Schell, O. (eds) (2018) *China's Influence & American Interests: Promoting Constructive Vigilance*, Stanford: The Hoover Institute.

Diamond, L.J. (2003) 'The Illusion of Liberal Autocracy', *Journal of Democracy*, 14(4):167–71.

Diaz, I.I. and Mountz, A. (2020) 'Intensifying Fissures: Geopolitics, Nationalism, Militarism, and the US Response to the Novel Coronavirus', *Geopolitics*, 25(5): 1037–44.

Dimitrov, M.K. (2023) *Dictatorship and Information: Authoritarian Regime Resilience in Communist Europe and China*, New York: Oxford University Press.

Ding, X. (2020) 'Tianjin guniang de zhefu manhua huole "wo zuixiang hua quanguo meishi jie reganmian chuyuan" [cartoon by Tianjin girl went viral: "hoping to draw it when all specialty dishes across the country welcome reganmian home from the hospital"]', *Tonight News Paper*, [online] 31 January, Available from: https://www.sohu.com/a/369826586_571524 [Accessed 31 August 2023].

Diop, C.A. [M. Cook, (trans)] (1974) *The African Origin of Civilization: Myth or Reality?*, New York and Westport: Lawrence Hill & Co.

Disteihorst, G. and Fu, D. (2019) 'Performing Authoritarian Citizenship: Public Transcripts in China', *Perspectives on Politics*, 17(1): 106–21.

diZerega, G., (2020) 'Liberalism for the Twenty-First Century: From Markets to Civil Society, from Economics to Human Beings', in D. Hardwick and L. Marsh (eds), *Reclaiming Liberalism. Palgrave Studies in Classical Liberalism*, Cham: Palgrave Macmillan, pp 163–78.

Doerr, N. (2020) 'Political Translation and Civic Translation Capacities for Democracy in Post-migrant Societies', in M. Ji and S. Laviosa (eds) *The Oxford Handbook of Translation and Social Practices,* New York: Oxford University Press, pp 109–27.

Dougherty, R.J. (2019) 'The Psychological Management of the Poor: Prescribing Psychoactive Drugs in the Age of Neoliberalism', *Social Issues*, 75(1): 217–37.

Downs, E.S. and Saunders, P.C. (1999) 'Legitimacy and the Limits of Nationalism: China and the Diaoyu Islands', *International Security*, 23(4): 114–46.

Doyle, N.J. (2013) 'Islam, Depoliticization and the European Crisis of Democratic Legitimacy', *Politics, Religion & Ideology*, 14(2): 265–83.

Du Bois, W.E.B. (2015 [1903]) *The Souls of Black Folk*, New Haven, Connecticut: Yale University Press.

Du, S. (2019) 'Xi Jinping: I will be non-me', *Xinhua Net*, [online] 24 March, Available from: http://www.xinhuanet.com/world/2019-03/24/c_1124275623.htm [Accessed 31 August 2023].

Dumm, T.L. (1996) *Michel Foucault and the Politics of Freedom*, Thousand Oaks, CA: Sage.

Dupré J. (2020) 'Making Hong Kong Chinese: State Nationalism and its Blowbacks in a Recalcitrant City', *Nationalism and Ethnic Politics*, 26(1): 8–26.

Duruz, J., Luckman, S. and Bishop, P. (2011) 'Bazaar Encounters: Food, Markets, Belonging and Citizenship in the Cosmopolitan City', *Continuum*, 25(5): 599–604.

Easton, D. (1950) 'Harold Lasswell; Political Scientist for a Democratic Society', *Journal of Politics*, 12: 450–77.

Easton, D. (1953) *The Political System*, Chicago: Chicago University Press.

Easton, D. (1965) *A Framework for Political Analysis*, Englewood Cliffs: Prentice-Hall.

Editorial Office (2012) *Xi Jinping's Seven Years of Educated Youth*, Beijing: Central Party School Press.

Editors (2014) 'Xi Jinping in Fujian', *People's Net*, [online] 6 November, Available from: http://politics.people.com.cn/n/2014/1106/c1001-25986542.html [Accessed 31 August 2023].

Editors (2015) 'Talk to the Third Plenary of the 18th Central Disciplinary Committee', in Xi Jinping's Quotes of Classics in His Anti-Corruption Narratives, *The Chinese Communist Party News Net*, [online] 18 June, Available from: http://cpc.people.com.cn/xuexi/n/2015/0618/c385474-27173822-4.html [Accessed 31 August 2023].

Einwohner, R.L., Kelly-Thompson, K., Sinclair-Chapman, V. et al (2021) 'Active Solidarity: Interpersonal Solidarity in Action', *Social Politics*, 28(3): 704–29.

Elvin, M. (1973) *The Pattern of the Chinese Past*, Stanford: Stanford University Press.

Emerton, R.H. (2018) 'The Mass-Line, 1917 to 1989: Chinese Experience', *Journal of Global Faultlines*, 4(2): 110–22.

Erica, F. and Elizabeth S. (2017) 'Countering Coups: Leadership Succession Rules in Dictatorships', *Comparative Political Studies*, 50(7): 1–29.

Erlanger, S. (2020) 'Global backlash builds against China over coronavirus', *New York Times*, [online] 3 May, Available from: https://www.nytimes.com/2020/05/03/world/europe/backlash-china-coronavirus.html [Accessed 20 January 2024].

Escobar, P. (2020) 'COVID-19: Confucius is winning the coronavirus war', *Consortium News*, 29, [online] 16 April, Available from: https://consortiumnews.com/2020/04/16/covid-19-confucius-is-winning-the-coronavirus-war/ [Accessed 31 August 2023].

Etzioni, A. (1993) *The Spirit of Community: Rights, Responsibilities, and the Communitarian Agenda*, New York: Crown.

Etzioni, A. (2004) 'The Responsive Communitarian Platform: Rights and Responsibilities', in A. Etzioni, A. Volmert and E. Rothschild (eds) *The Communitarian Reader: Beyond the Essentials*, Lanham: Rowan & Littlefield, pp 13–23.

Fanon, F. (1967) *Black Skin, White Masks*, New York: Grove Press.

Fanoulis, E. and Song, W. (2022) 'Cooperation between the EU and China: A Post-liberal Governmentality Approach', *Review of International Studies*, 48(2): 346–63.

Fatenkov, A.N. (2005) 'Who Should Rule: People or Laws? Masses or Personalities? (Apologia of Existential Autocracy)', *Polis. Political Studies*, 2: 158–71.

Fatke, M. (2017) 'Personality Traits and Political Psychology: A First Global Assessment', *Political Psychology*, 38(5): 881–99.

Federico, C.M. (2022) 'The Personality Basis of Political Preferences', in D. Osborne and C.G. Sibley (eds) *The Cambridge Handbook of Political Psychology*, Cambridge: Cambridge University Press, pp 68–88.

Federico, C.M. and Malka A. (2018) 'The Contingent, Contextual Nature of the Relationship between Security and Certainty and Political Preferences: Evidence and Implications', *Political Psychology*, 39(1): 3–48.

Feng, E. (2019) 'Hong Kong announces housing reforms as government faces ongoing protests', *National Public Radio*, [online] 16 October, Available from: https://www.npr.org/2019/10/16/770560183/hong-kong-announces-housing-reforms-as-government-faces-20th-week-of-protests [Accessed 31 August 2023].

Fewsmith, J. (2019) 'Authoritarian Resilience Revisited', *Journal of Contemporary China*, 28(116): 167–79.

Fifield, A. (2019) 'China thinks 'patriotic education' built a loyal generation. But in Hong Kong? Not so fast', *The Washington Post*, [online] 29 November, Available from: https://www.washingtonpost.com/world/china-thinks-patriotic-education-built-a-loyal-generation-but-in-hong-kong-not-so-fast/2019/11/28/80f4d586-0c2c-11ea-8054-289aef6e38a3_story.html [Accessed 31 August 2023].

Finchelstein, F. (2022) 'The Authoritarian Personality and the History of Fascism', *Polity*, 54(1): 107–23.

Fong, B.C.H. (2017) 'One Country, Two Nationalisms: Center-Periphery Relations between Mainland China and Hong Kong, 1997–2016', *Modern China*, 43(5): 523–56.

Foucault, M. [R. Hurley (trans)] (1978) *The History of Sexuality Volume 1: An Introduction*, New York: Patheon Books.

Foucault, M. (1979) 'On governmentality', *Ideology and Consciousness*, 6, 5–21.

Foucault, M. (1982) 'The Subject and the Power', in H. Dreyfus and P. Rabinow (eds) *Michel Foucault: Beyond Structuralism and Hermeneutics*, Brighton: Harvester, pp 208–26.

Foucault, M. (1988) 'The Political Technology of Individuals', in L.H. Martin, H. Gutman and P.H. Hutton (eds) *Technologies of the Self: A Seminar with Michel Foucault*, Amherst: University of Massachusetts Press, pp 145–62.

Foucault, M. [R. Braidotti, (trans), C. Gordon, (revised)] (1991) 'Governmentality', in G. Burchell, C. Gordon and P. Miller (eds), *The Foucault Effect: Studies in Governmentality*, Chicago: University of Chicago Press, pp 87–104.

Foucault, M. [A. Sheridan (trans)] (1995) *Discipline and Punish: The Birth of the Prison*, New York: Vintage.

Foucault, M. (1997) '14, January 1976', in M. Bertani and A. Fontana (eds) [D. Macey (trans)] *"Society Must Be Defended" Lectures at the Collège de France, 1975–76*, London: Penguin, pp 23–42.

Foucault, M. (2008a) '23 February, 1983', in F. Ewald and A. Fontana (eds) [G. Burchell (trans)] *The Government of Self and Others: Lectures at the Collège de France, 1982–1983*, New York: Palgrave Macmillan, pp 285–97.

Foucault, M. (2008b) '5 January, 1983', in F. Ewald and A. Fontana (eds) [G. Burchell (trans)] *The Government of Self and Others: Lectures at the Collège de France, 1982–1983*, New York: Palgrave Macmillan, pp 25–40.

Foucault, M. (2008c) '23 February, 1983', in F. Ewald and A. Fontana (eds) G. Burchell (trans) *The Government of Self and Others: Lectures at the Collège de France, 1982–1983*, New York: Palgrave Macmillan, pp 285–97.

Foucault, M. (2009a) '15 February 1978', in F. Ewald and A. Fontana (eds) [G. Burchell (trans)] *Security, Territory, Population: Lectures at the Collège de France, 1977–1978*, New York: Palgrave Macmillan, pp 186–220.

Foucault, M. (2009b) '25 January 1978', in F. Ewald and A. Fontana (eds) [G. Burchell (trans)] *Security, Territory, Population: Lectures at the Collège de France, 1977–1978*, New York: Palgrave Macmillan, pp 83–110.

Foucault, M. (2009c) '8 February 1978', in F. Ewald and A. Fontana (eds) [G. Burchell (trans)] *Security, Territory, Population: Lectures at the Collège de France, 1977–1978*, New York: Palgrave Macmillan, pp 161–75.

Foucault, M. (2011) *The Courage of Truth (The Government of Self and Other II): Lectures at the Collège de France, 1983–1984*, Basingstoke, UK: Palgrave Macmillan.

Foucault, M., Sheridan, A. and Kritzman, L.D. (1988) 'Politics and Reason', in L.D. Kritzman (ed) *Politics, Philosophy, Culture: Interviews and Other Writings 1977–1984*, London: Routledge, pp 57–85.

Fourie, E. (2015) 'China's Example for Meles' Ethiopia: When Development "Models" Land', *Journal of Modern African Studies*, 53(3): 289–316.

Frenkiel, E. (2019) 'The Evolution of Representative Claim-Making by the Chinese Communist Party: From Mao to Xi (1949–2019)', *Politics and Governance*, 7(3): 208–19.

Friedman, E. (1995) *National Identity and Democratic Prospects in Socialist China*, London: Routledge.

Friend, C. (2020) 'Social Contract Theory', *Internet Encyclopedia of Philosophy*, Available from: https://iep.utm.edu/soc-cont/#SH2a [Accessed 30 January 2024].

Fromm, E. (1941) *Escape from Freedom*, New York: Farrar & Rinehart.

Fromm, E. (1942) *The Fear of Freedom*, London: Routledge & Kegan Paul.

Fromm, E. (1956) *The Sane Society*, London: Routledge & Kegan Paul.

Fromm, E. (1957) *The Art of Loving*, London: Thorsons.

Fukuyama, F. (2012) 'China and East Asian Democracy: The Pattern of History', *Journal of Democracy*, 23(1): 14–26.

Fukuyama, F. (2014) *Political Order and Political Decay: From the Industrial Revolution to the Globalization of Democracy*, New York: Farrar, Straus and Giroux.

Fukuyama, F. (2020a) 'The Pandemic and Political Order: The World After the Pandemic', *Foreign Affairs*, 99(4): 26–32.

Fukuyama, F. (2020b) 'What Kind of Regime Does China Have?', *The American Interests*, 15(6), https://www.the-american-interest.com/2020/05/18/what-kind-of-regime-does-china-have/ [Accessed 21 January 2024].

Galway, M. (2010) 'From the Claws of the Tiger to the Jaws of the Crocodile: Pol Pot, Maoism, and Ultra-Nationalist Genocide in Cambodia, 1975–1979', *uOttawa Theses*, http://dx.doi.org/10.20381/ruor-12597

Galway, M. (2017) 'From Revolutionary Culture to Original Culture and Back: On "New Democracy" and the Kampucheanization of Marxism-Leninism, 1940–1965', *Cross-Currents*, 24, http://cross-currents.berkeley.edu/e-journal/issue-24.

Galway, M. (2022) *The Emergence of Global Maoism: China's Red Evangelism and the Cambodian Communist Movement, 1949–1979*, Ithaca: Cornell University Press.

Gan, Y. (2019) 'Unifying the Three Traditions in the New Era (selection) (2005)', in J. Fogel, T. Cheek and D. Ownby (eds) *Voices from the Chinese Century: Public Intellectual Debate from Contemporary China*, New York: Columbia University Press, pp 29–42.

Gandesha, S. (2018) 'Identifying with the Aggressor: From the "Authoritarian" to the "Neo-Liberal" Personality', *Constellations*, 25(1):147–64.

Gandesha, S. (2019) 'The "Authoritarian Personality" Reconsidered: The Phantom of "Left Fascism"', *The American Journal of Psychoanalysis*, 79(4): 601–24.

Gao, S. and Walayat, A.J. (2021) 'Confucianism and Democracy: Four Models of Compatibility', *Journal of Chinese Humanities*, 6(2-3): 213–34.

Gao, Z. (2022) 'Is China Repressing or Moulding Religion? "Religious Freedom", Post-coloniality, and the Chinese State Building', *Politics, Religion & Ideology*, 23(1): 1–22.

Gerber, A.S., Huber, G.A., Doherty, D. et al (2010) 'Personality and Political Attitudes: Relationships across Issue Domains and Political Contexts', *American Political Science Review*, 104(1): 111–33.

Gerschewski, J. (2018) 'Legitimacy in Autocracies: Oxymoron or Essential Feature?', *Perspectives on Politics*, 16(3): 652–65.

Gilley, B. (2012) 'Authoritarian Environmentalism and China's Response to Climate Change', *Environmental Politics*, 21(2): 287–307.

Glass, J. (1989) *Private Terror/Public Life: Psychosis and the Politics of Community*, Ithaca: Cornell University Press.

Glass, J. (1993) *Shattered Selves: Multiple Personalities in a Postmodern World*, Ithaca: Cornell University Press.

Glass, J. (1995) *Psychosis and Power: Threats to Democracy in the Self and the Group*, Ithaca: Cornell University Press.

Gleiss, M.S. (2016) 'From Being a Problem to Having Problems: Discourse, Governmentality and Chinese Migrant Workers', *The Journal of Chinese Political Science*, 21(1): 39–55.

Goes Aragão Santana, I. (2020) *The Source of Self-restraint? How Domestic Politics and International Markets Shape Natural Resource Policy in the Developing World?*, PhD dissertation, The University of Texas at Austin.

Goh, E. (2011) 'Institutions and the Great Power Bargain in East Asia: ASEAN's Limited "Brokerage" Role', *International Relations of the Asia-Pacific*, 11(3): 373–401.

Goldman, M. (2005) *From Comrade to Citizen: The Struggle for Political Rights in China*, Cambridge: Harvard University Press.

Goodman, B. (2021) *The Suicide of Miss Xi: Democracy and Disenchantment in the Chinese Republic*, Cambridge: Harvard University Press.

Goto-Jones, C. (2005) *Political Philosophy in Japan: Nishida, the Kyoto School and Co-Prosperity*, London: Routledge.

Goto-Jones, C. (ed) (2008) *Re-politicising the Kyoto School as Philosophy*, Oxon: Routledge.

Gotsis, G. (2022) 'Humanistic Leadership in the Confucian Context: Philosophical Foundations and Empirical Implications', in M.C. Vu, N. Singh, N. Burton and I. Chu (eds) *Faith Traditions and Practices in the Workplace. Vol. II. The Role of Spirituality in Unprecedented Times*, London: Palgrave MacMillan, pp 109–33.

Gottlieb, T. (1977) *Chinese Foreign Policy Factionalism and the Origins of the Strategic Triangle*, Santa Monica, CA: RAND.

Gover, A.R., Harper, S.B. and Langton, L. (2020) 'Anti-Asian Hate Crime During the COVID-19 Pandemic: Exploring the Reproduction of Inequality', *American Journal of Criminal Justice,* 45: 647–67.

Grande, E. (2022) 'Civil Society, Cleavage Structures, and Democracy in Germany', *German Politics*, 32(3): 420–39.

Greenfeld, L. (1992) *Nationalism: Five Roads to Modernity*, Cambridge: Harvard University Press.

Greenstein, F.I. (1968) 'Harold D. Lasswell's Concept of Democratic Character', *The Journal of Politics*, 30(3): 696–709.

Gregory, B.S. (2022) 'The End of Macro-Narratives of Progress? History, Christian Theology, and the Anthropocene', *Modern Theology* 39(4): 657–81.

Gries, P. and Yam, P.P.C. (2020) 'Ideology and International Relations', *Current Opinion in Behavioral Sciences*, 34: 135–41.

Grosfoguel, R. (2015) 'Epistemic Racism/Sexism, Westernized Universities and the Four Genocides/Epistemicides of the Long Sixteenth Century', in M. Araújo and S.R. Maeso (eds) *Eurocentrism, Racism and Knowledge: Debates on History and Power in Europe and the Americas*, New York: Palgrave MacMillan, pp 23–46.

Guardian News (2020) 'Boris Johnson invokes wartime language amid coronavirus crisis: "This enemy can be deadly"', *Guardian News*, [online] 17 March, Available from: https://youtu.be/1p3Ibx2dDVY [Accessed 31 August 2023].

Guimón, J. and Narula, R. (2020) 'Ending the COVID-19 Pandemic Requires More International Collaboration', *Research-Technology Management,* 63(5): 38–41.

Gülseven, E. (2021) 'Identity, Nationalism and the Response of Turkey to COVID-19 Pandemic', *Chinese Political Science Review*, 6(1): 40–62.

Gunnell, J. (1988) 'American Political Science, Liberalism, and the Invention of Political Theory', *American Political Science Review*, 82(1): 71–87.

Guo, X. (2019) *The Politics of the Core Leader in China: Culture, Institution, Legitimacy, and Power*, Cambridge: Cambridge University Press.

Guriev, S. and Treisman, D. (2022) *Spin Dictators*, Princeton University.

Gutmann, A. and Thompson, D.F. (2004) *Why Deliberative Democracy*, Princeton: Princeton University Press.

Habermas, J. [M. Pensky, (trans)] (2001) *The Postnational Constellation: Political Essays*, Cambridge: The MIT Press.

Habich-Sobiegalla, S. and Rousseau, J.-F. (2020) 'Responsibility to Choose: Governmentality in China's Participatory Dam Resettlement Processes', *World Development,* 135, 105090, doi.org/10.1016/j.worlddev.2020.105090

Hacking, N. and Flynn, A. (2018) 'Protesting against Neoliberal and Illiberal Governmentalities: A Comparative Analysis of Waste Governance in the UK and China', *Political Geography* 63: 31–42.

Hadded, M.A. (2010) 'The State-in-society Approach to the Study of Democratization with Examples from Japan', *Democratization*, 17(5): 997–1023.

Hadenius, A. and Teorell, J. (2007) 'Pathways from Authoritarianism', *Journal of Democracy*, 18(1): 143–56.

Hailey, J. (2008) *Ubuntu: A Literature Review*, London: Tutu Foundation.

Halabi, E.E. (2022) 'Coexistence: Citizenship and Democracy in Dialogue', *The Ecumenical Review*, 74(5): 698–706.

Hall, D. (2011) *A Reforming People: Puritanism and the Transformation of Public Life in New England*, New York: Knopf.

Hall, D.L. and Ames, R.T. (2003) 'A Pragmatist Understanding of Confucian Democracy', in D.A. Bell and H. Chaibong (eds) *Confucianism for the Modern World*, Cambridge: Cambridge University Press, pp 124–60.

Hammond, M. (2019) 'Deliberative Democracy as a Critical Theory', *Critical Review of International Social and Political Philosophy*, 22(7): 787–808.

Han, J.-w. (2013) *Power, Place, and State-Society Relations in Korea: Neo-Confucian and Geomantic Reconstruction of Developmental State and Democratization*, Lanham, MD: Lexington Press.

Han, R. (2019) 'Patriotism without State Blessing: Chinese Cyber Nationalists in a Predicament', in T. Wright (ed) *Handbook of Protest and Resistance in China*, Cheltenham: Edward Elgar, pp 346–60.

Han, X. (2021) 'Disciplinary Power Matters: Rethinking Governmentality and Policy Enactment Studies in China', *Journal of Education Policy*, 38(3): 408–31.

Hansson, R.O., Jones, W.H. and Carpenter, B.N. (1984) 'Relational Competence and Social Support', in L. Wheeler (ed) *Review of Personality & Social Psychology*, London: Sage, pp 5, 265–84.

Harding, J. (2014) 'Corruption or *Guanxi*? Differentiating Between the Legitimate, Unethical, and Corrupt Activities of Chinese Government Officials', *UCLA Pacific Basin Law Journal*, 31(2): 127–46.

Harell, A., Banting, K., Kymlicka, W. and Wallace, R. (2022) 'Shared Membership beyond National Identity: Deservingness and Solidarity in Diverse Societies', *Political Studies*, 70(4): 983–1005.

Harms, P.D. (2018) 'Autocratic Leaders and Authoritarian Followers Revisited: A Review and Agenda for the Future', *The Leadership Quarterly*, 29(1): 105–22.

Hartman, T.K., Stocks, T.V.A., McKay, R. et al (2020) 'The Authoritarian Dynamic During the COVID-19 Pandemic: Effects on Nationalism and Anti-Immigrant Sentiment', *Social Psychological and Personality Science*, 12(7): 1274–85.

Hartwell, R.M. (1982) 'Demographic, Political, and Social Transformations of China, 750–1550', *Harvard Journal of Asiatic Studies*, 42(2): 365–442.

Harvey, D. (2006) 'Neo-Liberalism as Creative Destruction', *Swedish Society for Anthropology and Geography*, 88(2):145–58.

Harvey, C., Gordon, J. and Maclean, M. (2021) 'The Ethics of Entrepreneurial Philanthropy', *Journal Business Ethics*, 171(1): 33–49.

Hauck, B. (2020) 'The Shared Time of the Mass Line: Economics, Politics and Participation in a Chinese Village', *Javnost – The Public*, 27(2): 186–99.

Haugaard, M. (2021) 'The Four Dimensions of Power: Conflict and Democracy', *Journal of Political Power*, 14(1): 153–75.

He, B. (2004) 'Confucianism Versus Liberalism over Minority Rights: A Critical Response to Will Kymlicka', *Journal of Chinese Philosophy*, 31(1): 103–23.

He, B. (2006) 'Village Elections and Three Discourses on Democracy', in C. Derichs and T. Heberer (eds) *The Power of Ideas: Intellectual Input and Political Change in East and Southeast Asia*, Copenhagen: NIAS Press, pp 150–65.

He, K. (2013) 'Xi Jinping's Operational Code Beliefs and China's Foreign Policy', *Chinese Journal of International Politics*, 6(3): 209–23.

He, B. and Warren, M.E. (2011) 'Authoritarian Deliberation: The Deliberative Turn in Chinese Political Development', *Perspectives on Politics*, 9(2): 269–89.

He, Z. and Chen, Z. (2021) 'The Social Group Distinction of Nationalists and Globalists amid COVID-19 Pandemic', *Fudan Journal of the Humanities and Social Sciences*, 14(1): 67–85.

Heinö, A.J. (2009) 'Democracy between Collectivism and Individualism: De-nationalisation and Individualisation in Swedish National Identity', *International Review of Sociology*, 19(2): 297–314.

Helman, R., Malherbe, N. and Kaminer, D. (2019) 'Young People's Reproductions of the "Father as Provider" Discourse: Intersections of Race, Class, Culture and Gender Within a Liberal Democracy', *Community, Work & Family*, 22(2): 146–66.

Helms, L. (2020) 'Leadership Succession in Politics: The Democracy/Autocracy Divide Revisited', *The British Journal of Politics and International Relations* 22(2): 328–46.

Hendriks, C.M., Ercan, S.A. and Boswell, J. (2020) *Mending Democracy: Democratic Repair in Disconnected Times*, Oxford: Oxford University Press.

Hernández, J.C. (2020) 'China spins coronavirus crisis, hailing itself as a global leader', *New York Times*, [online] 28 February, Available from: https://www.nytimes.com/2020/02/28/world/asia/china-coronavirus-response-propaganda.html [Accessed 31 August 2023].

Hesig, J. and Maraldo, J. (eds) (1995) *Rude Awakenings: Zen, the Kyoto School and the Question of Nationalism*, Honolulu: University of Hawai'i Press.

Heurlin, C. (2016) *Responsive Authoritarianism in China: Land, Protest, and Policy Making*, Cambridge: Cambridge University Press.

Hilsum, L. (2006) 'Africa's Chinese Love Affair', *Channel 4 News*, Available from: https://www.channel4.com/news/articles/politics/international_politics/africas+chinese+love+affair/171520.html [Accessed 29 February 2024]

Hobbes, T. (2019) *Leviathan*, Cambridge: Cambridge University Press.

Hodzi, O. (2018) 'China and Africa: Economic Growth and a Non-transformative Political Elite', *Journal of Contemporary African Studies*, 36(2): 191–206.

Hoffman, L. (2006) 'Autonomous Choices and Patriotic Professionalism: On Governmentality in Late-Socialist China', *Economy and Society*, 35(4): 550–70.

Hofstede, G. (2001) *Culture's Consequences: Comparing Values, Behaviors, Institutions, and Organizations across Nations*, Thousand Oaks: Sage.

Hofstede, G. and Bond, M.H. (1988) 'The Confucius Connection: From Cultural Roots to Economic Growth', *Organizational Dynamics*, 16(4): 5–21.

Holbig, H. (2013) 'Ideology after the End of Ideology. China and the Quest for Autocratic Legitimation', *Democratization*, 20(1): 61–81.

Holbig, H. (2022) 'Inside "Chinese Democracy": The Official Career of a Contested Concept under Xi Jinping', *Journal of Politics and Law*, 15(2): 21–31.

Holliday, I., Ngok, M. and Yep, R. (2008) 'A High Degree of Autonomy? Hong Kong Special Administrative Region, 1997–2002', *The Political Quarterly*, 73(4): 455–64.

Hong, C. (2022) 'Service and Reciprocity: Confucian Political Authority', *Journal of Chinese Philosophy*, 49(3): 295–307.

Hsu, C.L. (2001) 'Political Narratives and the Production of Legitimacy: The Case of Corruption in Post-Mao China', *Qualitative Sociology*, 24: 25–54.

Hsu, S.-c., Tsai, K.S. and Chang, C.-c. (eds) (2021) *Evolutionary Governance in China: State-Society Relations under Authoritarianism*, Cambridge: Harvard University Press.

Hu, F. (1998) 'Zhengi wenhua de yihan yu guancha [Concepts and Studies of Political Culture]', in *Zhengzhixue de kexue tanjiu, di er juan, zhengzhi yu wenhua* [*Scientific Inquiry of Politics, Vol. II. Politics and Culture*], Taipei: Sanmin Bookstore, pp 1–38.

Hu, S. (2013) 'The Natural Law in the Chinese Tradition', in C.-P. Chou (ed) *English Writings of Hu Shih: Chinese Philosophy and Intellectual History (Volume 2)*, Beijing: Foreign Language Teaching and Berlin: Research Publishing and Springer-Verlag, pp 217–34.

Hu, T.-W. (1927) 'The Chinese Version of the Law of Nature', *Ethics*, 38(1): 27–43.

Hu, X. (2019) 'Perpetuating Chaos in Hong Kong Strengthens Five Important Assessments of Chinese Inland Communities 香港持续动荡，强化了中国内地社会的五个重要认知', *Huanqiuwang*, [online] 10 October, Available from: https://china.huanqiu.com/article/9CaKrnKnlTH [Accessed 31 August 2023].

Hu, X. (2020) 'Huxijin: Fandui Chaonong Oumei Zaonan Guojia, Fandui Ziwopengzhang [Xijin Hu: Against the Mockery of America and European Countries That Are Suffering, against Self Aggrandisement]', *Huanqiuwang*, [online] 21 March, Available from: https://world.huanqiu.com/article/3xVoNcA0PHS [Accessed 31 August 2023].

Hu, Y. (2020) 'Serbia attracts Chinese online fans as joint fight on virus enhances ties', *The Global Times*, [online] 25 March, Available from: https://www.globaltimes.cn/content/1183654.shtml [Accessed 31 August 2023].

Huang, C.-c. (2006) *Taiwan in Transformation: 1895–2005: The Challenge of a New Democracy to an Old Civilization*, New Brunswick and London: Transaction Publishers.

Huang, C. and Shih, C.-y. (2014) *Harmonious Intervention: China's Quest for Relational Security*, Surrey: Ashgate.

Huang, G., Xue, D. and Wang, Y. (2019) 'Governmentality and Spatial Strategies: Towards Formalization of Street Vendors in Guangzhou, China', *International Journal of Urban and Regional Research*, 43(3): 442–59.

Huang, H., Intawan, C. and Nicholson, S. (2023) 'In Government We Trust: Implicit Political Trust and Regime Support in China', *Perspectives on Politics*, 21(4): 1357–75.

Huang, P.C.C. (1993) '"Public Sphere"/"Civil Society" in China? The Third Realm between State and Society', *Modern China*, 19(2): 216–40.

Huang, Q. (2021) 'The Pandemic and the Transformation of Liberal International Order', *Journal of Chinese Political Science*, 26(1): 1–26.

Huang, Y. (1994) 'Political Solidarity and Religious Plurality: A Rortian Alternative to Liberalism and Communitarianism', *Journal of Law and Religion*, 11(2): 499–534.

Huang, Y. (2023) *The Rise and Fall of the EAST: How Exams, Autocracy, Stability, and Technology Brought out China Success, and Why They Might Lead to Its Decline*, New Heaven: Yale University Press.

Hubbard, J. and Swanson, P.L. (eds) (1997) *Pruning the Bodhi Tree: The Storm Over Critical Buddhism*, Honolulu: Hawaii University Press.

Huntington, S. (1968) *Political Order in Changing Societies*, New Haven: Yale University Press.

Huntington, S. (1996) *The Clash of Civilizations and the Remaking of World Order*, New York, NY: Simon and Schuster.

Huntington, S. (2005) *Who Are We? The Challenges to America's National Identity*, New York: Simon and Schuster.

Hwang, K.-k. (2012) *Foundations of Chinese Psychology*, New York: Springer.

Hyde, S. and Saunders, E. (2020) 'Recapturing Regime Type in International Relations: Leaders, Institutions, and Agency Space', *International Organization*, 74(2): 363–95.

Ikenberry, G.J. (2001) *After Victory: Institutions, Strategic Restraint, and the Rebuilding of Order after Major Wars*, Princeton: Princeton University Press.

Illingworth, P., Pogge, T. and Wenar, L. (eds) (2011) *Giving Well: The Ethics of Philanthropy*, Oxford: Oxford University Press.

Immergut, E. (1998) 'The Theoretical Core of the New Institutionalism', *Politics & Society*, 26(1): 5–34.

Institute of Innovation Theory of Peking University (ed) (2017) *Young China Says: I Read Xi Jinping's Ideas of Governing*, Beijing: Chinese Youth Press.

Iorio, F.D. and Chen, S.-h. (2019) 'On the Connection between Agent-based Simulation and Methodological Individualism', *Social Science Information*, 58(2): 354–76.

Ivanhoe, P.J. (2009) Mencius, (trans.) *Irene Bloom*, New York: Columbia University Press.

Jackson, T. (2012) 'Postcolonialism and Organizational Knowledge in the Wake of China's Presence in Africa: Interrogating South-South Relations', *Organization*, 19(2): 181–204.

Jackson, T. (2014) 'Employment in Chinese MNEs: Appraising the Dragon's Gift to Sub-Saharan Africa', *Human Resource Management*, 53(6): 897–919.

Jackson, T. and Horwitz, F.M. (2018) 'Expatriation in Chinese MNEs in Africa: An Agenda for Research', *The International Journal of Human Resource Management*, 29(11): 1856–78.

Jacobs, A. (1991) 'Autocracy: Groups, Organizations, Nations, and Players', *Transactional Analysis Journal*, 21(4): 199–206.

Jacoby, S. and Cheng, J.C. (eds) (2020) *The Socio-spatial Design of Community and Governance: Interdisciplinary Urban Design in China*, Singapore: Springer.

Jacques, M. (2009) *When China Rules the World: The End of the Western World and the Birth of a New Global Order*, New York: The Penguin Press.

Jason, B. (2007) 'Hereditary Succession in Modern Autocracies', *World Politics*, 59(4): 595–628.

Jaworsky, B.N. and Qiaoan, R. (2020) 'The Politics of Blaming: The Narrative Battle between China and the US over COVID-19', *Journal of Chinese Political Science*, 26(2): 295–315.

Jay, M. (2022) 'The Authoritarian Personality and the Problematic Pathologization of Politics', *Polity*, 54(1): 124–45.

Jeffrey, E. (2011) *China's Governmentalities: Governing Change, Changing Government*, London: Routledge.

Jerónimo, P. (2020) 'COVID-19 Nationalism and Its Toll on Citizenship and Mobility Rights in European Union', *UNIO EU Law Journal The Official Blog*, [online] 20 April, Available from: https://officialblogofunio.com/2020/04/20/covid-19-nationalism-and-its-toll-on-citizenship-and-mobility-rights-in-the-european-union/ [Accessed 31 August 2023].

Jessen, H.M. and Eggers, N.v. (2020) 'Governmentality and Stratification: Towards a Foucauldian Theory of the State', *Theory, Culture & Society*, 37(1): 53–72.

Jian, G. (2022) 'From Empathic Leader to Empathic Leadership Practice: An Extension to Relational Theory', *Human Relations*, 75(5): 931–55.

Jiang, J. (2022) 'A Question of Human Rights or Human Left: The "People's War against COVID-19" under the "Gridded Management" System in China', *Journal of Contemporary China*, 31(136): 491–504.

Jiang, Q. and Bell, D. (2012) 'A Confucian Constitution for China', *New York Times,* 11 July, A25.

Jiang, T. (2021) *Origins of Moral-Political Philosophy in Early China: Contestation of Humaneness, Justice, and Personal Freedom*, Oxford: Oxford University Press.

Jie, S. (2020) '40 million online "overseers" watch Wuhan speed building new hospitals for coronavirus patients', *The Global Times*, [online] 30 January, Available from: https://www.globaltimes.cn/content/1177963.shtml [Accessed 31 August 2023].

Jin, Z. (2020) 'Zhongguo kangyi "chaozuoye" zhishuo de chuxian yu xiaoshi [The appearance and disappearance of "copy the homework" in China's COVID response]', *VOA News Chinese*, [online] 28 March, Available from: https://www.voacantonese.com/a/china---appearance-and-sudden-disappearance-of-copy-the-success-slogan/5349250.html [Accessed 31 August 2023].

Joffé, G. (2022) 'Authoritarian Resilience and the Absence of Democratic Transition: The Implication of 2011', *Journal of Islamic Studies*, 33(1): 72–94.

Johnson, D. (1966) *The Medieval Chinese Oligarchy*, Boulder: Westview Press.

Joseph, J. (2012) *The Social in the Global: Social Theory, Governmentality and Global Politics*, Cambridge: Cambridge University Press.

Kailitz, S. (2013) 'Classifying Political Regimes Revisited: Legitimation and Durability', *Democratization*, 20(1): 39–60.

Kallio, J. (2022) 'The Dialogue between Confucianism and its Translations', *Diogenes*, 64(1-2): 47–51.

Kalmoe, N.P. (2020) 'Uses and Abuses of Ideology in Political Psychology', *Political Psychology*, 41(4): 771–93.

Kamoche, K. and Siebers, L.Q. (2015) 'Chinese Managers' Practices in Kenya: Toward a Post-colonial Critique', *The International Journal of Resource Management*, 26(21): 2718–43.

Kang, L. (2022) 'Metamorphosis of the Dragon: The Collectivist Reconfiguration of Hong Kong-Taiwan Pop in the Reform Era', *Inter-Asia Cultural Studies*, 23(2): 288–301.

Kang, X. (2018) 'Moving Toward Neo-Totalitarianism: A Political-Sociological Analysis of the Evolution of Administrative Absorption of Society in China', *Nonprofit Policy Forum*, 9(1): 1–8.

Karl, T.L. (2019) 'Extreme Inequality and State Capture: The Crisis of Liberal Democracy in the United States', *Chinese Political Science Review*, 4(2): 164–87.

Kautz, S. (1995) *Liberalism and Community*, Ithaca: Cornell University Press.

Kearns, D. (1983) 'A Theory of Justice – And Love: Rawls on the Family', *Politics*, 18(2): 36–42.

Kendall-Taylor, A., Frantz, E. and Wright, J. (2020) 'The Digital Dictators: How Technology Strengthens Autocracy', *Foreign Affairs*, 99(2): 103–15.

Kennedy, J.F., (1963) 'Remarks of President John F. Kennedy at the Rudolph Wilde Platz, Berlin', [online] 26 June, Available from: https://www.jfklibrary.org/archives/other-resources/john-f-kennedy-speeches/berlin-w-germany-rudolph-wilde-platz-19630626 [Accessed 31 August 2023].

Kennedy, K.J. (2021) 'Asian Students' Citizenship Values: Exploring Theory by Reviewing Secondary Data Analysis', in B. Malak-Minkiewicz and J. Torney-Purta (eds) *Influence of the IEA Civic and Citizenship Education Studies: Practice, Policy, and Research across Countries and Regions*, Cham, Switzerland: Springer Nature, pp 233–45.

Kershaw, C., Rast III, D.E., Hogg, M.A. et al (2021) 'Divided Groups Need Leadership: A Study of the Effectiveness of Collective Identity, Dual Identity, and Intergroup Relational Identity Rhetoric', *Journal of Applied Social Psychology*, 51(1): 53–62.

Kevin, O'B. and Li, L. (2006) *Rightful Resistance in Rural China*, Cambridge: Cambridge University Press.

Kim, J. (2020) 'The Chinese People Step up to Enforce China's Nationalist Propaganda', *The Diplomat*, [online] 5 May, Available from: https://thediplomat.com/2020/05/the-chinese-people-step-up-to-enforce-chinas-nationalist-propaganda/ [Accessed 31 August 2023].

Kim, S. (2008) 'Transcendental Collectivism and Participatory Politics in Democratized Korea', *Critical Review of International Social and Political Philosophy*, 11(1): 57–77.

Kim, S. (2019) *Theorizing Confucian Virtue Politics: The Political Philosophy of Mencius and Xunzi*, Cambridge: Cambridge University Press.

Kimani, M. (2022) 'Kenya's ambassador to UN Martin Kimani's speech on Ukraine-Russia crisis wows the world!!', *Kenya Digital News*, [online] 22 February, Available from: https://www.youtube.com/watch?v=ZxZlaiuicYM [Accessed 31 August 2023].

King, A. (1975) 'Administrative Absorption of Politics in Hong Kong: Emphasis on the Grass Roots Level', *Asian Survey*, 15(5): 422–39.

King, B. (2020) 'Moral Concern in the Legalist State', *Dao,* 19: 391–407.

Kirkpatrick, M.D. (2022) 'The Emasculation of President José María Reyna Barrios: Manliness and Economic Crisis in Fin-de-Siècle Guatemala', *Estudios Interdisciplinarios De América Latina Y El Caribe*, 33(1): 89–113.

Kitschelt, H. (2000) 'Linkages between Citizens and Politicians in Democratic Polities', *Comparative Political Studies*, 33(6/7): 845–79.

Kloet, J.d., Lin, J. and Chow, Y.F. (2020) '"We Are Doing Better": Biopolitical Nationalism and the Covid-19 Virus in East Asia', *European Journal of Cultural Studies*, 23(4): 635–40.

Kluwer, E.S., Karremans, J.C., Riedijk, L. et al (2020) 'Autonomy in Relatedness: How Need Fulfillment Interacts in Close Relationships', *Personality and Social Psychology Bulletin*, 46(4): 603–16.

Knab, N. and Steffens, M.C. (2021) 'Emotions for Solidarity: The Relations of Moral Outrage and Sympathy with Hierarchy-challenging and Prosocial Hierarchy-maintaining Action Intentions in Support of Refugees', *Peace and Conflict: Journal of Peace Psychology*, 27(4): 568–75.

Kohler, J.C. and Mackey T.K. (2020) 'Why the COVID-19 Pandemic Should Be a Call for Action to Advance Equitable Access to Medicines', *BMC Medicine*, 18(193): 1–3.

Kornreich, Y. (2019) 'Authoritarian Responsiveness: Online Consultation with "Issue Politics" in China', *Governance*, 32(3): 547–64.

Koschut, S. (2018) 'No Sympathy for the Devil: Emotions and the Social Construction of the Democratic Peace', *Peach and Conflict*, 53(3): 320–38.

Koschut, S. (2019) 'Communitarian Emotions in IR: Constructing Emotional Worlds', in E. Van Rythoven and M. Sucharov (eds) *Methodology and Emotion in International Relations: Parsing the Passions*, London: Routledge, pp 79–96.

Kostka, G. and Zhang, C. (2018) 'Tightening the Grip: Environmental Governance under Xi Jinping', *Environmental Politics*, 27(5): 769–81.

Kramer, M.H. (1997) *John Locke and the Origins of Private Property: Philosophical Explorations of Individualism, Community, and Equality*, Cambridge: Cambridge University Press.

Kroenig, M. (2020) *The Return of Great Power Rivalry: Democracy versus Autocracy from the Ancient Word to the U.S. and China*, Oxford: Oxford University Press.

Krolikowski, A. (2018) 'Shaking up and Making up China: How the Party-state Compromises and Creates Ontological Security for Its Subjects', *Journal of International Relations and Development*, 21(4): 909–33.

Ku, A.S.-m. (2019) 'The Umbrella Movement as a Street Theater of Generational Change', *The China Journal* 82(1): 111–32.

Kubat, A. (2018) 'Morality as Legitimacy under Xi Jinping: The Political Functionality of Traditional Culture for the Chinese Communist Party', *Journal of Current Chinese Affairs*, 47(3): 47–86.

Kundnani, H. (2020) 'Coronavirus and the Future of Democracy in Europe', *Chatham House*, [online] 31 March, Available from: https://www.chathamhouse.org/expert/comment/coronavirus-and-future-democracy-europe [Accessed 31 August 2023].

Kurunmäki, J. and Marjanen, J. (2018) 'Isms, Ideologies and Setting the Agenda for Public Debate', *Journal of Political Ideologies*, 23(3): 256–82.

Kwak, J.-H. (2022) 'Confucian Role-ethics with Non-Domination: Civil Compliance in Times of Crisis', *Ethical Theory and Moral Practice,* 25: 199–213.

Laffin, M. (2020) 'The Conscience and Political Agency in Martin Luther and Hannah Arendt', *Political Theology*, 21(8): 705–22.

Lake, D. (2007) 'Escape from the State of Nature: Authority and Hierarchy in World Politics', *International Security*, 32(1): 47–79.

Lasswell, H. (1948) *Power and Personality*, New York: W.W. Norton.

Laszlo, E. (1963) *Collectivism and Political Power*, The Hague: Martinus Nijhoff.

Lauchlan, I. (2013) 'Guardians of the People's Total Happiness: The Origins and Impact of the Cult of the Cheka', *Politics, Religion & Ideology*, 14(4): 522–40.

Laurent, M. (2020) 'Filial Nationalism in Global Competition: The 2001 Reform of Mandarin Textbooks', *Pacific Affairs*, 93(3): 543–66.

Laville, J.-L. and Eynaud, P. (2019) 'Rethinking Social Enterprise through Philanthropic and Democratic Solidarities', in P. Eynaud, J. Laville, L. dos Santos et al (eds) *Theory of Social Enterprise and Pluralism: Social Movements, Solidarity Economy, and Global South*, New York: Routledge, pp 18–43.

Lee, D.S. and Schuler, P. (2019) 'Testing the "China Model" of Meritocratic Promotions: Democracies Reward Less Competent Ministers Than Autocracies?', *Comparative Political Studies*, 53(3-4): 531–66.

Lee, H. (2014) *The Stranger and the Chinese Moral Imagination*, Stanford: Stanford University.

Lee, S.-H. (2017) 'Confucianism as an Antidote for Liberal Self-Centeredness: A Dialogue between Confucianism and Liberalism', in R.T. Ames and P.D. Hershock (eds) *Confucianisms for a Changing World Cultural Order*, Honolulu: University of Hawai'i Press, pp 29–42.

Lee, T.C. (2018) 'Can Xi Jinping Be the Next Mao Zedong? Using the Big Five Model to Study Political Leadership', *Journal of Chinese Political Science*, 23(4): 473–97.

Lee, T.-m. (2020) 'Ideological Orthodoxy, State Doctrine, or Art of Governance? The "Victory of Confucianism" Revisited in Contemporary Chinese Scholarship', *Contemporary Chinese Thought*, 51(2): 79–95.

Lejeune, J. (2015) 'Ruling Parties as Communities of Practice and Collective Identity in China-Ethiopia Relations', *AFRASO Working Papers*, 1: 1–15.

Lerner, M. (2002) 'Pursuing the Justice Motive', in M. Ross and D.T. Miller (eds) *The Justice Motive in Everyday Life*, Cambridge: Cambridge University Press.

Leung, K.-H. (2019) 'The Inalienable Alien: Giorgio Agamben and the Political Ontology of Hong Kong', *Educational Philosophy and Theory*, 51(2): 175–84.

Levitsky, S. (2022) *Revolution and Dictatorship*, Princeton University Press.

Lew, S.-C., Choi, W.-Y. and Wang, H.S. (2011) 'Confucian Ethics and the Spirit of Capitalism in Korea: The Significance of Filial Piety', *Journal of East Asian Studies*, 11(2): 171–96.

Li, H. (2020) 'Mistreatment of Africans in Guangzhou Threatens China's Coronavirus Diplomacy', *The Conversation*, [online] 17 April, Available from: https://theconversation.com/mistreatment-of-africans-in-guangzhou-threatens-chinas-coronavirus-diplomacy-136348 [Accessed 31 August 2023].

Li, H.T.G. and Xiao, H. (2016) 'The Perception of Anti-corruption Efficacy in China: An Empirical Analysis', *Social Indicators Research*, 125(3): 885–903.

Li, J. (2020) 'China is being accused of mistreating coronavirus nurses for propaganda', *Quartz*, [online] 19 February, Available from: https://qz.com/1804040/chinas-coverage-of-coronavirus-nurses-provokes-backlash/ [Accessed 31 August 2023].

Li, L. (2010) 'Rights Consciousness and Rules Consciousness in Contemporary China', *The China Journal*, 64: 47–68.

Li, T. (2013) 'Ask the Masses about Cleaning the Four Tendencies', *The Life in the Party*, [online] 26 July, Available from: http://dangjian.people.com.cn/BIG5/n/2013/0726/c117092-22341144.html [Accessed 31 August 2023].

Li, X., Bo, L., Shen, D. and Soobaroyen, T. (2022) 'Bridging "Home" Political Economic Rationalities with "Host" Demands and Constraints: The Case of Regional Chinese State-owned Multinational Corporations', *British Journal of Management*, 34(2): 1042–61.

Li, Y. (2018) 'The Formation, Characteristics, and Spiritual Foundation of Buddhist Culture with Chinese Characters according to the Series of Important Remarks by President Xi Jinping', *Buddhism on Line*, [online] 6 December, Available from: http://www.fjnet.com/shishi/nr/201812/t20181206_271896.htm [Accessed 31 August 2023].

Liao, K.-s. (1990) *Antiforeignism and Modernization in China*, Hong Kong: The Chinese University of Hong Kong Press.

Limb, P. (2022) 'The Constitution, the People and the Reinvention of a Royal Autocracy', *Journal of Southern African Studies*, 48(1): 215–19.

Lifton, R.J. (1968) *Revolutionary Immortality: Mao Tse-tung and the Chinese Cultural Revolution*, New York: Vintage.

Lin, L. and Gullotta, D. (2022) 'Disarticulating Qingnian: Chinese Youth beyond "Rising Tides" and "Lying Flat"', *Made in China Journal*, 6(3): 20–30, http://hdl.handle.net/1885/275747.

Linda, C.L. and Wang, C.X. (2019) 'Collectivism and Individualism: The Differentiation of Leadership', *TechTrends*, 63(3): 353–6.

Ling, L.H.M. (2017) 'World Politics in Colour', *Millennium: Journal of International Studies*, 45(3): 473–91.

Ling, L.H.M. (2000) 'The Limits of Democratization for Women in East Asia', in R.J. Lee and C. Clark (eds) *Democracy and the Status of Women in East Asia*, Boulder: Lynne Rienner, pp 169–82.

Ling, L.H.M. (2020) 'Squaring the Circle: China's "Belt and Road Initiative" (BRI) and the Ancient Silk Roads', in A. Chong and Q.M. Pham (eds) *Critical Reflections on China's Belt & Road Initiative*, Singapore: Palgrave Macmillan, pp 24–40.

Ling, L.H.M. and Agathangelou, A.M. (2009) *Transforming World Politics: From Empire to Multiple Worlds*, New York: Routledge.

Linkhoeva, T. (2020) *Revolution Goes East*, Ithaca: Cornell University Press.

Linklater, A. (2021) *Violence and Civilization in the Western States-System*, Cambridge: Cambridge University Press.

Lipset, S.M. and Rokkan S. (1967) 'Introduction', in S.M. Lipset and S. Rokkan (eds) *Party Systems and Voter Alignments*, New York: Free Press.

Lisa, H. (2006) 'Autonomous Choices and Patriotic Professionalism: On Governmentality in Late-Socialist China', *Economy and Society*, 35(4): 550–70.

Liu, H.-h., Peng, F., Zeng, X.-h. et al (2019) 'Authoritarian Personality and Subjective Well-being in Chinese College Students: The Moderation Effect of the Organizational Culture Context', *Personality and Individual Differences*, 138(1): 79–83.

Liu, J. (2020) 'From Social Drama to Political Performance: China's Multi-front Combat with the Covid-19 Epidemic', *Critical Asian Studies*, 52(4): 473–93.

Liu, J. (2021) 'The Traditional Sources of Whole-Process People's Democracy, 全過程人民民主的傳統思想淵源', *Political Studies*, 4: 18–26.

Liu, Q. and Palmer, D.A. (2021) 'Chinese NGOs at the Interface between Governmentality and Local Society: An Actor-Oriented Perspective', *China Information*, 35(2): 158–78.

Lo, H.K.K. (2020) 'Who are Macro-Community Members: An Answer From the Viewpoint of Confucianism', *Safer Communities*, 19(3): 131–43.

Lo, S.-h. (1997) *The Politics of Democratization in Hong Kong*, London: Macmillan.

Locard, H. (2004) *Pol Pot's Little Red book, the Sayings of Angkar, Chiang Mai*, Thailand: Silkworm Books.

Loh, C. (1996) 'The Commonwealth and Hong Kong', *The Round Table*, 338: 231–7.

Lorch, J. and Bunk, B. (2017) 'Using Civil Society as an Authoritarian Legitimation Strategy: Algeria and Mozambique in Comparative Perspective', *Democratization*, 24(6): 987–1005.

Lu, S. (2019) 'How Do People in China Really Feel about Hong Kong? It's Complicated', *The Nation*, [online] 6 September, Available from: https://www.thenation.com/article/china-hong-kong-media/ [Accessed 31 August 2023].

Lueders, H. (2022) 'Electoral Responsiveness in Closed Autocracies: Evidence from Petitions in the former German Democratic Republic', *American Political Science Review*, 116(3): 827–42.

Lührmann, A. and Lindberg, S.I. (2019) 'A Third Wave of Autocratization Is Here: What Is New about It?', *Democratization*, 26(7): 1095–113.

Luo, Z. (2021) 'Discipline the Party: From Rectification Campaigns to Intra-Party Educational Activities in China', *China: An International Journal*, 19(4): 52–74.

Luttig, M.D. (2018) 'The 'Prejudiced Personality' and the Origins of Partisan Strength, Affective Polarization, and Partisan Sorting', *Political Psychology*, 39(S1): 239–56.

Lutz, D.W. (2009) 'African *Ubuntu* Philosophy and Global Management', *Journal of Business Ethics*, 84(3): 313–28.

Luyaluka, K.L. (2020) 'An African Alternative to Western Cosmological Argument: Hopeless Reliance on Ontological Argument', *Randwick International Social Science Journal*, 1(1): 33–41.

Lynch, K. and Kalaitzake, M. (2018) 'Affective and Calculative Solidarity: The Impact of Individualism and Neo-liberal Capitalism', *European Journal of Social Theory*, 23(2): 238–57.

MacIntyre, A. (1981) *After Virtue*, London: Duckworth.

Mamdani, M. (2015) 'Beyond Nuremberg: The Historical Significance of the Post-Apartheid Transition in South Africa', *Politics and Society*, 43(1): 61–88.

Mangena, F. (2020) 'Hunhu/Ubuntu in the Traditional Thought of Southern Africa', *The Internet Encyclopedia of Philosophy*, [online], Available from: https://iep.utm.edu/hunhu/ [Accessed 31 August 2023].

Manners, I. (2013) 'European Communion: Political Theory of European Union', *Journal of European Public Policy*, 20(4): 473–94.

Marcus, R.R. (2001) 'Madagascar: Legitimizing Autocracy', *Current History*, 100(646): 226–31.

Martin, J.T. (2020) 'Weak Police, Strong Democracy: Civic Ritual and Performative Peace in Contemporary Taiwan', *Current Anthropology*, 61(6): 657–85.
Massey, R. (2022) 'Reforming Masculinity: The Politics of Gender, Race, Militarism, and Security Sector Reform in the Democratic Republic of Congo', *International Feminist Journal of Politics*, 24(4): 586–607.
Matthews, J. (2020) '"Cultural Exceptionalism" in the Global Exchange of (Mis)Information around Japan's Responses to Covid-19', *Media and Communication*, 8(2): 448–51.
Mauk, M. (2020) *Citizen Support for Democratic and Autocratic Regimes*, Exon: Routledge.
Mawdsley, E., Fourie, E. and Nauta, W. (2019) *Researching South-South Development Cooperation: The Politics of Knowledge Production*, London and New York: Routledge.
Mayer, M. (2018) 'China's Historical Statecraft and the Return of History', *International Affairs*, 94(6): 1217–35.
Mazlish, B. (1976) *The Revolutionary Ascetic: Evolution of a Political Type*, New York: Basic Books.
Mazrui, A.A. (1994) 'Africa: In Search of Self-Pacification', *African Affairs*, 93(370): 39–42.
Mbembe, A. (2015) 'Decolonizing Knowledge and the Question of the Archive', Available from: https://wiser.wits.ac.za/system/files/Achille%20Mbembe%20-%20Decolonizing%20Knowledge%20and%20the%20Question%20of%20the%20Archive.pdf [Accessed 30 January 2024].
Mbiti, J.S. (1969) *African Religions and Philosophy*, Portsmouth, NH: Heimann.
McAdam, D. and Kloos, K. (2014) *Deeply Divided: Racial Politics and Social Movements in Post-War America*, Oxford: Oxford University Press.
McDermott, K. (2007) 'Stalinism "From Below"?: Social Preconditions of and Popular Responses to the Great Terror', *Totalitarian Movements and Political Religions*, 8(3-4): 609–22.
McIlvenny, P., Klausen, J.Z. and Lindegaard, L.B. (2016) *Studies of Discourse and Governmentality: New Perspectives and Methods*, Amsterdam: John Benjamins Publishing Company.
McMurtry, J. (2013) 'The Moral Decoding of 9-11: Beyond the U.S. Criminal State', *The Journal of 9/11 Studies*, 35: 1–67, http://www.journalof911studies.com/resources/2013McMurtryVol35Feb.pdf
Meijen, J. (2020) 'Exporting European Values? Political Myths of Liberal Democracy and Cultural Diversity in Creative Europe's Literary Translation', *International Journal of Cultural Policy*, 26(7): 942–58.
Meinhof, M. (2018) 'Contesting Chinese Modernity? Postcoloniality and Discourses on Modernisation at a Chinese University Campus', *Postcolonial Studies*, 21(4): 469–84.

Meinhof, M. (2020) 'Othering the Virus', *Discover Society*, [online] 21 March, Available from: https://archive.discoversociety.org/2020/03/21/othering-the-virus/ [Accessed 22 January 2024].

Merkel, W. (2014) 'Is Capitalism Compatible with Democracy?', *Zeitschrift für Vergleichende Politikwissenschaft*, 8(2): 109–12.

Metz, T. (2007a) 'The Motivation for "Toward an African Moral Theory"', *South African Journal of Philosophy*, 26(4): 331–5.

Metz, T. (2007b) 'Toward an African Moral Theory', *The Journal of Political Philosophy*, 15(3): 321–41.

Metz, T. (2012) 'An African Theory of Moral Status: A Relational Alternative to Individualism and Holism', *Ethical Theory and Moral Practice: An International Forum*, 15(3): 387–402.

Metz, T. (2022) *A Relational Moral Theory: African Ethics in and Beyond the Continent*, Oxford: Oxford University Press.

Meyskens, C.F. (2021) 'Rethinking the Political Economy of Development in Mao's China', *Positions*, 29(4): 809–34.

Miao, Y. (2021) 'Romanticising the Past: Core Socialist Values and the China Dream as Legitimisation Strategy', *Journal of Current Chinese Affairs*, 49(2): 162–84.

Migdal, J.S. (1988) *Strong Societies and Weak States: State-Society Relations and State Capabilities in the Third World*, Princeton: Princeton University Press.

Migdal, J.S. (2001) *State in Society: Studying How States and Societies Transform and Constitute One Another*, Cambridge: Cambridge University Press.

Migdal, J.S. (2021) 'The Question of Authority', *Journal of Chinese Governance*, 6(3): 333–50.

Mills, C.W (2022) *The Racial Contract*, New York: Cornell University Press.

Mistreanu, S. and Pan, J. (2022) 'Watch: The reason students in China Are crawling around in circles on campus', *The Telegraph*, [online] 21 November, Available from: https://www.telegraph.co.uk/world-news/2022/11/21/watch-reason-students-china-crawling-around-circles-campus/ [Accessed 31 August 2023].

Mizoguchi, Yuzo. (1989) *Hoho to shite no Chugoku* [China as Method], Tokyo: The University of Tokyo Press.

Mizoguchi, Yuzo. (2001) 'A Search for the Perspective on the Studies of East Asia: Centering on Chinese Studies', *Sungkyun Journal of East Asian Studies*, 1(1): 7–15.

Modongal, Shameer (2016) 'Development of Nationalism in China', *Cogent Social Sciences*, 2(1), https://doi.org/10.1080/23311886.2016.1235749

Monroe, J.C. (2020) 'Sovereignty after Slavery: Universal Liberty and the Practice of Authority in Postrevolutionary Haiti', *Current Anthropology*, 61(S22): 232–47.

Moore, B., Jr. (1966) *Social Origins of Dictatorship and Democracy: Lord and Peasant in the Making of the Modern World*, Boston: Beacon Press.

Morefield, J. (2022) 'More Things in Heaven and Earth: Liberal Imperialism and *The End of History*', *Polity*, 54(4): 781–93.

Motsamai, M. (2019) *An African Philosophy of Personhood, Morality, and Politics*, Switzerland: Palgrave Macmillan.

Mounk, Y. (2021) 'Democracy on the Defense: Turning Back the Authoritarian Tide', *Foreign Affairs*, 100(2): 163–73.

Mu, M. (2020) 'The Prevalence and Antecedents of Nationalism Conspiracy Theories During Covid-19 in China: Advances in Social Science', *Education and Humanities Research*, 466: 334–41.

Mudimbe, V.Y. (1991) *Parables and Fables: Exegesis, Textuality, and Politics in Central Africa*, Madison: University of Wisconsin Press.

Munoz-Dardé, V. (1998) 'Rawls, Justice in the Family and Justice of the Family', *The Philosophical Quarterly*, 48(192): 335–52.

Murove, M.F. (2012) 'Ubuntu', *Diogenes*, 59(3–4): 36–47.

Murove, M.F. (2020) 'African Traditional Humanism and the Ethic of Collectivism', *African Politics and Ethics*, Cham: Palgrave Macmillan.

Murray, C. (2020) 'Imperial Dialectics and Epistemic Mapping: From Decolonisation to Anti-Eurocentric IR', *European Journal of International Relations*, 26(2): 419–42.

Myers, S.L. (2021) 'An alliance of autocracies? China wants to lead a New World Order', *New York Times*, [online] 15 June, Available from: https://www.nytimes.com/2021/03/29/world/asia/china-us-russia.html [Accessed 21 November 2023].

Naito, K. (1983) [J. Vogel (trans)] *Naitō Konan and the Development of the Conception of Modernity in Chinese History*, Armonk, NY: M.E. Sharpe.

Nandy, A. (1983) *The Intimate Enemy: Loss and Recovery of Self Under Colonialism*, New Delhi: Oxford India Paperbacks.

Nathan, A. (2003) 'China's Changing of the Guard: Authoritarian Resilience', *Journal of Democracy*, 14(1): 6–17.

Naude, P. (2019) 'Decolonising Knowledge: Can *Ubuntu* Ethics Save Us from Coloniality?', *Journal of Business Ethics*, 159(1): 23–37.

Ndlovu-Gatsheni, S.J. (2018) *Epistemic Freedom in Africa: Deprovincialization and Decolonization*, Oxon, UK, and New York, USA: Routledge.

Ndlovu-Gatsheni, S.J. (2020) *Decolonization, Development and Knowledge in Africa: Turning Over a New Leaf*, Oxon, UK, and New York, USA: Routledge.

Neck, R. (2021) 'Methodological Individualism: Still a Useful Methodology for the Social Sciences?', *Atlantic Economic Journal*, 49(4): 349–61.

Needham, J. (1956) *Science and Civilization in China, Vol II: History of Scientific Thought*, New York: Columbia University Press.

Neumann, I.B. and Sending, O.J. (2010) *Governing the Global Polity: Practice, Mentality, Rationality*, New York: The University of Michigan Press.

Neundorf, A., Gerschewski, J. and Olar, R.-B. (2020) 'How Do Inclusionary and Exclusionary Autocracies Affect Ordinary People?', *Comparative Political Studies*, 53(12): 1890–925.

Neustadt, R. (1980) *Presidential Power: The Politics of Leadership from FDR to Carter*, New York: John Wiley & Sons Inc (first edition).

Neustadt, R. (1991) *Presidential Power and the Modern Presidents: The Politics of Leadership from Roosevelt to Ronald Reagan*, New York: The Free Press.

Newman, E. and Zhang, C. (2021) 'The Mass Line Approach to Countering Violent Extremism in China: The Road from Propaganda to Hearts and Minds', *Asian Security*, 17(2): 262–78.

Nicolaisen, J. (2020) 'Protecting Life in Taiwan: Can the Rights of Nature Protect All Sentient Beings?', *Interdisciplinary Studies in Literature and Environment*, 27(3): 613–32.

Nilsson, A. and Jost, J.T. (2020) 'The Authoritarian-Conservatism Nexus', *Current Opinion in Behavioral Sciences*, 34: 148–54.

Nkrumah, K. (1971) *Africa Must Unite*, London: Heinemann.

Nordin, A. (2016) 'Future Beyond "the West"? Autoimmunity in China's Harmonious World', *Review of International Studies*, 42(1): 156–77.

Nordin, A.H.M. and Smith, G.M. (2019) 'Relating Self and Other in Chinese and Western Thought', *Cambridge Review of International Affairs*, 32(5): 636–53.

Nyberg, D. (2021) 'Corporations, Politics, and Democracy: Corporate Political Activities as Political Corruption', *Organization Theory,* 2(1): 1–24.

O'Brien, K. and Li, L. (2006) *Rightful Resistance in Rural China*, Cambridge: Cambridge University Press.

O'Dwyer, S. (2019) *Confucianism's Prospects: A Reassessment*, Albany: State University of New York Press.

O'Flynn, I. (2007) 'Divided Societies and Deliberative Democracy', *British Journal of Political Science*, 37(4): 731–51.

Obama, B. (2012) 'Transcript of President Obama's election night speech', [online] 7 November, Available from: http://www.nytimes.com/2012/11/07/us/politics/transcript-of-president-obamas-election-night-speech.html?pagewanted=all&_r=0 [Accessed 31 August 2023].

Office of Literature Research (2013) *Selected Narratives on Achieving the Chinese Dream of Great Rejuvenation of the Chinese Nation*, Beijing: Central Literature Press.

Oguejiofor, J.O. (2009) '"Negritude" as Hermeneutics: A Reinterpretation of Léopold Sédar Senghor's Philosophy', *American Catholic Philosophical Quarterly*, 83(1): 79–94.

Oleinikova, O. (2019) 'Democratic Transition Research: From Western to Post-Soviet East European Scholarship', *East/West: Journal of Ukrainian Studies*, 6(1): 147–67.

Ollerenshaw, T. and Johnston, C.D. (2022) 'The Conditional Relationship of Psychological Needs to Ideology: A Large-Scale Republication', *Public Opinion Quarterly*, 86(2): 369–80.

Olson, M. (1991) 'Autocracy, Democracy, and Prosperity', in R.J. Zeckhauser (ed) *Strategy and Choice*, Cambridge: MIT Press, pp 131–57.

Ong, L.H. (2022) *Outsourcing Repression: Everyday State Power in Contemporary China*, Oxford: Oxford University Press.

Onwuegbuchulam, S.P.C. (2022) 'State-Civil Society Relations in Nigeria: A State-in-Society Approach Interrogation', in O. Tella (ed) *A Sleeping Giant: Nigeria's Domestic and International Politics in the Twenty-First Century*, Singapore: Springer, pp 31–44.

Ortmann, S. (2015) 'The Umbrella Movement and Hong Kong's Protracted Democratization Process', *Asian Affairs*, 46(1): 32–50.

Osborne, D., Satherley, N. and Sibley, C.G. (2021) 'Personality and Ideology: A Meta-analysis of the Reliable, but Non-Causal, Association Between Openness and Conservatism', in A. Mintz and L.G. Terris (eds) *Oxford Handbook on Behavioral Political Science*, Oxford: Oxford University Press, pp 1–43.

Overing, J. (1993) 'The Anarchy and Collectivism of the "Primitive Other": Marx and Sahlins in the Amazon', in C.M. Hann (ed) *Socialism: Ideals, Ideologies, and Local Practice*, London: Routledge, pp 20–37.

Owen, C. (2020) 'Participatory Authoritarianism: From Bureaucratic Transformation to Civic Participation in Russia and China', *Review of International Studies*, 46(4): 415–34.

Owen, J. (2005) 'The Tolerant Leviathan: Hobbes and the Paradox of Liberalism', *Polity*, 37(1): 130–48.

Pai, H.-H. (2020) 'The coronavirus crisis has exposed China's long history of racism', *The Guardian*, [online] 25 April, Available from: https://www.theguardian.com/commentisfree/2020/apr/25/coronavirus-exposed-china-history-racism-africans-guangzhou. [Accessed 21 January 2024].

Palmer, A.W. (2018) 'The case of Hong Kong's missing booksellers', *New York Times*, [online] 3 April, Available from: https://www.nytimes.com/2018/04/03/magazine/the-case-of-hong-kongs-missing-booksellers.html [Accessed 31 August 2023].

Palmer, D.A. and Winiger, F. (2019) 'Neo-socialist Governmentality: Managing Freedom in the People's Republic of China', *Economy and Society*, 48(4): 554–78.

Pan, C. (2012) *Knowledge, Desire and Power in Global Politics: Western Representations of China's Rise*, UK: Edward Elgar Publishing.

Pan, D. (2017) 'Cosmopolitanism, Tianxia, and Walter Benjamin's "The Task of the Translator"', *Telos*, 180: 26–46.

Pane, E.E. (2019) 'A Comparative Study: Original Sin on the View Between Augustine and Neo-Platonism', *Abstract Proceedings International Scholars Conference*, 7(1): 2065–83.

Pang, L. (2022) 'China's Post-Socialist Governmentality and the Garlic Chives Meme: Economic Sovereignty and Biopolitical Subjects', *Theory, Culture & Society*, 39(1): 81–100.

Park, C.-M. and Shin, D.C. (2006) 'Do Asian Values Deter Popular Support for Democracy in South Korea?', *Asian Survey*, 46(3): 341–61.

Parry, K., Cohen, M., Bhattacharya, S. et al (2019) 'Charismatic Leadership: Beyond Love and Hate and Toward a Sense of Belonging', *Journal of Management & Organization*, 25(3): 398–413.

Partaken, J. (2017) 'Listening to Students about the Umbrella Movement of Hong Kong', *Educational Philosophy and Theory*, 51(2): 212–22.

Pei, M. (1991) 'A Discussion on Authoritarianism with Samuel Huntington, the Pioneer of the Theory of Authoritarianism', *Chinese Sociology and Anthropology*, 23(4): 67–75.

Peng, F. (2020) '"Xinguan Feiyan" Yiqing Fangkong Beijing Xia De Zhonghua Minzurentong Yu Minzuzhuyi De Yingdui [Identity to the Chinese Nation and Response to Nationalism within the Context of the Prevention and Control of Covid-19]', *Minzu Xuekan [Journal of Ethnology]*, 11(1): 1–7, 119–20.

People's Court News and Media Headquarters (2020) 'Zhongyang zhengfawei yinfa tongzhi yaoqiu: fajue zhan"yi" dianxing jifa shehui zhengnengliang [Central Political and Legal Affairs Commission issued notice to explore typical examples of fighting the novel coronavirus and stimulate positive energy in society]', [online] 18 February, Available from: http://www.court.gov.cn/zixun-xiangqing-220051.html [Accessed 31 August 2023].

People's Daily (2020) 'Suowei "Feizhouren Zai Guangzhou Zaoshou Qishi" Yu Shishi Yanzhong Bufu [So-called "Africans face discrimination in Guangzhou" is seriously untrue]', *People's Daily (Johannesburg)*, [online] 16 April, Available from: http://world.people.com.cn/n1/2020/0416/c1002-31676666.html [Accessed 31 August 2023].

Perry, E. (1994) 'Trends in the Study of Chinese Politics: State-Society Relations', *China Quarterly*, 139: 704–13.

Perry, E. (2011) *Mao's Invisible Hand: The Political Foundations of Adaptive Governance in China*, Cambridge: Harvard University Press.

Perry, E. (2021) 'Epilogue', in S.-c. Hsu, K.S. Tsai, C.-c. Chang (eds) *Evolutionary Governance in China: State-Society Relations Under Authoritarianism*, Cambridge: Harvard University Press, pp 387–96.

Perry, E.J. (2008) 'Chinese Conceptions of "Rights": From Mencius to Mao – and Now', *Perspectives on Politics*, 6(1): 37–50.

Perry, E.J. (2009) 'A New Rights Consciousness?', *Journal of Democracy*, 20(3): 17–20.

Perry, S.L., Whitehead, A.L. and Grubbs, J.B. (2020) 'Culture Wars and COVID-19 Conduct: Christian Nationalism, Religiosity, and Americans' Behavior During the Coronavirus Pandemic', *Journal for the Scientific Study of Religion*, 59(3): 405–16.

Peys, C. (2021) 'On the Global Politics of "Decency" and "Restraint"', *Journal of International Political Theory*, 17(3): 553–65.

Peys, C. and Steele, B.J. (2021) 'Restraint in International Politics: A Conversation between Brent Steele and Christopher Peys', *Contemporary Voices: St Andrews Journal of International Relations*, 2(1): 1–21.

Pieterse, J.N. and Parekh, B. (1995) *The Decolonization of the Imagination: Culture, Knowledge and Power*, London: Zed Books.

Pillsbury, M. (2016) *The Hundred-Year Marathon: China's Secret Strategy to Replace America as the Global Superpower*, New York: St. Martin's Griffin.

Pils, E. (2018) *Human Rights in China: A Social Practice in the Shadows of Authoritarianism*, Cambridge, UK: Polity.

Pina e Cunha, M., Rego, A. and Clegg S. (2011) 'Pol Pot, alias Brother Number One: Leaders as Instruments of History', *Management & Organizational History*, 6(3): 268–86.

Posen, A.S. (2020) 'Containing the Economic Nationalist Virus through Global Coordination', in R. Baldwin and B.W. di Mauro (eds) *Mitigating the COVID Economic Crisis: Act Fast and Do Whatever It Takes*, London: Centre for Economic Policy Research, pp 203–12.

Pow, C.P. (2018) 'Building a Harmonious Society through Greening: Ecological Civilization and Aesthetic Governmentality in China', *Annals of the American Association of Geographers*, 108(3): 864–83.

Przeworski, A. and Sprague, J. (1986) *Paper Stones: A History of Electoral Socialism*, Chicago: The University of Chicago Press.

Putnam, R.D. (1993) *Making Democracy Work: Civic Traditions in Modern Italy*, Princeton: Princeton University Press.

Pye, L. (1968) *The Spirit of Chinese Politics: A Psychocultural Study of the Authority Crisis in Political Development*, Cambridge: MIT Press.

Pye, L. (1981) *The Dynamics of Chinese Politics*, Cambridge, MA: Oelgeschlager, Gunn & Hain.

Pye, L. (1985) *Asian Power and Politics: The Cultural Dimensions of Authority*, Cambridge: Harvard University.

Pye, L. (1988) *The Mandarin and the Cadre: China's Political Culture*, Ann Arbor: Center for Chinese Studies, University of Michigan.

Qiaoan, R. and Teets, J.C. (2020) 'Responsive Authoritarianism in China: A Review of Responsiveness in Xi and Hu Administrations', *Journal of Chinese Political Science*, 25(1): 139–53.

Qin, J. (2022) 'Challenges Faced by Individualism under Confucian Role Ethics', *Frontiers in Business, Economics and Management*, 4(2): 79–80.

Qin, Y. (2018) *A Relational Theory of World Politics*, Cambridge: Cambridge University Press.

Rao, G. and Wang, Z. (2008) 'Hong Kong's 'One Country, Two Systems Experience under the Basic Law: Two Perspectives from Chinese Legal Scholars', *The Journal of Contemporary China*, 16(52): 341–58.

Rathbun, B. (2020) 'Towards a Dual Process Model of Foreign Policy Ideology', *Current Opinion in Behavioral Sciences*, 34: 211–16.

Redman, E. (1973) *The Dance of Legislation: Accounts of the Workings of the United States Senate*, New York: Simon & Schuster.

Reigadas, C. (2022) 'Multiple Ways to Democracy in Contemporary China', *International Critical Thought*, 12(2): 225–36.

Richburg, K.B. (2020) 'Covid-19 will permanently alter China's relations with the world', *Australian Strategic Policy Institute (ASPI)*, [online] 24 April, Available from: https://www.aspistrategist.org.au/covid-19-will-permanently-alter-chinas-relations-with-the-world/ [Accessed 31 August 2023].

Richey, J.L. (2013) *Confucius in East Asia: Confucianism's History in China, Korea, Japan and Vietnam*, Ann Arbor, MI: Association of Asian Studies.

Riedl, R.B., Slater, D., Wong, J. and Ziblatt, D. (2020) 'Authoritarian-Led Democratization', *Annual Review of Political Science*, 23(3): 315–32.

Roach, S.C. (2019) *Decency and Difference: Humanity and the Global Challenge of Identity Politics*, Ann Arbor: University of Michigan Press.

Roberts, M.E. (2018) *Censored: Distraction and Diversion Inside China's Great Firewall*, Princeton University Press.

Rocha, Z.L. (2014) '"Stretching out the Categories": Chinese/European Narratives of Mixedness, Belonging, and Home in Singapore', *Ethnicities*, 14(2): 279–302.

Rolf, J.N. (2014) 'The State of Nature Analogy in International Relations Theory', *International Relations*, 28(2): 150–82.

Rorty, R. (1989) *Contingency, Irony, Solidarity*, Cambridge: Cambridge University Press.

Rorty, R. (1997) 'Justice as a Larger Loyalty', *Ethical Perspectives*, 4(2): 139–49.

Rosta, M. and Tóth, L. (2021) 'Is There a Demand for Autocracies in Europe? Comparing the Attitudes of Hungarian and Italian University Students toward Liberal Democratic Values Inspired by János Kornai', *Public Choice*, 187: 217–33.

Rothchild, D. and Chazan, N. (ed) (1988) *The Precarious Balance: State and Society in Africa*, Boulder: Westview.

Rowen, H.S. (2007) 'When Will the Chinese People Be Free?', *Journal of Democracy*, 18(3): 38–52.

Sabelo, J.N.-G. (2018) *Epistemic Freedom in Africa: Deprovincialization and Decolonization*, New York: Routledge.

Sabelo, J.N.-G. (2023) 'Memory, Knowledge and Freedom: From Dismemberment and Re-Membering', in M. Nkondo (ed) *Social Memory as a Force for Social and Economic Transformation*, London: Routledge, Chapter 7.

Sabelo, J. N.-G. (2022) *Decolonization, Development and Knowledge in Africa: Turning Over a New Leaf*, New York: Routledge.

Salter, R. (2000) 'Time, Authority, and Ethics in the Khmer Rouge: Elements of the Millennial Vision in the Year Zero', in C. Wessinger (ed) *Millennialism, Persecution, and Violence*, Syracuse: Syracuse University Press, pp 281–98.

Salvatore, A. (2013) 'Islam and the Quest for a European Secular Identity: From Sovereignty through Solidarity to Immunity', *Politics, Religion & Ideology*, 14(2): 253–64.

Sandel, M.J. (1998) *Democracy's Discontent: America in Search of a Public Philosophy*, Cambridge: Harvard University Press.

Sanders, P. (2019) 'Leadership and Populism: A Parallel Reading of Hannah Arendt and Franz Neumann', *Leadership*, 15(6): 750–67.

Sangiovanni, A. (2013) 'Solidarity in the European Union', *Oxford Journal of Legal Studies*, 33(2): 213–41.

Schaff, P. (2022) *History of Christian Church, Volume 2*, Frankfurt am Main: Salzwasser Verlag.

Schell, O. and Shirk, S.L. (co-chairs) (2019) 'Course Correction: Toward an Effective and Sustainable China Policy', *Task Force Report*, [online] February, Available from: https://asiasociety.org/sites/default/files/inline-files/CoursEcorrection_FINAL_2.7.19_1.pdf [Accessed 31 August 2023].

Schertzer, R. and Woods, E.T. (2020) 'How Nationalism Can be a Force for Good in the Struggle against Covid-19', *USAPP-American Politics and Policy Blog*, [online] 9 April, Available from: https://bit.ly/2XsOtPj [Accessed 31 August 2023].

Schlesinger, A. (1998) *The Disuniting of America: Reflections on a Multicultural Society*, New York: W.W. Norton & Company.

Schlesinger, A.M. (1986) *The Cycle of American History*, Boston: Houghton Mifflin Company.

Schmitt, C. [G.D. Schwab (trans)] (1996) *The Concept of the Political*, Chicago: University of Chicago Press.

Schneider, F. (2022) 'Political Communication in Xi's China: Mao and the Cultural Revolution as Analogies for PRC Current Affairs', in C.-y. Shih, S. Singh and R. Marwah (eds) *Studies of China and Chineseness Since Cultural Revolution: Reinterpreting Ideologies and Ideological Reinterpretations*, Singapore: World Scientific, pp 91–114.

Schoenhals, M. (1993) *The Paradox of Power in a People's Republic of China Middle School*, Armonk: M.E. Shape.

Schramm, K. (2020) 'Diasporic Citizenship under Debate: Law, Body, and Soul', *Current Anthropology*, 61(S22): s210–19.

Scudder, M.F. (2023) 'Deliberative Democracy, More than Deliberation', *Political Studies*, 71(1): 252 (238–55).

Shaki, D. and Ascione, G. (2016) 'Rethinking the Absence of Post-Western International Relations in India: "Advaitic Monism" as an Alternative Epistemological Resource', *European Journal of International Relations*, 22(2): 313–34.

Shan, W. (2019) *Out of the Gobi: My Story of China and America*, New York: Wiley.

Share News Japan (2020) '【伊】麻生大臣「『"何の関係もない。あれは黄色人種の病気で俺達の病気じゃない"と誰が言ったんだ。お前じゃないか』と言ったのが第一回の会議」', [online] 24 March, Available from: https://snjpn.net/archives/187001 [Accessed 31 August 2023].

Sharon, A. (2019) 'Populism and Democracy: The Challenge for Deliberative Democracy', *European Journal of Philosophy*, 27(2): 359–76.

Sheets, P., Domke, D.S., Wells, C. et al (2011) 'America, America: National Identity, Presidential Debates, and National Mood', *Mass Communication and Society*, 14(6): 765–86.

Shen, L.C. (2017) 'Between Localism and Cosmopolitanism: A Look at Zhou Zuoren's Early Construction of the Individual', *Telos*, 180: 121–46.

Shi, T. (1997) *Political Participation in Beijing*, Cambridge: Harvard University Press.

Shih, C.-y. (1995) *State and Society in China's Political Economy: Dynamics of Socialist Reform*, Boulder: Lynne Rienner.

Shih, C.-y. (1999) *Collective Democracy: Political and Legal Reform in China*, Hong Kong: University Press of Hong Kong.

Shih, C.-y. (2007) *Democracy Made in Taiwan: The "Success" State as a Political Theory*, Lanham, MD: Lexington.

Shih, C.-y. (2011) 'The West That is Not in the West: Identifying the Self in Oriental Modernity', *Cambridge Review of International Affairs*, 23(4): 537–60.

Shih, C.-y. (2012) *Self, Nation, and Modernity in East Asia*, London: Routledge.

Shih, C.-y. (2017) 'From Nothingness to Great Sympathy: Chinese Non-interventionism from Buddhist Perspectives', *QUEST: Studies on Religion and Culture in Asia*, 2, https://www.theology.cuhk.edu.hk/quest/index.php/quest/article/view/46.

Shih, C.-y. (2019) 'Post-Chinese Reconnections through Religion: Buddhism, Christianity, and Confucianism', in G. Shani and T. Kibe (eds) *Religion and Nationalism in Asia*, London: Routledge, pp 168–85.

Shih, C.-y. (2020) 'Re-Worlding China: Notorious Tianxia, Critical Relationality', *E-International Relations*, [online] 2 September, Available from: https://www.e-ir.info/2020/09/02/re-worlding-china-notorious-tianxia-critical-relationality/ [Accessed 31 August 2023].

Shih, C.-y. (2022) *Eros of International Relations: Self-feminization and the Claiming of Postcolonial Chineseness*, Hong Kong: University of Hong Kong Press.

Shih, C.-y. and Yu, P.-t. (2015) *Post-Western International Relations Reconsider: The Pre-modern Thought of Gongsun Long*, London: Palgrave.

Shih, C.-y. and Huang, C.-c. (2020) 'Competing for a Better Role Relation: International Relations, Sino-US Rivalry and Game of Weiqi', *Journal of Chinese Political Science*, 25(1): 1–19.

Shih, C.-y., Huang, C.-c., Yeophantong, P. et al (2019) *China and International Theory: The Balance of Relationships*, Oxon: Routledge.

Shilliam, R. (2021) *Decolonizing Politics: An Introduction*, Cambridge: Polity Press.

Shimizu, K. (2015) 'Materialising the "Non-Western": Two Stories of Japanese Philosophers on Culture and Politics in the inter-war Period', *Cambridge Review of International Affairs*, 28(1): 3–20.

Shimizu, K. (2021) 'Buddhism and the Question of Relationality in International Relations', *Uluslararasi Iliskiler*, 18(70): 29–44.

Shimizu, K. (2022) *The Kyoto School and International Relations: Non-Western Attempts for a New World Order*, London: Routledge.

Shimizu, K. and Noro, S. (2023) 'An East Asian Approach to Temporality, Subjectivity and Ethics: Bring Mahāyāna Buddhist Ontological Ethics of *Nikon* into International Relations', *Cambridge Review of International Affairs*, 36(3): 372–90.

Shin, D.C. (2011) *Confucianism and Democratization in East Asia*, Cambridge: Cambridge University Press.

Shirk, S.L. (2018) 'China in Xi's 'New Era': The Return to Personalistic Rule', *Journal of Democracy*, 29(2): 22–36.

Shue, V. (1988) *The Reach of the State: Sketches of the Chinese Body Politic*, Stanford: Stanford University Press.

Sigley, G. (2006) 'Chinese Governmentalities: Government, Governance and the Socialist Market Economy', *Economy and Society*, 35(4): 487–508.

Simon, S. (2020) 'Subtle Connections: Pandemic and the Authoritarian Impulse', *Survival*, 62(3): 103–11.

Singh, S. (2022) 'Cultural Revolution and the Making of Xi Jinping', In C.-y. Shih, M. Tanigaki and T. Clemente (eds) *Studies of China and Chineseness Since the Cultural Revolution Micro Intellectual History through Den-central Lenses*, Singapore: World Scientific, pp 155–82.

Skaaning, S.-E. (2020) 'Waves of Autocratization and Democratization: A Critical Note on Conceptualization and Measurement', *Democratization*, 27(8): 1533–42.

Skinner, G.W. (1964–5) 'Marketing and Social Structure in Rural China', *The Journal of Asian Studies*, 24(1–3): 3–43.

Skinner, G.W. (1985) 'Presidential Address: The Structure of Chinese History', *Journal of Asian Studies'*, 44(2): 271–92.

Skocpol, T. (1979) *States and Social Revolutions: A Comparative Analysis of France, Russia, and China, Canto Classics*, Cambridge, England: Cambridge University Press.

Smart, A. and Smart, J. (2017) 'Formalization as Confinement in Colonial Hong Kong', *International Sociology*, 32(4): 437–53.

Smidt, C., den Dulk, K. and Froehle, B. (2010) *The Disappearing God Gap? Religion in the 2008 Presidential Election*, Oxford: Oxford University Press.

Smith, A. (1759) *The Theory of Moral Sentiments*, https://en.wikisource.org/wiki/The_Theory_of_Moral_Sentiments

Smith, K. (2012) 'Contrived Boundaries, Kinship and *Ubuntu*: A (South) African View of "The International"', in A.B. Tickner and D.L. Blaney (eds) *Thinking International Relations Differently*, New York: Routledge.

Smith, K. (2017) 'Reshaping International Relations: Theoretical Innovations from Africa', *All Azimuth*, 7(2): 81–92.

Smith, C.W. and Mayorga-Gallo, S. (2017) 'The New Principle-Policy Gap: How Diversity Ideology Subverts Diversity Initiatives', *Sociological Perspectives*, 60(5): 889–911.

Solinger, D. (ed) (1984) *Three Visions of Chinese Socialism*, New York: Routledge.

Solinger, D. (1999) *Contesting Citizenship in Urban China: Peasant Migrants, the State, and the Logic of Market*, Berkeley: University of California Press.

Solinger, D. (2009) *States' Gains, Labor's Losses: China, France, and Mexico Choose Global Liaisons, 1980–2000*, Ithaca: Cornell University Press.

Solomon, R. (1971) *Mao's Revolution and the Chinese Political Culture*, Berkeley: University of California Press.

Somin, I. (2010) 'Deliberative Democracy and Political Ignorance', *Critical Review*, 22(2–3): 253–79.

Sonny, L. (2015) *Hong Kong's Indigenous Democracy. The Theories, Concepts and Practices of Democracy*, London: Palgrave Macmillan.

Spragens, T.A. (1999) *Civic Liberalism: Reflections on Our Democratic Ideals*, Oxford: Rowman & Littlefield.

Staff Writer, Central News Agency (2020) 'Protest to decry Chinese student rules', *Taipei Times*, [online] 7 August, Available from: https://www.taipeitimes.com/News/front/archives/2020/08/07/2003741257 [Accessed 31 August 2023].

Stavridis, J. (2018) 'Democracy isn't perfect, but it will still prevail', *Time*, 23 July: 32–9, Available from: https://time.com/5336615/democracy-will-prevail/ [Accessed 21 January 2024].

Steele, B.J. (2019) *Restraint in International Politics*, Cambridge: Cambridge University Press.

Steffensen, K.N. (2017) 'The Political Thought of the Kyoto School: Beyond "Questionable Footnotes" and "Japanese-style Fascism"', in M. Yusa (ed) *Contemporary Japanese Philosophy*, London: Bloomsbury, pp 65–104.

Steinberg, M.P. (2022) *The Afterlife of Moses: Exile, Democracy, Renewal*, Stanford: Stanford University Press.

Stone, J. (1999a) *Original Enlightenment and the Transformation of Medieval Japanese Buddhism*, National City, CA: The Kuroda Institute.

Stone, J. (1999b) 'Some Reflections on Critical Buddhism', *Japanese Journal of Religious Studies*, 26(1–2) (Spring):159–88.

Su, R. and Shen, W. (2021) 'Is Nationalism Rising in Times of the COVID-19 Pandemic? Individual-level Evidence from the United States', *Journal of Chinese Political Science*, 26(1): 169–87.

Su, Y. (2020) 'Coronavirus in Wuhan: Residents shout 'stay strong' from windows', *The Conversation*, [online] 31 January, Available from: https://theconversation.com/coronavirus-in-wuhan-residents-shout-stay-strong-from-windows-130851 [Accessed 31 August 2023].

Sun, J. and Sun, K. (2023) 'The Way of Nature from the Perspective of Laozi, Confucius, and Sunzi', *Philosophies*, 8(2): 18.

Sun, T. and Zhao, Q. (2021) 'Delegated Censorship: The Dynamic, Layered, and Multistage Information Control Regime in China', *Politics and Society*, 50(2): 191–221.

Svetelj, T. (2018) '"Weak Thought" in the Face of Religious Violence: Perplexing Dimensions of Modernity and Globalization', *Philosophy and Theology*, 30(1): 235–54.

Talmon, J.L. (1952) *The Rise of Totalitarian Democracy*, Boston: Beacon Press.

Tamir, Y. (1993) *Liberal Nationalism*, Princeton: Princeton University Press.

Tan, S.-H. (2009) 'A Confucian Response to Rorty's Postmodern Bourgeois Liberal Idea of Community', in Y. Huang (ed) *Rorty, Pragmatism, and Confucianism: With Responses by Richard Rorty*, Albany: State University of New York Press.

Tarkhan, Q. (2020) 'The Cosmological Grounds of Lifestyle and Its Implications for Political Life', *Journal of Islamic Political Studies*, 2(3): 117–42.

Taylor, C. (1992) *Multiculturalism and the Politics of Recognition*, Princeton: Princeton University Press.

Taylor, C. (1999) 'Conditions of an Unforced Consensus on Human Rights', in J.R. Bauer and D. Bell (eds) *The East Asian Challenge for Human Rights*, New York: Cambridge University Press.

Taylor, C. (2007) *A Secular Age*, Cambridge: Harvard University Press.

Tava, F. (2023) 'Justice, Emotions, and Solidarity', *Critical Review of International Social and Political Philosophy*, 26(1): 39–55.

Tetlock, P.E. (1983) 'Cognitive Style and Political Ideology', *Journal of Personality and Social Psychology*, 45(1): 118–26.

Thakur, V. (2015) 'Africa and the Theoretical Peace in IR', *International Political Sociology*, 9(3): 213–29.

Thomas, N. (2018) *Democracy Denied: Identity, Civil Society and Illiberal Democracy in Hong Kong*, Oxon: Routledge.

Thompson, S. (2019) 'Hate Speech and Self-Restraint', *Ethic Theory Moral Practice*, 22(3): 657–71.

Thornton, P.M. (2023) 'The A4 Movement: Mapping Its Background and Impact', *China Leadership Monitor*, 75, [online] 1 March, Available from: https://www.prcleader.org/thornton-spring-2023 [Accessed 31 August 2023].

Tian, I.L. (2020) 'Vampiric Affect: The Afterlife of a Metaphor in a Global Pandemic', *Social Text Online*, [online] 17 June, Available from: https://socialtextjournal.org/periscope_article/vampiric-affect-the-afterlife-of-a-metaphor-in-a-global-pandemic/ [Accessed 31 August 2023].

Tieku, T.K. (2008) 'The Challenge of Africa's Embedded Personhood to Global Studies', *49th Annual Congress of the International Studies Association*, March, San Francisco.

Tieku, T.K. (2012) 'Collectivist Worldview: Its Challenge to International Relations', in S. Cornelissen, F. Cheru and T.M. Shaw (eds) *Africa and International Relations in the 21st Century*, London: Palgrave Macmillan, pp 36–50.

Time Weekly, The (2020) '"chaozuoye" zheyang de chunhua, wo buxiang zaiting dierci [I don't want to listen to stupid comments like "chaozuoye" again]', *The Time Weekly (WeChat Public Account)*, [online] 29 February, Available from: https://finance.sina.com.cn/wm/2020-02-29/doc-iimxyqvz6762015.shtml [Accessed 31 August 2023].

Toepfl, F. (2020) 'Comparing Authoritarian Publics: The Benefits and Risks of Three Types of Publics for Autocrats', *Communication Theory*, 30(2): 105–25.

Tong, L., Toppinen, A. and Wang, L. (2021) 'Cultural Motives Affecting Tea Purchase Behavior under Two Usage Situations in China: A Study of *Renqing, Mianzi*, Collectivism, and Man-Nature Unity Culture', *Journal of Ethnic Food*, 8(15): 2–10.

Torigian', J. (2018) 'Historical Legacies and Leaders' Worldviews: Communist Party History and Xi's Learned (and Unlearned) Lessons', *China Perspectives*, 1–2: 7–15.

Trey, G. (1998) *Solidarity and Difference: The Politics of Enlightenment in the Aftermath of Modernity*, Albany: State University of New York Press.

Trownsell T., Tickner, A.B., Querejazu Escobari, A. et al (2021) 'Differing about Difference: Relational IR from around the World', *International Studies Perspectives*, 22(1): 25–64.

Trownsell, T., Behera, N.C. and Shani, G. (2022) 'Introduction to the Special Issue: Pluriversal Relationality', *Review of International Studies*, 48(5): 787–800.

Truex, R. (2016) *Responsiveness in Modern China*, Cambridge University Press.

Tsai, K.S. (2021) 'Introduction', in S.-c. Hsu, K.S. Tsai and C.-c. Chang (eds) *Evolutionary Governance in China: State-Society Relations Under Authoritarianism*, Cambridge: Harvard University Press, pp 3–37.

Tsang, M. (2018) 'Who's the Egg? Who's the Wall? Appropriating Haruki Murakami's "Always on the Side of the Egg" Speech in Hong Kong', in F. Rösch and A. Watanabe (eds) *Modern Japanese Political Thought and International Relations*, Lanham: Rowman and Littlefield, pp 221–40.

Tsang, S. and Cheung, O. (2022) 'Has Xi Jinping Made China's Political System More Resilient and Enduring?', *Third World Quarterly*, 43(1): 225–43.

Tseng, R. (2023) *Confucian Liberalism: Mou Zongsan and Hegelian Liberalism*, Albany: State University of New York Press.

Tsourapas, G. (2021) 'Global Autocracies: Strategies of Transnational Repression, Legitimation, and Co-optation in World Politics', *International Studies Review*, 23(3): 616–44.

Tu, W. (2000) 'Implications of the Rise of "Confucian" East Asia', *Daedalus* 129(1): 195–218.

Unger, J. (1987) 'The Struggle to Dictate China's Administration: The Conflict of Branches vs Areas vs Reform', *Australian Journal of Chinese Affairs*, 18: 15–45.

Vaccaro, A. (2021) 'Comparing Measures of Democracy: Statistical Properties, Convergence, and Interchangeability', *European Political Science*, 20: 666–84.

Valdez, I. (2016) 'Nondomination or Practices of Freedom? French Muslim Women, Foucault, and the Full Veil Ban', *American Political Science Review*, 110(1): 18–30.

Van Klinken, G. and Barker, J. (eds) (2009) *State of Authority: The State in Society in Indonesia*, Ithaca: Cornell University Southeast Asia Program.

Vasilache, A. (2019) 'Security in the Sovereignty-Governmentality Continuum', *Cambridge Review of International Affairs*, 32(6): 681–711.

Verma, R. (2020) 'China's Diplomacy and Changing the Covid-19 Narrative', *International Journal*, 75(2): 248–58.

Vieira, M.B. (2020) 'Representing Silence in Politics', *American Political Science Review*, 114(4): 976–88.

Villa, D.R. (1992) 'Postmodernism and the Public Sphere', *American Political Science Review*, 86(3): 712–21.

Vucetic, S. (2011) *The Anglosphere: A Genealogy of a Racialized Identity in International Relations*, Stanford: Stanford University Press.

Wahman, M., Teorell, J. and Hadenius, A. (2013) 'Authoritarian Regime Types Revisited: Updated Data in Comparative Perspective', *Contemporary Politics*, 19(1): 19–34

Wai, Z. (2020) 'Resurrecting Mudimbe', *International Politics Review*, 8: 57–78.

Walden, D. (1974) 'Dubois' Pan-Africanism, a Reconsideration', *Negro American Literature Forum*, 8(4): 260–2.

Walder, A. (2019) *Agents of Disorder: Inside China's Cultural Revolution*, Cambridge: Harvard University Press.

Walder, A.G. (1994) 'Collective Behavior Revisited: Ideology and Politics in the Chinese Cultural Revolution', *Rationality and Society*, 6(3): 400–21.

Waltz, K. (1979) *Theory of International Politics*, Long Grove, IL: Waveland Press.

Walzer, M. (1992) 'The New Tribalism', *Dissent*, 39(Spring): 164–71.

Wang, B. (2018) 'Confucianism and Nature: Ecological Motifs in Kang Youwei's Great Community', *Telos*, 183: 47–67.

Wang, F. (2017) *The China Order: Centralia, World Empire, and the Nature of Chinese Power*, Albany: State University of New York Press.

Wang, F. (2019) *The China Order: A Challenge for the U.S. and the World*, Albany: State University of New York Press.

Wang, J. and Nahm, K. (2019) 'From Confucianism to Communism and Back', *Journal of Asian Sociology*, 48(1): 91–114.

Wang, J., Zhu, E. and Umlauf, T. (2020) 'How China built two coronavirus hospitals in just over a week', *The Wall Street Journal*, [online] 6 February, Available from: https://www.wsj.com/articles/how-china-can-build-a-coronavirus-hospital-in-10-days-11580397751 [Accessed 31 August 2023].

Wang, S. (2022) 'The Chinese Communist Party's Atheistic Approach to Religious Freedom in China', *Politics, Religion & Ideology*, 23(2): 204–225.

Wang, V. and Qin, A. (2020) 'As coronavirus pandemic fades in China, nationalism and xenophobia flare', *The New York Times*, [online] 16 April, Available from: https://www.nytimes.com/2020/04/16/world/asia/coronavirus-china-nationalism.html [Accessed 31 August 2023].

Wang, Y. (2016) *Tying the Autocrat's Hands: The Rise of The Rule of Law in China*, Cambridge: Cambridge University Press.

Wang, Y. (2017) 'Betting on a Princeling', *Studies in Comparative International Development*, 52(4): 395–415.

Wang, Y. (2020) 'Zhongzheng xinguanfeiyan huanzhe zhiliaofei chao baiwan, doushi guojia maidan [Medical expenses for each critically ill coronavirus patient cost over million, all covered by the country]', *Sohu News*, [online] 16 March, Available from: https://www.sohu.com/a/380474648_359980 [Accessed 31 August 2023].

Wang, Y. (2021) 'State-in-Society 2.0: Toward Fourth Generation Theories of the State', *Comparative Politics*, 54(1): 175–98.

Wang, Y. (2022a) *The Rise and Fall of Imperial China: The Social Origins of State Development*, Princeton: Princeton University Press.

Wang, Y. (2022b) *Pension Policy and Governmentality in China: Manufacturing Public Compliance*, London: LSE Press.

Wang, Y. and Klein, T. (2022) 'Representing the Victorious Past: Chinese Revolutionary TV Drama between Propaganda and Marketization', *Media, Culture and Society*, 44(1): 105–20.

Warren, M.E. (2017) 'A Problem-Based Approach to Democratic Theory', *American Political Science Review*, 111(1): 39–53.

Wasserstrom, J. (2017) 'Hong Kong and Shanghai, 1987–2017: A Convergence, a Reversal, and Two Ironies', *Telos*, 179: 213–17.

Weber, C. (2019) 'Ideology and Values in Political Decision Making', *Oxford Research Encyclopedias of Politics*, https://doi.org/10.1093/acrefore/9780190228637.013.998

Wei, L., Yao, E. and Zhang, H. (2021) 'Authoritarian Responsiveness and Political Attitudes during COVID-19: Evidence from Weibo and a Survey Experiment', *Chinese Sociological Review*, 55(1): 1–37.

Weiss, J.C. (2020) 'China's self-defeating nationalism – brazen diplomacy and rhetorical bluster undercut Beijing's influence', *Foreign Affairs*, [online] 16 July, Available from: https://www.foreignaffairs.com/articles/china/2020-07-16/chinas-self-defeating-nationalism [Accessed 21 January 2024].

Wells, C. (2020) 'Nationalism in the wake of Covid-19 hurts China's international appeal, says Cornell University Professor Jessica Chen Weiss', *Freeman Spogli Institute for International Studies*, [online] 3 June, Available from: https://fsi.stanford.edu/news/nationalism-wake-covid-19-hurts-china%E2%80%99s-international-appeal-says-cornell-university-professor [Accessed 31 August 2023].

West, T.G. and Jeffrey, D.A. (2006) *The Rise and Fall of Constitutional Government in America: A Guide to Understanding the Principle of the American Founding*, Claremont, CA: The Claremont Institute.

White, C.M. (2021) 'Human Nature and Globalization's Discontents: What the Antecedents of Ideology Tell Us about the Obstacles to Greater Global Interconnectedness', *Research in Globalization*, 3, 100038, https://doi.org/10.1016/j.resglo.2021.100038

White, G. (1987) 'The Impact of Economic Reforms in the Chinese Countryside: Towards the Politics of Social Capitalism', *Modern China*, 13(4): 411–40.

White, G. (1993) *Riding the Tiger: The Politics of Economic Reform in Post-Mao China*, Stanford: Stanford University Press.

White, T.J. (2010) 'The Impact of British Colonialism on Irish Catholicism and National Identity: Repression, Reemergence, and Divergence', *Varia*, 35(1): 21–37.

Winter, T. (2020) 'Silk Road Diplomacy: Geopolitics and Histories of Connectivity', *International Journal of Cultural Policy*, 26(7): 898–912.

Winter, T. (2021) 'Geocultural Power: China's Belt and Road Initiative', *Geopolitics*, 26(5): 1376–99.

Wolf, B. (2022) 'Adam Smith's Cosmopolitan Liberalism: Taste, Political Economy, and Objectification', *Polity*, 54(4): 709–33.

Wolin, R. and Rockmore, T. (1992) 'The Heidegger Controversy: A Critical Reader', *Ethics*, 103(1): 178–81.

Wong, B. (2020) 'How Chinese nationalism is changing', *The Diplomat*, [online] 26 May, Available from: https://thediplomat.com/2020/05/how-chinese-nationalism-is-changing/ [Accessed 31 August 2023].

Woods, E.T., Schertzer, R., Greenfeld, L. et al (2020) 'COVID-19, Nationalism, and the Politics of Crisis: A Scholarly Exchange', *Nations and Nationalism*, 26(4): 807–25.

Wright, J. (2008) 'Do Authoritarian Institutions Constrain? How Legislatures Affect Economic Growth and Investment?', *American Journal of Political Science*, 52(2): 322–43.

Wright, J. (2021) 'The Latent Characteristics That Structure Autocratic Rule', *Political Science Research and Method*, 9(1): 1–19.

Wu, C. (2020) 'How Chinese citizens view their government's coronavirus response', *The Conversation*, [online] 5 June, Available from: https://theconversation.com/how-chinese-citizens-view-their-governments-coronavirus-response-139176 [Accessed 31 August 2023].

Wu, C., Shi, Z., Wilkes, R. et al (2021) 'Chinese Citizen Satisfaction with Government Performance during COVID-19', *Journal of Contemporary China*, 30(132): 930–44.

Wu, Q. (2022) 'The CCP is losing people's hearts ['The Communist Party is losing China's people' in the English edition]', *New York Times* Chinese edition, [online] 12 December, Available from: https://cn.nytimes.com/opinion/20221202/china-protests/zh-hant/ [Accessed 31 August 2023].

Wu, Y. and Acharya, K. (2023) 'The Blank White Paper as a Disobedient Object', in S. Holmlid, V. Rodrigues, C. Westin et al (eds) *Nordes 2023: This Space Intentionally Left Blank*, 12–14 June, Linköping University, Norrköping, Sweden.

Xi, J. (2003) 'Interview', in the Association for Alumni of Universities outside Fujian Province (ed) *Elegant Doctors of Philosophy in Fujian*, Fuzhou: Haichao Photo Art Press, Chapter 2.

Xi, J. (2007) *New Words upon Arriving in Zhejiang*, Hangzhou: Zhejiang People's Press.

Xi, J. (2012a) 'Talk to the 1st Plenary of the 18th Party Congress', *China Association for Promoting Democracy*, [online] 11 November, Available from: https://www.mj.org.cn/mjzt/xxsj/2014-05/22/content_144220.htm [Accessed 31 August 2023].

Xi, J. (2012b) 'Achieving the great rejuvenation of the Chinese nation is its greatest dream since the modern times', *Chinese Communist Party News Net*, [online] 29 November, Available from: http://cpc.people.com.cn/xuexi/n/2015/0717/c397563-27322292.html [Accessed 31 August 2023].

Xi, J. (2013) 'Talk to the 1st Meeting of the 12th National People's Congress', 中國共產黨新聞網, [online] 17 March, Available from: http://cpc.people.com.cn/xuexi/n/2015/0717/c397563-27322349.html [Accessed 31 August 2023].

Xi, J. (2014a) 'Let us become partners in pursuit of our dreams (Recorded by the Ministry of Foreign Affairs, Sri Lanka)', *Daily News*, [online] 16 September, Available from: https://mfa.gov.lk/exclusive-xi-jinping-president-peoples-republic-of-china-to-daily-news-readers-let-us-become-partners-in-pursuit-of-our-dreams/ [Accessed 31 August 2023].

Xi, J. (2014b) 'Young people should consciously practice the core values of socialism', 共產黨員網 [webpage for Communist Party Members], [online] 4 May, Available from: https://syss.12371.cn/2015/06/15/ARTI1434355638326518.shtml [Accessed 31 August 2023].

Xi, J. (2015) 'Must remain heart-to-heart with the people, taste the sweet and bitter together, and struggle in unity', *The People's Net*, [online] 15 November, Available from: http://cpc.people.com.cn/18/n/2012/1115/c350821-19590515.html [Accessed 31 August 2023].

Xi, J. (2017) 'Talk to the 2nd Plenary Session of the 6th Central Committee of the 18th National Party Congress', [online] 1 January, Available from: http://www.xinhuanet.com//politics/2017-01/01/c_1120228200.htm [Accessed 31 August 2023].

Xi, J. (2018) 'Talk to Central Politburo about Improving the Work Style and Maintaining Close Contacts with the Masses on December 4, 2012', *The Life of Party*, [online] 21 May, Available from: https://zuzhibu.nwpu.edu.cn/info/1030/3956.htm [Accessed 31 August 2023].

Xi, J. (2021) 'Talks to the Central Investigation on October 16, 2014', *The Party Construction Net*, [online] 12 October, Available from: http://www.dangjian.com/shouye/dangjianyaowen/202110/t20211012_6199453.shtml [Accessed 31 August 2023].

Xia, M. (2020) 'Fang Fang's Wuhan diaries are a personal account of shared memory', *The Conversation*, [online] 19 May, Available from: https://theconversation.com/fang-fangs-wuhan-diaries-are-a-personal-account-of-shared-memory-138007 [Accessed 31 August 2023].

Xie, E. (2020) 'Coronavirus journal Wuhan Diary continues to upset Chinese nationalists', *South China Morning Post*, [online] 3 May, Available from: https://www.scmp.com/news/china/society/article/3082575/coronavirus-journal-wuhan-diary-continues-upset-chinese [Accessed 31 August 2023].

Xie, S. (2017) 'Chinese Beginnings of Cosmopolitanism: A Genealogical Critique of Tianxia Guan', *Telos*, 180: 8–25.

Xing, Y., Liu, Y., Tarba, S.Y. et al (2014) 'Intercultural Influences on Managing African Employees of Chinese Firms in Africa: Chinese Managers HRM Practices', *International Business Review*, 25(1): 28–41.

Xinhua News (2020) 'Chinese netizens put their noodles together for virus-hit Wuhan', *Xinhua News*, [online] 1 February, Available from: http://www.xinhuanet.com/english/2020-02/01/c_138747797.htm [Accessed 22 January 2024].

Xiuhui, L. (2020) 'Wuhanfeiyan "chuishaoren" Liwenliang guoshi: "yanlunziyou" cheng weibo resou, wangyou zhiyi ta "budehaosi" [Wuhan pneumonia "whistle-blower" Liwenliang passed away: "freedom of speech" became Weibo hot topic, netizens raise doubts about his "miserable death"', *The News Lens*, [online] 7 February, Available from: https://www.thenewslens.com/article/130955 [Accessed 31 August 2023].

Xu, K. (2006) 'Early Confucian Principles: The Potential Theoretical Foundation of Democracy in Modern China', *Asian Philosophy*, 16(2): 135–48.

Xu, Y. (2018) 'Human Rights by Virtue of Ancestry: A Principle of Ontological Construction Originating from Consanguineous Rationality', *Social Sciences in China*, 39(1): 114–135 & 206–7.

Xu, Y. (2022) 'The Greatest Politics Is about the People's Hearts', Guangmimg Ribao (19 September) http://theory.people.com.cn/BIG5/n1/2022/0919/c40531-32528894.html [Accessed 19, November 2023]

Xue, Y., Gao, S. and Ma, W. (2020) 'Huoshenshan shiri qiji, waiguo "yunjiangong" jinghu: zhiyou zhongguo keyi [Huoshenshan ten-day miracle: foreign "online supervisors" exclaimed: only China can!]', *Xinhua News*, [online] 6 February, Available from: http://www.xinhuanet.com/politics/2020-02/06/c_1125536113.htm [Accessed 31 August 2023].

Yan, F. (2020) 'Managing 'Digital China' During the Covid-19 Pandemic: Nationalist Stimulation and its Backlash', *Postdigital Science and Education*, 2(3): 639–44.

Yan, X. (2014) 'From Keeping a Low Profile to Striving for Achievement', *Chinese Journal of International Politics*, 7(2): 153–84.

Yan, Y. (2021) 'The Politics of Moral Crisis in Contemporary China', *The China Journal*, 85(1): 96–120.

Yang, F., Wang, S. and Zhang, Z. (2022) 'State-enlisted Voluntarism in China: The Role of Public Security Volunteers in Social Stability Maintenance', *China Quarterly*, 249: 47–67.

Yang, H. (1990) *The History of Pre-Qin Legal Thought* (先秦法律思想史), Beijing: China University of Political Science and Law Press.

Yang, S. and Rosenblatt, P.C. (2008) 'Confucian Family Value and Childless Couples in South Korea', *Journal of Family Issues*, 29(5): 571–91.

Yang, Y. and Chen, X. (2020) 'Globalism or Nationalism? The Paradox of Chinese Official Discourse in the Context of the COVID-19 Outbreak', *Journal of Chinese Political Science*, 26(1): 89–113.

Yeoh, B.S.A., Acedera, K. and Rootham, E. (2019) 'Negotiating Postcolonial Eurasian Identities and National Belong in Global-city Singapore', *Social Identities*, 25(3): 294–309.

Yi, J. and Lee, W. (2020) 'Pandemic Nationalism in South Korea', *Society*, 57(4): 446–51.

Yu, X. and Li, Z. (2020) 'Tuidong goujian renlei minyun gongtongti de zhongguo dandang [China's responsibility in promoting the construction of a community with shared future for mankind]', *Chinese Central Government*, [online] 27 May, Available from: http://www.gov.cn/xinwen/2020-05/27/content_5515232.htm [Accessed 31 August 2023].

Zafirovski, M. (2021) 'The Protestant Ethic and the Spirit of Political Power: Sociopolitical Conditions Underlying the Development of Calvinism', *Journal for the Academic Study of Religion*, 34(2): 131–54.

Zakaria, F. (1997) 'The Rise of Illiberal Democracy', *Foreign Affairs*, 76(6): 22–43.

Zakaria, F. (2003) *The Future of Freedom: Illiberal Democracy at Home and Abroad*, New York: Norton.

Zeng, J. (2014) 'The Debate on Regime Legitimacy in China: Bridging the Wide Gulf between Western and Chinese Scholarship,' *Journal of Contemporary China*, 23(88): 612–35.

Zeng, Y. (2020) 'Home, Work, Homework, And Field', *Anthropology News*, [online] 12 June, Available from: https://anthropologynews.report/home-work-homework-and-fieldwork/ [Accessed 31 August 2023].

Zhang, C. (2018) 'Governing Neoliberal Authoritarian Citizenship: Theorizing hukou and the Changing Mobility Regime in China', *Citizenship Studies*, 22(8): 855–81.

Zhang, C. (2020a) 'Governing (through) Trustworthiness: Technologies of Power and Subjectification in China's Social Credit System', *Critical Asian Studies*, 52(4): 565–88.

Zhang, C. (2020b) 'Covid-19 in China: From "Chernobyl Moment" to Impetus for Nationalism', *Made in China Journal*, 5(2): 162–5.

Zhang, J.J. and Savage, V.R. (2020) 'The Geopolitical Ramifications of COVID-19: The Taiwanese Exception', *Eurasian Geography and Economics*, 61(4–5): 464–81.

Zhang, P. (2020) 'China's communist youth idols get the thumbs down in coronavirus crisis', *South China Morning Post*, [online] 19 February, Available from: https://www.scmp.com/news/china/society/article/3051224/chinas-communist-youth-idols-get-thumbs-down-coronavirus-crisis [Accessed 31 August 2023].

Zhang, Q. and Chow, Y.F. (2021) 'COVID-19 and Sonic Governmentality: Can We Hear the Virus Speak', *China Information*, 35(3): 325–45.

Zhang, Y. (1988) 'The Reasons for and Basic Principles in Formulating the Hong Kong Special Administrative Region Basic Law and Its Essential Contents and Mode of Expression', *Journal of Chinese Law*, 2(1): 5–19.

Zhang, Y., Schoonjans, Y. and Gantois, G. (2022) 'Re-uncovering the Collectivism in Mao's China, 1950–1970s: The Workers' Villages in Northeast China', *International Planning History Society Proceedings*, 19(1): 131–44.

Zhang, Y.B., Lin, M.-c., Nonaka, A. et al (2005) 'Harmony, Hierarchy and Conservatism: A Cross-Cultural Comparison of Confucian Values in China, Korea, Japan, and Taiwan', *Communication Research Reports*, 22(2): 107–15.

Zhao, S. (2020) 'Rhetoric and Reality of China's Global Leadership in the Context of Covid-19: Implications for the US-led World Order and Liberal Globalization', *Journal of Contemporary China*, 30(128): 233–48.

Zhao, S. (2022) *The Dragon Roars Back: Transformational Leaders and Dynamics of Chinese Foreign Policy*, Stanford: Stanford University Press.

Zhao, T. (2019) *Redefining a Philosophy for World Governance*, London: Palgrave/Macmillan.

Zhao, X., Shang, Y., Lin, J. et al (2016) 'Leader's Relational Power: Concept, Measurement and Validation', *European Management Journal*, 34(5): 517–29.

Zhaxi, D. (2019) 'Housing Subsidy Projects in Amdo: Modernity, Governmentality, and Income Disparity in Tibetan Areas of China', *Critical Asian Studies*, 51(1): 31–50.

Zhou, M. (2015) 'Under Non-Western Eyes: Chinese Values and Western Values in a Twenty-First-Century Media Ecology', *Telos*, 171: 124–30.

Zhou, R. and Li, X. (2020) '"Fanquanhua" Fansi – zainan zhong xuyao taiduo ziwo gandong he jiti kuanghuan ma? [Reflecting on "fandomisation" – do we need much self- and collective celebration amid disasters?]', *Chawang [CWZG]*, [online] 10 February, Available from: http://m.cwzg.cn/theory/202002/54950.html?page=full [Accessed 31 August 2023].

Zi, Z. (2020) '1900 & 2020 – an old anxiety in a new era', *China Heritage*, [online] 28 April, Available from: http://chinaheritage.net/journal/1900-2020-an-old-anxiety-in-a-new-era/?utm_medium=email&utm_content=6LhsAQ-CeP5HFTZuvJBfGrrvICUeFPUb-khVCWrSeQvnv2EgEbUnLuObh2kffS9O [Accessed 31 August 2023].

Zmigrod, L. (2020) 'The Role of Cognitive Rigidity in Political Ideologies: Theory, Evidence, and Future Directions', *Current Opinion in Behavioral Sciences*, 34: 34–9.

Zou, S. (2020) '"SARS hero" follows leads on illness', *China Daily*, [online] 23 January, Available from: http://global.chinadaily.com.cn/a/202001/23/WS5e28dd3ca310128217272df3.html [Accessed 31 August 2023].

Index

A

accountability 39, 40, 46–7, 80
Adorno, Theodor 57
Agathangelou, A.M. 132
Agriculturalism 42, 52
Ai Guo Zhe (AGZ) 65, 67, 70
al-Bashir, Omar 138
Almond, G.A. 45
Analects, The 60–1
ancestry 28–9, 111, 135, 137
Ang, Yuenyuen 25
anti-corruption 13, 100–1, 105
anti-imperialism 37
arrogance 32, 79
authoritarian personality 89, 90, 91
Authoritarian Personality, The (Adorno) 57
authoritarian resilience 22, 36, 41, 55
autocracy 1–2, 10–11, 15–16, 40, 146
  and Chinese Communist Party 19, 82
  and counter-governmentality 11, 19, 36, 37
  and democracy 33, 147, 149
  and disengagement 27
  governmentality 26
  modern 35
  modern and premodern/classic, differences between 34
  and monopoly 24, 108
  and nationalism 73
  ownership of resources for controlling 36
  postmodern 34
  and rights of people 6
  role of the people within 5–7
  and selflessness 150
  Xi's governmentality 100–3
autocrats
  -as-society 26–8
  bad 148
  care for their people 5, 28–9, 35
  naturalness of 11, 127
  personality level 47–8
  readiness of the people to follow 26
  and self-discipline 19
  self-roles 88
  as unit 6

B

Babones, S. 129
Balkans 58, 114
Banqiao, Zheng 97
Bao, Shusun 31
Basic Law 66, 68
behaviouralism 45
Beijing Olympics in 2008 22, 82
'being special' and 'being different,' distinguishing between 4
Belgrade, bombing of the Chinese embassy in 82
Bell, Daniel 114–15, 138
belonging 10, 73, 77, 107–8, 134–7, 148
  and benevolence 43, 56, 111
  to communities 2–3, 4, 58, 71
  and dominance 5, 8, 146–51
  failure of 15
  and governmentality 14
  mutual 4, 49, 56, 57, 69, 106, 134, 135, 151, 152
  One Country Two Systems (OCTS) as a system of 67–71
  and self-restraints 111
  and unity 64
Belt & Road Initiative (BRI) 98, 102–3, 104
benevolence 31, 37, 43–4, 55, 69, 70, 108, 143, 148, 149
  of autocrats 18, 37, 54
  and belonging 43, 56, 111
  collective 15
  and kings 28–9
  and kinship 134, 135–6
  and leadership 34
  and princes 9, 64
  quarantine as 77
  and Tianxia 132, 141
benevolent love 12, 44, 60, 64, 67–8, 70–1, 108
  between the autocrat and their claimed population 12
  and Confucianism 60–4
  hierarchical nature of 68

INDEX

'One Country, Two Systems' as 64–7
and universal love 56–7
Bērziņa-Čerenkova, U.A. 92
Bhambra, G. 139
Bieber, Florian 86
Book of Changes, The 60
Book of Rites 43, 62
Book of Zhou, The 33
boundary consciousness 68
Bowers, Fergal 83
Breslin, S. 76
Brown, K. 92
Buck, Pearl 21, 81
Buddhism 89, 97–8, 101, 103
  see also Zen
Buddhist nationalism 93
Bunskoek, Raoul 25
Burlingame, Anson 81

C

capitalism 6, 20, 21, 24, 68, 109
  and civil society 22
  modern 58, 147, 149
  and socialism 65
Carter, Jimmy 47
case-sensitive agendas 89, 91
censorship 78, 80
checks and balances (C&B) 106–8, 107, 115–18, 121, 125
Chinese Communist Party (CCP) 11, 20, 21, 34, 42, 48, 50, 74, 94, 96, 104, 150
  autocracy 19
  and nationalism 84
  selflessness 101
  unresponsive autocracy during the pandemic 82
Chinese cultural cultivation 70–1
Chinese nationalisms
  binaries 81
  compared and reconsidered 80–2
  see also nationalism
Chinese Text Project 30, 43
Chow, Y.F. 76
Christianity 39, 44, 45, 48, 52, 53, 110, 136
Chronicle of Zuo, The 31
churches 7, 21, 44, 51–4, 147, 150
civic nationalism 7, 13, 54, 108–12, 109, 113–14, 125, 151
civil society 16, 22–3, 25, 132–3
  and capitalism 22
  in Japan 85
civil war 49
Collection of Literature Arranged by Categories, The 32
collective benevolence 15
collective identity 130
collective volatility 48–9
collectivism 20, 83

colonialism 131
  and colonial division 59
  and democracy, impact on indigenous population 6
  and education 70–1
commoners 5, 48, 60, 61, 62–3, 64
communitarian democracy, and rights of the people 6
communitarianism 7, 137, 138
  and liberalism 3
  and love 67
  and solidarity 4, 45, 56, 147
communities 2–3, 59, 147–8
  disintegration of 58
  resilience 79
conduct of conduct 19–20, 21
Confucianism 27, 33, 39, 43, 54, 70, 89, 100, 103, 136
  and involution 5, 12, 55, 60–64, 83, 116, 125–6
  and leadership 3, 8, 9, 28, 48, 52, 115, 147
  and people 22, 36, 46, 88, 99
  as idea 1, 16, 18, 30, 35, 44, 45, 67, 91–95, 146
  as relationality 10, 11, 102, 104, 114, 134, 135, 142, 149, 151
  as self-restraint 13, 98, 101, 108, 110–1
Confucius 9, 27, 28, 36, 38, 42, 43, 48, 60, 62, 111
constitutional democracy 54, 109, 112–14, 115
constitutional liberalism 112–13
constitutionalism 13, 113, 114, 148
Convention for a Democratic South Africa (CODESA) 138
corruption 6, 36, 40, 46, 52, 55, 100, 114, 122, 124, 141
  corrupt relationship 69
  and monopoly 52
cosmological beliefs 7, 10, 111, 131, 148
cosmologies 7–8, 9, 127, 129–30, 133, 136, 139, 140, 144
counter-counter-governmentality 37
counter-governmentality 16–19, 35, 74, 124, 146, 152
  and autocracy 11, 19, 36, 37
  Chinese autocracy 37
  definition of democracy 35
  demand for and supply of 153
  diagrammatic logic of 152–7
  by induction 30–1
  and modern nationalism 37
  in modern times 34
  and nationalism 155
  and people's heart 27–30
  and people's well-being 36
  power, and union of resistance strength 34
  and revolution 36
  and rights consciousness 21
  and state-in-society 19

209

supply and demand, during involution under liberal democracy 154
and Xi 156
see also governmentality
counter-nationalism 85
COVID-19 pandemic 12–13, 150
  Chinese, literature on 75–7
  quarantine policy 50, 74
  unpredictable dynamics of solidarity and unity 74
  see also pandemic nationalism; Wuhan
critical translation 7–8
cross-boundary population 150
cultural continuity, in postmodern times 17, 33–7
cultural resemblance 69
Cultural Revolution 50, 57, 89–90, 92–4, 95

D

Daoism 42, 62, 134
de Sousa Santos, B. 131, 139
decentralization 50, 99
Declaration of Universal Human Rights 51
decolonization 8, 60, 138, 139
deliberative democracy 12, 40–1, 51–5, 151
democracy 2, 5, 9, 16, 146
  attempt to save the reputation of 83
  and autocracy 33, 147, 149
  and colonialism, impact on indigenous population 6
  communitarian 6
  and Confucian governmentality 15, 35
  constitutional 54, 109, 112–14, 115
  deliberative 12, 40–1, 51–5, 151
  democratic centralism 49
  democratic governability 123
  electoral 125
  illiberal 6, 13, 41, 83, 109, 114, 125
  and involution 46, 154
  liberal 6, 8, 39, 41, 107, 110, 131, 148, 151
  and monopoly 36
  in the pluriversal world 7–10
  recession 40–1
  relational 106, 118–19, 123–5, 146
  uniqueness 6
  whole-process 30, 51
democratization 22, 41, 65, 131–2
Deng Xiaoping 65, 95, 102, 122
Denghui, Li 113
descendants 135
Discourses of the Kingdoms, The 31
discursive othering 84
discursive people 18–19, 21, 28, 29–30, 33–4, 35, 123
disengagement, of people 27–8, 37, 55
Disteihorst, Greg 25
docile citizens 86–7
dominance and belonging, balancing 146

E

Easton, David 45
electoral systems 27, 55, 64, 70, 110
elites 20, 141
equal rights 2, 3, 4, 51–2, 148, 149
equality 3, 8, 44, 51–3, 55, 59, 62–3, 136, 141, 146
Escape from Freedom (Fromm) 57
ethnic politics 114
evolutionary governance 51
extravagance 32

F

failing states 131, 141
Fanon, Frantz 142
fascism 22, 45, 92
feudalism 24, 29, 65, 150
forgiveness 69, 138
Foucauldian 16
Foucauldian governmentality 11, 16, 17–18, 21
Foucauldian methodology of pain 18
Foucault, Michel 17–21, 18–19, 21, 33–4, 57, 58
Fromm, Eric 57, 58–9
Fu, Diana 25
Fukuyama, Francis 83

G

Galway, Matthew 93
general will 8, 9, 61
Germany 47, 128
gift-giving 69, 81, 85, 102
Glass, James 58–9
Global Barometer Survey 41
Goto-Jones, Christopher 92
Gottlieb, Thomas 25
governability 107, 118
  versus cash and balance (C&B) 118–19
  democratic 123
  failure of 124
  obliges the counter-governmentality of authorities 124
  obliges the governmentality of the people 124
  and relations 106–7
  as restraining extremism 118–23
  through relations and balances 107–8
governmentality 17–18, 25, 39, 146–7, 152
  application in the Chinese context 17–21
  instrumental 20
  intra-systemic 108
  and norms 39
  parallel 35
  pluriversal 144
  positive energy 78
  stable 42
  systemic-level 108
  see also counter-governmentality

Great Leap Forward 50, 89, 93
Greater East Asian Co-Prosperity Sphere (GEACPS) of WWII Japan 89, 91
Greenfeld, L. 76
group consciousness 4, 141

H

Halabi, E.E. 51
Han Dynasty 43, 48
happiness 17, 20
He, Baogang 23
heaven and earth 9, 14, 27, 28
  see also mandate of heaven
Heidegger, Martin 88
Hobbes, Thomas 8, 61–2, 133
holding, notion of 58, 64, 71, 72, 122
Holocaust 57, 58, 113
Hong Kong 12, 56–7, 64, 71–2, 153–4
  activists and activism 67, 72
  landing and housing reform 69
  perceived failure of the activists to understand the rise of China 70
  problematization of universal love 59–60
  residual power 68
Hong Kong Autonomy Act (2020), US 57, 72
Hong Kong Human Rights and Democracy Act (2019), US 57, 72
Houdun, Xia 32
Hu, Xijin 77
Huang, Philip 23
Hubei 80
Hughes/Hugues 75–6
human rights 3, 47, 54, 57, 82, 131, 135, 137, 147
Hunhu *see* Ubuntu
Huntington, Samuel 136
Huoshenshan hospital 79

I

illiberal democracy 6, 13, 41, 83, 109, 114, 125
illiberal politics 113–14
imagined resemblance 10, 123, 135
Inclusiveness 11, 13, 52, 108, 111, 115, 118, 122, 125
individual preferences 55
individualism 10, 12, 39, 44, 45, 92, 97, 109, 111, 132, 137, 138
individuality 3, 14, 43, 44–5, 136, 140
individualization 53, 58, 112
integrity, failing 31–2
involution 12, 54–5, 104, 153
  and caveat 103–4
  and democracy 46, 154
  and norms 39
  and violence 49
Israel 128

J

Japan 47, 84–5, 92
Jaworsky, B.N. 76
Jefferson, Thomas 51
Jiacheng, Liu 76
Jintao, Hu 82
Johnson, Boris 84
Joint Declaration on the Question of Hong Kong 65–6, 68
joint leadership 3

K

Kant, Immanuel 133
Khmer Rouge 88, 93
killing 28, 32, 62, 122, 134
Kimani, Martin 128–9
king, significance of 27–8, 29, 31, 32, 60
King of Wei 32
kinship 111, 114, 134–5
kinship love 60, 61, 62–3
Kissinger, Henry 21, 81
Kitaro, Nishida 92
Kloet, J.d. 76
Korea 83, 131
Kyoto School of Philosophy 91–2, 97

L

land rights 135
Lasswell, Harold 57
laws of nature 14, 61, 132, 133, 134, 135–6
legalism 42, 134
legislative activism 121
legitimacy, significance of 121–2
Leishenshan hospital 79
Lenin, Vladimir 49
Leninism 19
Leviathan, Hobbesian 6, 7, 9, 61, 62, 126, 133
Li, Lianjiang 25, 29
Li, Xiangxin 23
liberal democracy 6, 8, 39, 41, 107, 110, 131, 148, 151
liberal governmentality 14, 19–20, 23, 25–6, 35, 113
  and deliberate democracy 54
  and exclusion and discrimination 112
liberalism 1, 9, 12, 15, 44, 45, 46–7, 146
  communitarian 3
  and Confucianism 9, 35
  family within 61
  individualist 92
  and socialism 35–6
Lifton, Robert 57
Lin, J. 76
Ling, L.H.M. 132
Linkhoeva, Tatiana 92
living people 18, 25, 26, 27, 30, 33–8, 65, 77, 86, 89
Locard, Henri 93

Locke, John 3, 35, 126, 133
Loong, Lee Hsien 68
Lost Book of Zhou 31–2
love
  benevolent *see* benevolent love
  and communitarianism 67
  differential 12
  as emancipation, problematization of 57–60
  intuitive 61
  kinship 60, 61, 62–3
  role-embedded 63–4, 69, 70, 71
  solidarity as 67
  solidarity-love 68–9, 71–2
  universal 12, 56–7, 59–60, 67, 71–2, 134

M

Mamdani 128, 138
mandate of heaven 27–8, 33, 60–1, 62, 64
Mao Zedong 49, 50, 57, 90, 92–5, 93, 97
Maoism 90, 93
Marx, Karl 35
Marxism and Confucianism, intersection between 64
mass-line approach 12, 40, 49–51, 55, 94, 95–7, 100–1, 102, 104, 152
material redistribution 104
materialistic sensibilities 64
Mawdsley, E. 144
Mazlish, Bruce 57
Mazrui, Ali 138
Mbembe, A. 130, 144
Mbiti, J.S. 137
medical staff, national mobilization of 74
Mencius 34, 43, 61, 62
metaphorical kinship love 63
Metz, T. 138
Migdal, Joel 23, 24
migrants 6, 32, 65, 72, 109, 111, 122, 125, 150
Mills, C.W. 133
minzhu 17, 29, 30, 31
misdistribution of wealth 52
Mizoguchi, Yuzo 24
modernity 24, 25, 37
Mogae, Festus 142
Mohism (Moism) 42, 134
Mongolia 83
monopoly 9, 16, 35, 49, 52, 66, 70, 106, 120, 148–50
  autocratic 24, 108
  and corruption 52
  and democracy 36
  and governmentality 38, 117
  of state 27
moral theory (Metz) 138
Mu, Ming 75
Mudimbe, V.Y. 139
multiple networking 117

mutual belonging 4, 49, 56, 57, 69, 106, 134, 135, 151, 152
mutual nurturing 137, 141, 143, 144, 145, 150

N

national dignity 22
national identity 109, 116, 117, 118, 125
National People's Congress 66
national pride 77, 79
nationalism 3, 13, 19, 24, 37, 73–4, 99–100, 149, 155
  and antiWesternism 77
  biopolitical 76–7
  bottom-up 74, 78, 152, 155
  competitive 73
  and counter-governmentality 155
  disaster 77
  metaphoric prescription for 86–7
  relationally embedded 83–5
  statist 149, 150
  top-down 155
  see also Chinese nationalisms
natural contract 8–9, 28, 57, 61, 63
natural law 66, 134
natural rights 35, 59, 63, 66, 131, 134, 135
Naude, Piet 137–8
Nazis 47, 57, 58, 82
Ndlovu-Gathseni, S.J. 139
New Book 32
New Zealand 83
NGOs 37
non-interventionism 140–4
normative liberalism versus law-like Confucianism 41–5
normativity 53
nurturing 132, 137, 140–4, 145, 150
Nyerere, Julius 137

O

Obama, Barack 109
O'Brien, Kevin 25
One Country Two Systems (OCTS) 12, 56, 71–2
  as benevolent love 64–7
  as a system of belonging contested 67–71
oneness 62, 63, 68, 133, 134, 137
original sin 40, 53–4, 109, 133, 136, 141, 148, 151
othering 84–5
Owen, Catherine 23

P

Pan-Africanism 128
pandemic nationalism 73–5
  Chinese people tend to be accepting 75
  Chinese problem 76
  chronic phenome 76
  literature on 75–7

politically engineered 75–6
relationally embedded nationalism 83–5
and Wuhan 77–80
Parekh, B. 139
people not caring versus people not cared for 45–9
people's hardship, being indifferent to 32
people's hearts 19, 21, 26, 27–30, 33, 36–8, 42–4, 48, 49, 51, 55, 75, 87
People's Liberation Army 70
people's master 29, 30–3, 61
Perry, Elizabeth 23
personality
  and ideas 91
  political 89
  ruler's 13
  totalitarian 59, 93
personhood, African notion of 137
Pieterse, J.N. 139
pluriversalism 35, 127, 132, 138, 144–5, 150–1
  approach to relational worlds 130
  and democracy 7–10
  mini-pluriversalism 140, 152
  relations between governmentalities 157
  and social processes 139
Pol Pot regime 88, 93, 94
political consultation 50–1
political correctness 6, 47, 50–1, 52, 53, 64, 150
political sub-nationalism 149
postcolonialism 37
  conformity 83
  education 70–1
Power and Personality (Lasswell) 57
Practice of the 'One Country, Two Systems' Policy, The 66
princes 61, 62–3, 64, 134
Principles of Governing from Many Books, The 32–3
prior resemblance 143
propaganda 78, 80
public goods 3
public opinion 80
public versus private dichotomy 24–5
Putnam, Robert 47
Pye, Lucien 25, 49, 57, 92

Q

Qiaoan, R. 76

R

racism 6, 75, 113, 139
radical dependence 58
Rawls, John 61
rebels, defecting to 32
Records of the Three Kingdoms, The 32
reforms 36, 49
reganmian 78

regime of regimes 15, 19, 26–7, 33, 36, 38, 62, 75, 86, 88, 106, 126, 148, 150
relational cosmology 129
relational democracy 106, 146
  balance of relationships in 123–5
  governability versus C&B 118–19
relational networks 26, 75
relational skills 148–9
relationally embedded nationalism 83–5
relations and balances (R&B) 13, 107–8, 118, 119, 125, 150
relations and governability 106–7
repressed aggression, collective personality of 92
rights consciousness 21, 68, 114, 115
rights of nature 1, 7, 11, 14, 22, 54, 61, 62, 127, 130, 131, 132–7, 140–5
Roberts, M.E. 78
role-embedded love 63–4, 69, 70, 71
role-taking 15, 135
Rousseau, Jean-Jacques 6, 8, 61, 133
Russia, invasion of Ukraine 128–9
Rwanda 58

S

sacrifices 111, 147–8
sanctions 24, 69
Santos, B. 139
Schaff, Philip 44
Schlesinger, Arthur, Jr 40
School of Nomenclature 42, 43, 52
secularism 54
self-assertion 110
self-disintegration 58
self-fulfilment 46, 59, 60, 63–4, 100
self-governing citizens 35
self-in-relation 13, 90
self-interests 4, 21, 49, 126, 141, 144, 145
self-involvement, committing 32–3
selflessness 2, 4, 36, 64, 115, 148, 149
self-othering 85
self-preparation 13, 78, 90
self-regulation 25, 26
self-restraint 26, 27, 107–8, 110, 113–14
  as governmentality in relational democracy 156
  liberal 110
  as relational democracy 114–18
self-sacrifice 74, 92, 110, 145, 148
self-security 59, 60
setting a bad example to the people 33
Shih, Chih-yu 23, 25
Shikai, Yuan 113
Shimizu, Kosuke 91
Shin, Doh Chull 118
Shue, Vivienne 23
Shun, Emperor 62
Sikhi 59
Singapore 83

Smith, Adam 3, 35
Snow, Edgar 21, 81
social contract theory 8, 28, 54, 57, 61, 63, 133, 135, 136
social democrats 46
social regression 15, 54, 71, 109
solidarity 22, 54, 63, 69, 71, 78–9, 86, 106, 110, 124, 147–8, 149
   culture of 3–4, 12, 107, 154
   and equity 4
   as forms of love 67
   intra-systemic 112
   romanticized by civic nationalism 109
   and unity, difference between 108
   versus unity 3–5
solidarity-love 68–9, 71–2
Solinger, Dorothy 23
Solomon, Richard 57
South Africa 128, 138
South-South cooperation (SSC) 127
South-South relations 141
sovereignty 19, 20, 37, 80, 84
state
   capacity 83–4
   pupil 131
   revisionist 131
   rogue 131
   as a social network 25
state and society, perspectives of 11, 16, 17
   and autocracy 25–7
   generally 21–3
   state-as-society 23–7, 24, 35
   state-in-society 17, 21, 23–5, 37
state of nature 7
statist nationalism 149, 150
Steffensen, Kenn Nakata 92
strangeness 10, 56, 68, 135, 136
strategic patience 143, 145
survivor's justice 128
symbolic unity 115
system theory 45, 112
systemic identity 13, 106, 108, 112, 114, 122–3, 125

T

Taishao Democracy 47
Taiwan 83, 84–5, 112–13, 115–20, 121, 125
   R&B factor, restraint 121
   restraint factor in 120
   unity factor 120
Taro, Aso 82
Thomas, Neil 79
Tianxia 14, 59, 126, 127, 129, 140–2
   abstraction definition 130
   re-emergence of 131
Tieku, T.K. 132, 137
Timor, East 58
Trump, Donald 82, 84

Truth and Reconciliation Commission (South Africa) 138

U

Ubuntu 14, 59, 126, 128, 136
   abstraction definition 130
   as the cosmological necessity to nurture 137–40
   as a project of decolonization 138
   re-emergence of 131
   as unlearning 127–30
uncertainty 30, 34, 40, 46, 49, 118, 152
United States 24, 109, 113–14
   challenge to the nation-state 80–1
   and China 22, 56, 73
   Chinese embassy bombing by 82
   Declaration of Independence 51
   Hong Kong Acts 57, 72
   political science 45
   presidential elections 109
unity 64, 106–7, 110–11, 115, 124, 148, 149
   and solidarity, difference between 108
   symbolic 115
   through reciprocal role relations 63
universal love 12, 56–7, 59–60, 67, 71–2, 134
universal rights 133–4
unpredictability 30, 34, 36, 48, 74–5, 148, 152–3

V

values and institutions 130–1
Verba, S. 45
victims and perpetrators 128
Vietnam 83
volunteerism 23, 62, 76, 145
Vucic, Aleksandar 79
vulnerable, caring for 115

W

Wade, Abdoulaye 142
Wai, Z. 139
Walder, Andrew 24
Waltz, Kenneth 136
Wang, Yuhua 23, 25
Warren, Mark 23
Weimar Republic 47
Wenliang, Li 74, 77–8
Western colonization 142
White Paper Protests 34, 36, 50–1, 74
Wong, B. 77
Woods, E.T. 80
World Health Organization (WHO) 82
World Trade Organization 82
Wuhan
   emergence of voluntarism in 76
   and pandemic nationalism 12–13, 77–80, 81, 84
'Wuhan jiayou' 78
see also pandemic nationalism

INDEX

X

Xi Jinping 13, 24, 42, 76, 77, 79, 89–109, 90, 105
  alters-in-relation 13, 90, 91
  anti-corruption programmes 100–1
  autocratic governmentality 100–3
  belief system of 95
  Buddhist spirit 91, 94, 103
  'Chinese dream' 101–2
  collective selves 100
  Confucian thought 91, 94, 99–100
  conscious self-preparation 90–1
  counter-governmentality 156
  and discursive people 29
  emergence from the Cultural Revolution 94
  epistemological scheme 97
  mass line 13, 94, 95–7, 100–1, 102, 104
  nationalism 99–100
  peasants' admiration 96
  personality 13, 90
  personality reformation during the Cultural Revolution 94
  political discourses 91
  political ideas not for emancipation 90–4
  poverty-elimination plan 102
  self-discipline 93, 104
  and socialism 91, 94
  vulnerability, overcoming 104
  Zen thought 98
Xinjiang blaze 74
Xu Xing 42
Xunzi 49, 54

Y

Yan, Fei 75
Yang, F. 23
Yaobang, Hu 95
Yongyao, Lin 69

Z

Zen 59, 91, 98
  see also Buddhism
Zhang, J.J. 75
Zhang, Z. 23
Zhongxun, Xi 95
Zhongyan, Fan 97

www.ingramcontent.com/pod-product-compliance
Lightning Source LLC
Chambersburg PA
CBHW051541020426
42333CB00016B/2043